To Kimberly T
to a great
and compassionate &
appreciation, I really value y[our]
friendship
John B. Orts
Former U.S. Congress[man]
Texas

Remarkable

Journey

CATHY TRAVIS

ISBN-13: 978-1495254581
ISBN-10: 1495254585

* * * * * *

Cover image designed by Ricardo Lopez-Guerra

DEDICATION

For "Grandma" Martinez and the Cheerleaders, the generation that
dreamed of greater possibilities ... and for every Mexican American child
born in South Texas. Humble beginnings can lead to extraordinary things.

CONTENTS

Foreword   3

1   The Beginning   5

2   Military Service   14

3   Launching a Lifetime of Service   19

4   The Dream of his Childhood   33

5   Money Launderers Hit Back   46

6   First Campaign for Congress   62

7   Mr. Ortiz goes to Washington   71

8   Navigating Capitol Hill   79

9   South Texas Military Bases/BRAC   84

10 The Screwing of South Texas   94

11 Depot Warrior   102

12 Deficit Reduction   105

13 Sad Tale of Border Security   110

14 Iraq War and the Fight to Fix a Broken Military   119

15 Being Nice, Winning Friends   135

16 Diplomatic Journey   140

17 "Axis of Evil," Subsequent Diplomacy   148

18 Trying to Tame Libya   153

19 Weird Little World of North Korea   159

20 Redistricting, 21st Century's Sin   167

21 Politics, Not Journalism   179

22 Trade Diplomat   189

23 The Perfect Storm   194

24 Legacy   203

FOREWORD

I worked for U.S. Congressman Solomon Ortiz for 18 years before I retired from Capitol Hill in 2008.

This story is about his life and times – before, during, and after our professional association. But our relationship was never just about Capitol Hill and government.

He is my friend, like a favorite uncle. We were both political animals; we campaigned together from the 1990s until 2010 (the last election was after I'd left the Hill).

We are opposites. Congressman Ortiz is a little older than me. He's Hispanic and from Texas; I'm a big-mouth white girl from rural Arkansas.

We stood together in the midst of some colossal times on Capitol Hill – and some outsized moments in our national life.

Before I retired from Congress, I told the "Bossman" – as I called him – that when he was ready, I would write a book about his life, easily one of the most fascinating stories in Congress.

When we began talking about this in 2011, the earliest request he made was this: "Tell the whole story, Cathy, not just the good stuff."

So I did that. Solomon Ortiz is a great man, and a good man. But he is not faultless. He is incredibly human. Occasionally childish. Sometimes high maintenance. A man.

This is an authorized biography; the Bossman offered context for a ton of research … and we would talk at length for hours. I didn't think it was possible, but even I learned more about him than I knew in the beginning.

Most importantly, he never asked me to change or play down anything for this book.

While people were remarkably candid about using the names of those involved in the South Texas drug trade, most asked me not to reveal those names in association with what they told me for this biography.

Many of those involved in the vast drug world of the 1970s – the sellers, users or money launderers – have family still living in South

Texas today. So sources for much of this information saw no need to embarrass them for something their family did long ago.

I was lucky to have talked to my old friend, Noemi Martinez – "Grandma" to so many, the last living "Ortiz Cheerleader" from Robstown – for this book in 2011. Grandma passed away less than a year later. She would have liked this story.

As a long-time advisor to – and writer for – Congressman Ortiz, for much of the machinations of the last 20 years of Ortiz' congressional service, I had better than front row – daily – access to the Bossman and his decision-making process.

More often than not, I was in meetings where decisions were made and strategy was assembled. I knew his story in Congress from way inside.

I worked in his campaigns from the mid-1990s on ... and so much of the story of his congressional-political life I saw much closer up than most people might have imagined.

When I began this biography, I began with the premise that the Bossman lived an extraordinarily lucky life stumbling into opportunity after opportunity. In several instances, though, I found that he made his own luck ... as often as destiny jumped into his path.

For this book, I talked to the people who have known the Bossman the best and the longest ... people who were there for the highs and the lows, in Texas and on Capitol Hill.

They provided awesome insight.

Nearly all of the stories herein, before my association with the Bossman, are based on the memories of those who were there when events happened.

This gives all of us an extraordinary look inside some difficult moments in our national history ... as well as the very human insights associated with law enforcement, legislative, military and diplomatic circles.

Solomon Ortiz' life so far has been a remarkable journey.

– CT

1 – THE BEGINNING

THE ORDINARY LIFE of an extraordinary man began on June 3, 1937 in Robstown, Texas, as Solomon P. Ortiz screamed his way into the world. The son of Feliciana Ochoa, a maid, and Jose N. Ortiz, a gardener, the baby boy was the firstborn in a family of migrant workers.

It was during the Great Depression – and it was long before any social safety net existed. He remembers hearing the sirens and church bells that sounded when World War II ended; he was seven years old.

The neighborhood in which he grew up was known as Canta Ranas [Singing Frogs] because the area flooded so easily after heavy rains.

"My most enduring memories of family life in my childhood were the laughter and joy of our family," Ortiz said. "But the darker experiences loomed very large, too. We were poor migrant workers. We knew we were poor."

Ortiz' most lasting memory was hunger, a memory that still cuts very deep in his psyche.

"We were reminded that we were poor every day … with the ever-present hunger pain," he said slowly. "We were more acutely aware of it if we needed health care or clothes and other things for school."

"When we were kids, the only health insurance my family had was prayer; when Mother was sick, Dad would tell us to pray for her," he said. "That was our health care plan then … that was our insurance. Pray … and don't get sick."

"One of the things I remember very clearly – and very early – was the formal manners our parents taught us," Ortiz said. "It was about both discipline and dignity for them, for us. Mother and Dad were both teaching us about proper behavior, even when it seemed to us that there would never be a time we'd need it."

Every morning, all the Ortiz children had to offer a proper cultural greeting to each parent; they kissed their father's hand saying, "Good morning, Dad" … and then kissed both cheeks of their mother with the same greeting.

"Boys are always hungry, whatever their circumstances, but add to that we had to divide the little food we'd scrapped together to eat that day among the seven of us … and hunger is the thing I think of when somebody asks me what I remember most about growing up," Ortiz said. "Happy and loved, but always hungry."

"When I was training for the Army, I was the only one who was accustomed to working on an empty stomach," Ortiz said.

The dynamic for the times was different from the later 20th Century and beyond. Race relations today are more nuanced, more focused on economic progress, and a perennial fight over what taxpayers are willing to pay for in terms of assistance to the very poor.

But in the early-mid 20th Century, race relations worked exactly one way: if you were white, people who were Hispanic or black were required to show deference regardless of age.

"I loved my Granddaddy — he was so smart about the world," Ortiz said. "Plus his looks were interesting. He was a Mexican, but he was very light skinned, so much so that he was sometimes mistaken for being white."

But not always.

"I still remember walking down the street with Granddaddy," he said. "If a white person was walking toward you, you had to step off the narrow sidewalks into the street to show the proper respect for Anglos. He would tip his hat, step off the sidewalk, and look away. It was humiliating."

"Very early on when we were traveling and picking vegetables, I remember living in barns at whatever farm we were picking. Going to school as a little boy was a luxury," Ortiz said. "You did not work, you did not eat. That was drilled into us as they taught us to speak."

"We always saw interesting things on the road, things we wouldn't see in Robstown," Ortiz said. "Mountains, canyons, cities, people.

Once in Michigan – I don't remember the town – we were picking cucumbers in a field across the railroad tracks from where Eleanor Roosevelt was speaking."

Smiling as he remembered the very first time he saw a political figure, Ortiz said, "We were all little kids – talk about child labor, there were no laws then. My sister and I were picking together this particular time."

"On Saturdays, they would take us to town for supplies," Ortiz remembered. "We were on the side of the railroad tracks. Eleanor Roosevelt got off the train and we recognized her; she was probably about 50 feet away. She was visiting there – don't even know if it was an election year or not – but I'd seen her face when Mother and I would read paper together."

"I can still remember riding in the truck with tarp over the truck bed when we drove to find work picking fields," Ortiz said. "There were usually several families of us, traveling and staying together. We stayed in barns with blankets over ropes to divide the place into tiny rooms for whole families to sleep, and cook."

"One of the things I remember that still stings was seeing so many places with signs that read: 'no Mexicans or dogs allowed'," Ortiz said. "That does something to you as a kid. But my mother was a great lady of faith. When those hurtful things crossed our paths, she told us we were all God's children – just everybody didn't know that yet."

Ortiz remembers the pain of other children at school laughing at him because he wore the same clothes every day.

"Clothes for school were not a priority for us when eating and paying for the house were our main concern," Ortiz said. "When I was a little boy in school – we could only afford one outfit of clothes for me when I went to school: a red shirt and a pair of pants."

Those painful memories of poverty and being teased by classmates burned into the young boy's brain ... and they never went away.

"Mother washed the clothes every night so I would be clean at school the next day," he said, swallowing hard at the memory. "She said as long as we went to school clean, that was the most important thing – not how many clothes we had."

"She also used that experience to teach me – all of us – that life is a marathon, not a sprint," he said. "What happened at school in the hallways or on the playground didn't matter ... all that really mattered to her, to us, was to get an education."

"She told me this, and I've used this ever since," he said: "Getting an education is the single thing – the silver bullet – to finding a good job and a better life."

"Another thing I didn't have was shoes," Ortiz said. "Lots of other kids didn't have shoes either, but most did. That wasn't so bad in South Texas, but the winters were hard without shoes. I shined shoes when I was a little bitty kid, as young as 6. I'd go downtown with my shoeshine kit. Guess that was my first small business."

"If we weren't out picking crops and I wasn't in school, I was mowing grass or downtown shining shoes," Ortiz said. "That was where I was first introduced to law enforcement. I was so little. The bigger boys would see me getting money for the shine, then come and take it from me. The cops felt sorry for me, and liked that I was trying to earn money for the family."

"One of them in particular – Officer Ramirez – he kept an eye on me," Ortiz smiled. "He put an end to the bigger boys stealing my earnings ... and he kept the boys away after that. I admired the policemen so much. They had the power to help people, and they wore great uniforms – with shining shoes – and a gun. I wanted the power to serve and protect."

The power of a lawman to protect a little boy, and the few coins he earned, made a powerful impression on Ortiz. It was the first, most significant public service the little boy could imagine.

He wanted to protect others like that. His career of choice, even that young, was law enforcement.

The lack of shoes as a boy might have sparked Ortiz' lifelong interest in shoes. In Congress, many decades later, Ortiz was always noticing the type and condition of shoes people wore.

"I bought my first pair of shoes with my shoeshine money ... probably before I was 10," Ortiz said. "Well, they weren't actually shoes. I bought a pair of moccasins; they were much cheaper than real shoes – one dollar, I think. Down side of moccasins was when it rained, the water soaked through the seams. So I didn't wear them when it rained."

"Our childhood ... we were so poor, it's hard to quantify for today's generation," said Ortiz. "We were lucky we owned our little house. When you are that poor, you can't make much money, and there is nobody to borrow from. Your family is as poor as you are, and banks don't take a chance on people without money."

"There was a central shed located in town where people sorted vegetables that got picked that day, by size, and tossing out the soft or damaged ones into a pile just outside the door," he explained.

"We went by that trash pile several times a day and grabbed whatever unspoiled food we could to take home," Ortiz remembered, grimacing. "You could salvage a lot of food out of the vegetables they threw out in a day. We'd cut off the rotten or soft spot, and the rest of it was fine."

Typically, the Ortiz family meals consisted of beans, rice and chilies.

In Robstown, everybody is family – either several times removed, or they become extended family. In the case of Richard Borchard, this Ortiz extended family member followed him to the County Commissioners Court – then served as Nueces County Judge. In 2012, he was serving as a commissioner for the Port of Corpus Christi.

"We all grew up together – as one big family," Borchard said. "My earliest memories include Solomon and the Ortiz family and our church. We all went to our grandfather's church; Solomon's mother was my Sunday school teacher."

"No kidding, we literally grew up in the church. No drinking, no smoking, no dancing, no lipstick – none of those things," Borchard said. "Solomon was older than me. Our association growing up was entirely about the church. He was the president of the youth group. I really thought he'd grow up to be a preacher."

Even as a very young man, Ortiz drew people to him. "Everybody looked up to him; he was a good speaker, a leader already," Borchard said. "Solomon was very Christian, a very hard worker, always working. It was – well, it was a boring childhood. It was not a typical upbringing … very fundamentalist … no movies, no dancing."

"When I was 12 – Mother was pregnant with [the youngest sibling] Oscar," Ortiz said. "We hardly ever went to doctors, but she was very sick and was afraid for the baby. Since she was going, she took me with her."

"The doctor told Mother she should take vitamins – and pointed to me and said the boy needs to take vitamins, too, or his bones and muscles won't develop," Ortiz said.

"When we got outside, Mother started to cry – and she apologized to me," Ortiz grimaced. "She said we couldn't afford vitamins for me or for her, but she would take them while she was pregnant – for the baby. She was so upset. I told her I hadn't needed them yet – not to worry, I didn't need that."

It was the painful experiences of his youth that – decades later – most often informed Ortiz' choices in public office. He viewed the questions about poverty, federal spending and health care through the prism of his own painful personal experience.

Noemi Martinez – who died in 2012 – knew Ortiz all his life. In a small town like their hometown of Robstown, everybody knows everybody ... and lives intersect several times over.

For both families, the church was the center of their lives. Noemi's husband, Adam Martinez, was a member of Ortiz' church, and his longtime friend. Adam's father was the pastor.

One of the church's most active members was Ortiz' mother, Feliciana Ochoa.

Like most mothers in those days, while the men earned the money, the women kept the faith, parented their children, and earned what they could to help support the family.

The Ortiz and Martinez family followed that dynamic.

"I'd seen Solomon growing up, in the church, around town, so I knew him growing up as a little boy," said Noemi Martinez. "But the first chance I had to observe him up close, to see his nature, was as his Sunday School teacher."

"What struck me then was how much respect he had for other people, and how much respect he had for his mother," Martinez said. "He was a very smart, engaging young man. Even then, you could see that people listened to him, they liked him. I knew he would be a leader one day."

The way he behaved in church, Martinez said, was the way he behaved everywhere else she saw him around town.

At age 16, young Solomon's father, Jose, suddenly died of a heart attack, leaving his wife and five children without a provider for the family. As the eldest son, Solomon shouldered that responsibility.

"Dad died at age 43 in December," Ortiz said sadly. "We buried him on New Year's Eve; it was very surreal. We could hear everybody around us celebrating ... while we grieved for Dad and feared – even more – what would come."

Oscar Ortiz was 15 years younger than Solomon and the baby of the family, the "love child," Oscar said. "My earliest memories are of the church and the things we did there – those were our activities."

Oscar Ortiz remembers the painful poverty of their childhood. "Christmas gifts were the little bags of apples from the church," Oscar smiled. "In Mother's house, if you looked hard during the day at the walls, you could see the sunlight through the boards."

Oscar, eight years younger than the next oldest sibling, talked about growing up with the neighbors, in a mixed race neighborhood of blacks and Hispanics in Robstown.

"Neighborhood kids looked after each other," Oscar Ortiz said. "I don't remember Dad and grew up in the only single parent household in the neighborhood. I felt a little funny about not having a dad. Solomon frequently stood in for me as a father. He knew a lot of people, had many extended friendships, so the family was large."

"We were as poor as everybody else we knew, so we didn't feel particularly different in Robstown," Oscar Ortiz said. "All the houses did have a tiny porch – that's where we all gathered to talk and play. There were no TVs there yet."

Oscar smiled at the memory of the first TV in their neighborhood. "The first family that got a TV, it was easy to tell where it was – every young guy in the neighborhood sat on their front porch to see in the screen door and through the window to watch the TV."

"After Dad died and I had to leave school to earn a living for us – that was an especially difficult time for Mother, having emphasized the need for school above all else … then seeing me leave school to go to work," Ortiz said, his voice trailing off. "We had no other choice. But she said for the rest of her life how much that broke her heart."

"I wasn't a fool – we had very little money," Ortiz said. "And no way to get money. It wasn't so much a choice as a necessity. Most nights I went to sleep hungry. We would find food anyplace we could."

He dropped out of school and went to Fort Wayne, Indiana to work with an uncle who was a carpenter for two years.

Lonesome for home and not making enough money there to

justify being that far away, Ortiz returned home to work at the *Robstown Record*, the local newspaper, to provide an income for his mother and younger siblings.

"I first met Solomon at the *Robstown Record*," said Sam Keach, the former publisher of the *Robstown Record*. "I was still in junior high; he's a couple of years older than me."

"To know Solomon Ortiz is to know where he came from," Keach said. "At age 16, still in high school, suddenly he was the breadwinner for all these kids and his mother, he had all this responsibility ... responsibilities that should never fall on a child."

"My dad [Carroll Keach] said, 'you've got so much on your shoulders,' and he gave him a raise to help a little," Keach said. "Back then, we used letter press printing, and we'd go home sloppy with ink every day. I was just a little bit younger than Solomon and Joe Perez – they both worked at the paper, played jokes on me, treated me like a little brother."

"One day, there was a substantial storm, a mesquite tree where we lived, the tree had split, and fell over fence," Keach laughed. "Daddy told Solomon and Joe to go cut off the part that fell and chop it up for cooking mesquite barbecue. They cut down the whole tree. Daddy was mortified. So were they, but it came to be a big joke among us."

His mother was – quite simply – an outsized influence on the young teenager, Noemi Martinez said.

"Solomon was his mother's boy," Martinez said. "Remember, by age 16 he was both an orphan and – suddenly – the family breadwinner. Losing his father was so very hard. It probably would have been easy for him to turn away or look for comfort in unhealthy ways."

"But his mother was his champion, and after he lost his father, she made sure he was at the church, keeping the faith," Martinez said. "His mother was a very Christian lady – always praying for Solomon and Oscar, for all the children. She even organized a prayer chain so the church could pray for his first campaign."

Ortiz' job at The *Robstown Record*, his hometown newspaper, was as a "printer's devil."

"I'd come home filthy at the end of the day – covered with ink," Ortiz said of the newspaper job, explaining that printer's devils applied the ink to the letter press at the paper, a very dirty job. "I came home covered in ink every night. But it was best job I had back then and I met some people who would stand with me for the rest of my life."

Ortiz' earliest ambitions were simple and close to home: he wanted to make money to feed, clothe and house his family.

When he dreamed about the ideal job, he dreamed of law enforcement – or one day working at the Corpus Christi Army Depot, a long-time civilian-operated military base whose mission was repairing helicopters for the U.S. military and other U.S. security forces.

Working at CCAD – the local moniker for the helicopter depot – was, and remains, a common ambition for South Texans. CCAD offers great jobs for veterans, Hispanics, and others in the community.

But it remained law enforcement that tickled the fancy of young Solomon Ortiz.

He met many policemen and other officers as he lugged his little shoeshine kit around Robstown looking for people who regularly wanted their shoes shined.

"The police officers had great shoes," Ortiz smiled.

They all befriended him, regaling him with stories of good guys and bad guys and offering him advice about how to live his life. They made a deep impression on the young man who was defined by abject poverty and who would lose his father early in his life.

Talking to policemen made him think about law enforcement as a job; it was respectable and it was important. But for Ortiz, it was still pretty far down the road.

2 – MILITARY SERVICE

STILL SEEKING A job to bring in more money to his family, Ortiz tried another tact in his early 20s in 1959. He joined the Army. While on the one hand it would take him far from his family – something he did not want – it would provide a consistent income.

"When Dad died – we were heartbroken, we were lost, we had no idea how to go on," Ortiz said. "Between my parents, they held three to four jobs. Dad was gardener and took odd jobs; Mother was a maid and a babysitter for other families. Now we were minus one mouth to feed, but also minus two incomes."

"It was such a hard time for everybody," Ortiz mused. "The only thing we had going for us was Mother owned the house. But that was it. The overarching question was how to feed the family. I got a couple of odd jobs. Still, that came nowhere near making up for the income Dad was bringing in."

Desperate times called for desperate measures.

"One day I walked in to the Selective Service office at the bank – and volunteered for the draft," Ortiz said. "The lady said, 'Solomon, you don't have to do this; your daddy died.' But I had found out the Army would send an allotment check to Mother since I was now the family breadwinner."

Ortiz had found a job that would certainly be hard, but it meant that the Army would also send his mother a monthly stipend while he was away.

The stipend to his mother was enough to build a new kitchen in their tiny home. It was a lot of money for a penniless kid from a tiny town with no choices.

"It was the hardest – but the easiest – decision I'd made by that point in my life," Ortiz said. "There were zero options for me in terms of a job at CCAD, or in a company, or someplace near law enforcement. Those dreams were very far away."

"The decision was easier still because I could get my GED [high school equivalency] while in the Army," he said, an argument that finally swayed his mother to support the choice. "Plus I could take correspondence courses from there on police procedures. I hoped I'd be eating better, too."

The Army physical was traumatic for a kid who'd never had one. "My friend David Esquivel went to the Army with me; we went to San Antonio for the physical. We were in the same boat as far as medical care in our life," Ortiz stopped to laugh at the memory.

His face reddened. "I mean, the doctor said spread your cheeks and I put my hands on my face, pulling back my cheeks," he said. "The doctor had to tell me, 'not those cheeks.' It was just very traumatic. I'd had no idea what a medical physical consisted of."

"I was scared to death," Ortiz admitted. "I'd only been out of South Texas in the back of a truck during picking seasons as a migrant worker, and in Indiana. When we were picking, I'd seen Michigan, Arkansas, Oklahoma, Ohio and California where my family picked fields – and all the places in between. Saw it all from the road, in the back of a truck. But that was with family – and this was a different dynamic."

He was all alone.

"I'd never gone out on my own so far away from family," he said; he'd had family around when he was in Indiana. Even basic training at Fort Hood, Texas, seemed as far away as the moon. Already homesick and uncertain about his decision, Ortiz still plowed on, determined to see it through.

He knew he had no other choice. Plus, he'd promised his mother he would take advantage of the opportunity to get his high school equivalency diploma, in the Army.

The eight weeks of basic training at Fort Hood were very rough, Ortiz said, with a lot of harassment. Ortiz chose his Army specialty there. It was the first time he realized that the Army also had policemen. He chose the military police as his military specialty.

It was also where he learned to peel an orange.

He had not quite expected the military to offer that entre to law enforcement tools and procedures. He trained at Fort Hood, then got advanced training at Ft. Gordon, in Georgia.

"They tried to break us there," he said. "But that's how it works. All kinds of harassment. If you can survive, you're in. I survived. I had nowhere else to go."

"Most people complain about food in the Army," Ortiz said. "Not me. I didn't eat well until I got in the Army. We never had fruit at home, unless we'd found some in the trash pile beside the vegetable shed. But mostly that was vegetables. We couldn't afford fruit or meat."

"Mother cried a lot," he said quietly, eyes wet.

Private Ortiz deployed to France in 1960, for his tour of duty in Verdun and Vitry Le Francois. It was the first time in his life he flew on a plane, and it was a transatlantic flight to Europe.

"We landed in Paris, this guy from West Virginia – his name was Richard Hogan – and me, we had a room in a hotel; we were just there overnight," Ortiz said "But it was Paris, when were we going to be there again? We saw the Eifel Tower far away, and we walked and walked – all night long."

"It was kinda magical," he smiled. "We met up with another soldier and a young lady. It was another world. Hogan and I were wearing Army camouflage; we hadn't wasted time changing clothes. Then this French movie star stopped the car when she saw us; she wanted to take a picture with U.S. soldiers."

Still so lonesome for his family and South Texas, Ortiz nevertheless dug in for the European military adventure. He made good use of the time, getting his high school equivalency while he was serving there.

The profession that still both fascinated and eluded him was law enforcement. He was a MP wearing a uniform and carrying a gun, but not exactly solving crimes just yet. He was still hearing from his friends in South Texas who were policemen or worked for the Sheriff's office.

His first six-month duty in France was at Verdun, on a U.S. military base, and it consisted of policing traffic at base gates, investigating accidents, and following the black market. Later he was transferred to a patrol unit.

Almost a year into Ortiz' deployment, one day during a typical barracks inspection in Verdun, France, Ortiz' commanding officer, Captain Zook, found books on investigative procedures and police techniques with his gear.

Zook commanded the U.S. Army's 61ˢᵗ Military Police Company, Criminal Investigation Office.

Ortiz had been working on correspondence courses from the Institute of Applied Science, an investigative and identification school for police work in Chicago, Illinois.

"You interested in detective work, Private?" Captain Zook thundered.

"Yes, sir," Ortiz answered enthusiastically, so happy someone with power was interested in his professional goals.

That simple, seconds-long, conversation would launch the next phase of his professional life. Captain Zook reassigned Ortiz to the Criminal Investigation Division, where he was a "Provost Marshall Investigator," akin to a chief of police, Ortiz said.

At last, like the heroes of his childhood, Solomon Ortiz was a law enforcement officer. Even better, he was an investigator, not just chasing down drunken soldiers off base.

He remained an investigator for the duration of his two-year tour of duty.

Ortiz enjoyed the fulfilling investigative work. "Understand the mindset then, we were deathly afraid of what the Soviet Union was doing … the Berlin Wall was going up in Germany and the Cuban Missile Crisis was still very fresh in our minds," he said. "It was an exciting time, and a scary time."

Ortiz – and other MPs – directed traffic and policed the soldiers at the crossroads of Europe where the Berlin Wall would give illustration to the division of Europe. "Everything was coming right down the middle at us. We just knew there was going to be a war."

"I enjoyed my military service, even when I was so lonely for my home and family," Ortiz said candidly. "Had it not been for my stint in the Army, I would not be where I am today. Without the Army, I'm certain my life would have taken an altogether different path."

When his tour of duty was up, Army Specialist 4ᵗʰ Class Ortiz returned to South Texas a changed man. "After my discharge – through Brooklyn – I came home," he smiled. "I flew in late from New York, to Houston, where we got in so late I had to sleep in the airport. Now, nobody knew I was coming. Flew to Corpus, then went to my house, but nobody was home."

"I fell asleep on mother's couch, and my grandmother Vivian

woke me up," he said. "'God told me you were going to be here,' she said to me." Then, suddenly, he was overcome with the reality of being back in his family's arms, back home in Robstown. "My faith originated with her," he said of his grandmother.

Like so many young people, he went into the service as a child — but came out a confident man.

He brought back with him the skills he needed to be in law enforcement.

3 – LAUNCHING A LIFETIME OF SERVICE

BACK FROM FRANCE and his enlistment, Ortiz threw himself back into the community, serving as a mentor to young people around town and at the church.

"I was glad, and proud, when he joined the Army," Sunday School teacher Noemi Martinez said. "He wanted to learn new things, to have new opportunities. When he came home, he looked like a taller, more mature version of himself. He was more confident; he'd seen a world far from Robstown, beyond the state and the country."

The job market in South Texas was still bare, even with his newly acquired skills and contacts. That was burdened further by the social climate of the early 1960s across Texas and the American South.

Racial discrimination was as rampant as it traditionally had been, but the injustice of it was becoming more apparent through TV.

Many Americans at the time heard a sanitized version about it – then saw the unvarnished brutality and patent unfairness of it via the unblinking eye of a live TV camera; people who before were content to ignore the dark underbelly of U.S. society were appalled.

"Obviously, we were aware of the Civil Rights movement that had begun in the 1950s, and reached its zenith in the 1960s," Ortiz remembered. "What the country remembers about that time period is the experience of blacks in the deep South. There was a whole 'nother experience in South Texas."

The incident that laid bare the racism of some in the white community, when it came to the Hispanic community in South Texas, was the refusal of the funeral home in Three Rivers, Texas, to

19

bury Private Felix Longoria.

Army Pvt. Longoria, born in Three Rivers, was killed on a volunteer mission during the last days of World War II in the Philippines. His badly mangled remains were not recovered until 1948, when they were returned to his home in Texas.

The Three Rivers cemetery, like many across Texas, had a "Mexican" section separated from a "white section" by barbed wire.

The director of the funeral home refused to let the Longoria family use the chapel, alleging previous Mexican American services caused "disturbances," and because, most tellingly, "the whites would not like it."

"I was just a little kid when this happened," said Ortiz. "But I remember hearing about it – we all did. I was old enough to understand death and burying people – but I didn't understand then why in the world cemeteries separated Anglo and Hispanic dead."

"I certainly didn't understand why they felt the need to separate them by barbed wire," he added. "Really? Barbed wire to keep the dead people apart? I still don't understand the logic behind that."

"For us, the Civil Rights movement in South Texas revolved around Dr. Hector Garcia – who founded it – and the American G. I. Forum, a civil rights organization for Mexican Americans," Ortiz remembered.

"Dr. Hector taught us to fight racial discrimination with political pressure ... nonviolent political pressure," he said. "First, he called the funeral home himself to make a reasoned argument. 'Longoria had died fighting for his country.' They still refused."

So Dr. Hector convened the new organization he founded, the American G. I. Forum, and they began sending telegrams to congressmen, senators and the White House. Senator Lyndon Johnson answered quickly to offer his support.

Then Sen. Johnson surprised all sides by arranging for Longoria to be buried at Arlington National Cemetery, with full military honors.

That likely did not please the whites in Three Rivers either.

"On the day Dr. Martin Luther King, Jr. was killed in Memphis, we all heard about it ... but it just didn't affect us as much as finding a way to eat," Ortiz said quietly. "I was campaigning during the later years of the Civil Rights movement. By then, I'd been living with the black and Hispanic community my whole life, so we were family. What affected any of us affected all of us. His death was a national tragedy."

"Dr. King was a great man," he said. "We were all peripherally aware of the movement, but the more urgent task for everybody was making money for food, or to pay the bills."

CONSTABLE

The structure of county law enforcement in Texas includes several constables, also elected, for sections of the county.

"When I first met Roy de Alejandro [the incumbent constable who Ortiz defeated in 1964], it was his first campaign. I thought he was a good guy," said Ortiz. "He came by the *Robstown Record*, where I worked then. I even helped him with ads for the newspaper. He won that race, and I was headed off to the military."

"By time I got back from France, there were so many stories of him being politically controlled by the guys higher up," Ortiz said. "People wanted to be policed by a constable that answered to Robstown. Everybody was complaining about him, saying Roy was being manipulated by the local white police force. People wanted somebody to run against him and beat him. But there wasn't a natural candidate, and it was frustrating."

"My best friends then – my compadres – said that I should run against him, that I was somebody people knew, and that I was fresh back from the Army," Ortiz smiled. "I laughed. I was sure they were kidding me. But the faces looking back at me weren't laughing. They were smiling, but not joking. It scared me to death."

"I was just back from France and was trying to increase my law enforcement credentials," Ortiz said. "I wanted to get a job at the Army Depot, or the police department or sheriff's office – maybe the Rangers. But that was my direction, where I wanted to go.

So there was finally a moment in his young life when he had options. But he'd been away from Robstown for too long – in Indiana, then in Europe for his military service – and he wanted to help. He was selling insurance part time to pay the bills, but still dreaming about a career in law enforcement.

The core team of Ortiz' compadres in that first campaign included: Johnny Calderon, Adam Martinez, Esequiel Gonzalez, David Esquivel, Pete Montalvo, Jesus Luna, Abraham Enrriquez, Fred Serna and Fidencio Lopez.

Convinced by his friends and contemporaries to run for the office of Nueces County Constable, Ortiz eventually jumped at the chance to use his military law enforcement experience in the real world.

"My compadres kept at it until I agreed to do it, but I made them promise to be in it with me," he said. "I was sure I would lose. So I wanted to share the pain some."

What Ortiz feared most about running for constable was that in doing so, he might short-circuit his law enforcement career before it had begun.

"Besides losing and being embarrassed, it was possible I'd be tagged as a troublemaker – and that would keep me away from a law enforcement job," Ortiz said. "But I was young and stupid ... and idealistic. It was time for somebody to try. If you never try, you never know."

His first campaign for public office was the classic case of political and ideological naiveté whacked around by the political reality of 1964, the final election year before the Voting Rights Act of 1965 abolished literacy tests and poll taxes.

"After I decided to make the run for constable, I started making the rounds, talking to voters and trying to get support," Ortiz smiled. "Looking back, I was such a kid and I had no idea what I was doing."

"When I was out one day, telling people I was running for constable and asking them to vote for me, an old friend was excited for me and asked when I'd filed for the office," said Ortiz, who had no idea about the mechanics of a campaign. "Told him I was gonna file the next day. So I did. Even took some of my compadres with me for a show of support."

"I was so proud to file my candidacy with the Democratic Party," he shook his head. "I went up to the desk and told them I wanted to file for the office of County Constable. I filled out the papers while my friends there milled around. When I was done, the clerk asked me for the $600 filing fee."

"That surprised the heck out of me, and my friends who'd been chatting in the background were suddenly silent," Ortiz remembered, grimacing. "I couldn't afford supper that night, much less $600 to run for an office I might not win. It seemed like such a gamble, and I'm not a gambler. Plus I had no idea how to get that much money. Might as well have been $6 million."

Recovering just enough to smile and ask if he could bring the fee by later, Ortiz and his compadres took off and spent the rest of the day trying to think of a way to get the money.

Doing what he always did when he needed to make a decision and get straightforward advice; he went to his mother's house and outlined the situation, the facts, and money he would need for the filing fee and for a bare-bones campaign.

"My mother could care less about politics," Ortiz smiled. "For all the help she gave me and inspiration she gave me – because she believed in me – she really didn't care for politics."

The Ortiz family didn't own anything but their house. So, after the worry and the tears, Ortiz' mother kept his first campaign alive by taking out a $1,000 loan with their house as collateral – $600 for his filing fee, and the balance to help offset the poll tax for Hispanic voters whose priority was putting food on the table.

Motivated before, now Ortiz was strapped with the knowledge that if the campaign lost, his family would have lost $1,000 on a gamble he was taking.

And Ortiz didn't gamble with money.

That meant that he was going all day and all night, spending like a miser, running for the office.

When he got into the race for constable, most people were surprised, Noemi Martinez, the Sunday School teacher, said. "The most common reaction [to his candidacy] was shock. That a young Mexican American would run for office! How would he get money? We weren't part of the political landscape. How did a political campaign work?"

They made do with what they had, learning as they went along.

"We used our garage for a makeshift headquarters, making signs, making plans, making lists, asking people to take tasks," Martinez said, describing the evening campaign meetings at their tiny home.

The adults sat around the yard in chairs from the church; the women inside cooked supper for everyone; and the children played underfoot.

The core group of Ortiz volunteers was a group of young mothers in Robstown, including Noemi Martinez. Dubbed "The Ortiz Cheerleaders," these dozen or so women were the organizers who never stopped working to see Ortiz elected.

Led by the widely-loved, dynamic Crisanta Lopez, the Cheerleaders were the ones who made the phone calls, found space for the campaign's events, and raised money by selling menudo (a

Mexican soup) and other Mexican foods.

Other Robstown-based Cheerleaders included: Linda Flores, Maria Silva, Beatrice Perez, and Eva Gracia.

"Crisanta was the head Cheerleader, and she was so efficient, so hopeful, absolutely fearless," Martinez smiled. "She was so useful for Solomon. He always realized that – and always gave her, and all of us Cheerleaders, credit for the work we did."

If the Cheerleaders were not gathering at the Martinez house, they would gather at the fruit stand owned by Crisanta and her husband.

Ortiz and Jesus Luna, plus Jesus' little grandson, literally walked house to house in that first campaign around Robstown. "He was right there beside me, like we were connected at the hip for the months of that campaign."

"Solomon was the first Mexican we'd ever heard of running for political office. It was just a dream," Martinez said. "Everybody was happy, but scared… some were jealous. Just running for office was so audacious. Suddenly anything was possible."

Eventually one more candidate joined the incumbent and Ortiz in the primary, Jesus Trevino. Another candidate changed the political dynamic. Now the race was not one-to-one, with a winner needing over 50%.

The race would be to force the incumbent into a runoff. That could change the momentum heading into the runoff.

"In my first campaign, people knew me, but hardly anybody called me by my name," Ortiz smiled. "They either referred to me as 'Chanita's boy' [Chanita was his mother's nickname] … or 'el chamaco'– the kid. No kidding, conversations went like: who you gonna vote for? El chamaco, you know, Chanita's boy."

Ortiz' mother was much like a Mexican Rose Kennedy, writ smaller and in South Texas – her charm and relentless support drove the voters to Ortiz, despite the fact she was not enamored with politics.

By primary Election Day 1964, the easygoing former Army MP was riddled with anxiety about his campaign. He was certain he was going to lose and he was mortified by the prospect.

"On election day, I was completely surprised when I saw cars and cars of Anglos driving Mexicans to the polls, paying the poll tax, and telling them who to vote for," Ortiz winced. "None of us had expected that. I thought, 'I'm so very screwed'."

He discovered later that most of them were taking the money and voting for Ortiz anyway.

Right after the polls closed, Ortiz remembered what had been bugging him all day, something he was supposed to remember. He slapped his forehead.

He'd forgotten to vote. His stomach roiled even worse.

Ortiz was so nervous at the election party that night that he just couldn't stay there. He didn't want his friends to see his face when he lost. But he still wanted to hear the election returns.

He went to his car to listen to the returns on the radio, safely out of view of his friends and supporters to monitor election returns.

"I was so new to this" Ortiz remembered, smiling. "There I am, alone in my car, trying desperately to find election returns on the radio. I can't even find KROB. Suddenly, there's a huge racket on the back of my car – I thought it was hooligans or something."

"It was my compadres coming to tell me we'd won – sort of," he grinned. "Everybody was talking at once – it took me a minute to actually get the news I'd held the incumbent constable to under 50%. We'd succeeded by making it into the runoff!"

Ortiz had "won" about 900 votes, Roy de Alejandro got around 1200 votes, and the other candidate ended up with around 500 votes.

Two weeks later, the new darling of Nueces County politics was more and more confident he would win. The lousy showing of the incumbent in his primary sounded his political death knell.

The night of the election, Ortiz spent every minute of the party thanking supporters. When the results were complete, Ortiz had defeated the incumbent constable in the runoff election by winning 55% of the vote. That was the entire election; no Republican ran against him in the general election campaign that fall.

"When I won that first primary, Mother was sitting outside in the lawn chairs," Ortiz said. "I told her I won, and she said, 'That's good mihijto [my little boy].' She was proud ... and maybe a little unimpressed. Maybe like she expected it."

Or maybe she was just a little unimpressed with politics.

"He had to take on the traditional Anglo establishment," Keach smiled, shaking his head. "He made waves as a constable. Things were a mess; the drug trade was just awful, so he dug in. Solomon knew the guys that were part of the drug trade – he'd grown up with 'em."

"After he won, it was like the sun shined brighter, the world was prettier," Noemi Martinez said. "One of our own had won a political office, even when the powers were stacked against us. That single event meant the world to our little town – to all the people in it."

"I got my bonifides as a little bit of a bad ass with the Robstown community right after I was sworn in as constable," Ortiz said with a smile. "There was a gas station back then, McGee's, in Robstown, where everybody hung out. One night, a lady came to McGee's, frantic, disheveled, and with bullet holes in her car."

"She was screaming, crying, and said her husband was violently drunk, chased her out of the house, kept the children there, and shot up the car," Ortiz said. "So they called me. It was my first thing, to arrest a violent drunk holed up in his house with guns and two kids."

"I took Adam Martinez with me – he stayed in the backseat, praying the whole way," Ortiz said. "We were going to need it. It's the worst case scenario for law enforcement. A violent guy – armed and holed up with kids. I'd literally just taken office – hadn't even gotten my first paycheck yet."

"The wife he'd chased off led us back to their house, but she stayed at the gate, pointed to the house and said, 'good luck'," Ortiz smiled. "Adam and I were trying to decide if we should go in with great muster and show of force, or go quietly."

They went with the element of surprise.

"We went quietly, to surprise him. I went in front; Adam went in the back, in case he ran or in case Adam could get the kids out of the way," he said.

"When we got in, the stupid drunk was passed out, asleep; with the kids sleeping there too," Ortiz said. "I tiptoed over, took the gun and cuffed him before he woke up. He came out of the stupor angry and yelling. But we had him under control. He wouldn't shut up, threatening us, being loud."

"Before I took him to the pokey, we went to McGee's to fill up the car," Ortiz smiled broadly. "We actually went by McGee's to show the people hanging out there that we'd captured a violent offender right off the bat. We never said we caught him asleep. He was so drunk, he didn't even know."

"But that little event captured the imagination of the folks in Robstown, both supporters and opponents, and cemented my reputation as fearless, unafraid of dangerous situations," Ortiz said.

"I probably should have been a little afraid, but I was young, a little stupid, and awfully brash. The good Lord protected me in my stupidity."

The good Lord protected him quite a lot actually. Not long after disposing of the drunk who kidnapped his kids, Ortiz had another nut job to deal with – very publicly.

"I'd just been constable about a couple of months, and I got a call that a guy had a gun, and had lined his neighbor's family up against a wall," Ortiz said. "Flores was the guy with gun; he'd come to complain at my office for something silly, I can't remember now what the complaint was."

"So here I go, wading through the crowd – just me and a deputy sheriff, Ted Jolly," said Ortiz. "Hundreds of people had already gathered to watch the drama – to see the idiot who was waving his gun, making threats and terrorizing his neighbors. I asked him to put the gun down. I knew not to go for my gun; you become a threat to somebody unstable, then that forces them to act."

"I just stayed as calm as I could, never took my eyes off the guy with the gun, never trying to control the crowd," Ortiz said. "It took a while – probably about 30 minutes of talking to get him to put down the gun. When he did, I cuffed him, put him in the car, and called one of the two deputy sheriffs in Robstown – who weren't there to help me – and they took him over to the Nueces County jail."

"I was in high school, a sophomore or a junior when Solomon came back from the service and ran for constable. Then he bought a car," Borchard recalled. "I remember that car – it was a hot rod."

"When Solomon was constable, the story went out that Solomon was gonna shave the heads of the kids he picked up," Borchard laughed. "It was the 1960s and everybody had long hair. It was a psychological weapon – nobody wanted to lose their lovely locks. The threat of it probably kept a few people in line."

"In his first campaign for constable, Solomon rounded up me and my friends – we were his earliest advance team," said Oscar. "We knocked on doors, asking for votes and spreading information."

"When Solomon was constable, I was in junior high," said Oscar. "I remember lots of fights. People would be going at it, then somebody would say, 'here comes Solomon,' and everybody would scatter. For young guys, getting caught could be real bad. Kids' parents knew Solomon; kids knew he would punish them, then their parents would, too."

"There were beer joints in front of our house," said Oscar. "In cotton-picking season, people would go there to blow off steam. That frequently led to fights. Solomon always got called first since he was so close."

"The black people that came into town and got in fights or got in trouble, didn't know Solomon was family with area blacks, that we'd grown up together," Oscar laughed. "When the outsiders would throw down with the constable, they were always surprised when the blacks from Robstown stood with Solomon."

"That was when I became aware of domestic violence," Oscar said thoughtfully. "Lots of times people were at our house talking about their most personal issues. It never ceased to amaze me — sometimes he was cop, sometimes counselor ... all the tender young age of 25-26."

"I remember the constant flow at our house, and hearing people talking to him about all kinds of things ... problems, ideas, politics, whatever," Oscar said. "People would see his car at our house and stop to talk."

"Solomon knew what it's like to come from abject poverty – he's a remarkable politician," Keach said. "He wouldn't have been able to do what he did if he hadn't come from that background. It was a big deal when he ran for constable."

"In 1968 after Solomon beat Frank Gallagher in the Democratic Primary for commissioner, the establishment got another Hispanic who'd carry their water to run against Solomon as a Republican in the November election," said Keach. "Solomon cleaned his clock too."

Ortiz learned the fine art of South Texas politics at the county level in Nueces County over the next 12 years, serving as constable until 1968, when he successfully ran to serve on the Nueces County Commissioners Court.

In the late 1960s, Ortiz married Irme Roldan and they began a family. Their oldest, daughter Yvette, was born in 1971. Son Solomon Jr. was born in 1977. In what Ortiz has termed his greatest personal disappointment, their marriage began to disintegrate.

"Before we married, we talked about the nature of my life – how our life would be with me as a public official ... always on call, never with a dependable schedule," Ortiz ruminated. "That life is very hard on a young family. I worshiped my kids. They were amazing little people from the get-go. Still are."

"A lot of things happened between us, and we proceeded to a divorce," Ortiz said slowly. "My entire concern was for the kids. She fought me for them. She was so vindictive. Yvette was six or seven, and Sollie was just a baby."

"My lawyer said consider this: Yvette is old enough and brassy enough to tell you if she's hurt or lonesome or out of sorts, but the baby isn't," he said. "You take Sollie and have Yvette stay with Irme – get past this obstacle."

"Irme had already moved out and the kids and I were in the house," Ortiz said, wiping his eyes. "Yvette and her mother were out running errands, and when they came home, I had all of Yvette's little things in front room. Gawd, that was a painful moment."

"But neither one of us expected how our brassy daughter would weigh in," Ortiz smiled. "She was upset at seeing all her things there. She said, 'why is my bike, my stuff in here?' We told her – then she told us."

Young Yvette said, "I'm not leaving Sollie. Ya'll can leave each other, but we stay together."

They always did. Ortiz and his children lived together under the same roof – with Ortiz' cousin-in-law, Rosa Lopez – until they moved out as young adults.

A native of Guadalajara, Mexico, Rosa Lopez first met Solomon Ortiz when she came to Corpus Christi for his wedding to her cousin, Irme.

"They needed somebody," Lopez said. "Solomon and Irme owned a restaurant [The Tejano] and a bridal boutique." So Lopez remained in Corpus Christi, living with them as family during the nine years of the marriage.

His young children, Yvette and Sollie, were already very attached to Lopez. "It was a natural thing for Solomon to ask me to stay during their separation."

"When Yvette cried for her father, I'd call Solomon, who'd come to see her," Lopez said.

Her relationship with Ortiz, Lopez said, was sometimes family, sometimes friend.

Ortiz said the same about her, but added, "Nobody was a better sounding board for me than Rosa."

"My wife left me in such debt," Ortiz lamented. "I was paying her child support, and the kids were living with me."

"Irme and I met when I was constable, running for commissioner," Ortiz said. "She didn't like politics at all and was glad that I was running for commissioner; win or lose, that would get me out of law enforcement." He paused. "Maybe we just fell out of love," he said quietly.

Having tried marriage, Ortiz was determined not to enter into another relationship quickly or lightly. He never remarried.

Rosa was (and remains) a sounding board for Ortiz, and was a surrogate parent for Yvette and Sollie.

"Rosa was the key to letting me serve in Congress," Ortiz said. "I am so grateful to her. She practically raised the kids while I was back and forth to Washington."

Known affectionately as the "Rose Patrol" by young Sollie's teenage friends, Rosa was a firm hand in the children's lives.

When Solomon decided to run for Nueces County Commissioner four years later, now-Cheerleader Noemi Martinez said, the shock that he was running for higher office wasn't nearly so profound.

But there were still people who discouraged him, declaring that he should hold onto the gains of one Mexican American elected official in the county.

But this was another campaign, one with a larger constituency and more people-to-people work … plus the authority to speak to decisions of the county commission.

"Frank Gallagher was the incumbent commissioner," Ortiz said. "Some of the politicos told me not to run, that a Hispanic had never run for the Commissioners Court. The Hispanic politicos came to me said they'd help me get reelected for constable. But you won't win a race for commissioner."

Ortiz, who'd confounded expectations before, was respectful but unconvinced. There was also the desire of his family for him to get away from the moderate danger of working as a constable.

"Think I got about 1,600 votes in that election, he [Gallager] got about 1,200 votes," Ortiz remembered. Ortiz was getting new and more respectful looks from area political watchers and power brokers.

"I remember in his first [primary] race for county commissioner; his headquarters was a little store on Main Street," Oscar Ortiz said.

"His opponent walked in on election night to congratulate him. That impressed me. That would never happen now. Nobody's that classy."

In the November election, Ortiz ran against a Hispanic Republican, Beto Escobar.

"There was just so much excitement when Solomon ran for commissioner," Oscar Ortiz said. When his big brother was sworn in, he was officially the first Hispanic to serve on the Nueces County Commissioners Court.

"After Solomon was elected commissioner, he went to the church to thank everybody," Martinez said. Then she got quite a surprise. It was back in the day when husbands gave permission to wives in matters of important decisions.

"My husband, Adam, and I were very active in the church," Martinez said. "After church, Solomon said, 'Adam, I want Noemi to come work for me.' I said, wait, what? Wait … I need to pray about that," so surprised she was at the offer, and in overhearing it first posed to her husband.

"I finally said OK, and the Lord helped both of us," Martinez smiled, describing the work as largely clerical, including organizing jury summons and helping people apply for poverty programs.

"The people who came to the office … I never imagined the problems people had," Martinez said. "So I had to learn about the various troubles, and how to help them with paper work and applications."

From 1968 until 1976, Martinez toiled with Ortiz in the tiny, nondescript office on the outskirts of Robstown. She remembers that work as eye-opening for her, and considered it some of the most important work of her life.

"We were a movement, but we didn't really think of it that way at the time," Martinez said. "When I talk to kids today, I tell them how far we have come, how hard it was, and how much better their lives are because of those early efforts, and the courage of Solomon's first campaigns."

In 2011, Republican Nueces County Sheriff Jim Kaelin remembered fondly his friendship with Solomon Ortiz, a friendship that has spanned four decades.

"I met Solomon back in the late 1960s," Kaelin recalled. "In 1968, I came back from Vietnam, looking for work. I worked for

Sheriff Johnnie Mitchell, and Solomon was County Commissioner."

"We actually met in classes at Del Mar [college]," Kaelin said. "It was a funny position for me. As a County Commissioner, Solomon was my quasi-boss, with me working at the Sheriff's Department."

"But Solomon was great," Kaelin said. "We became really good friends and established a good working relationship that still remains. Then Solomon ran for sheriff, and won."

4 – THE DREAM OF HIS CHILDHOOD

ORTIZ SERVED AS county commissioner until 1976, when he was elected Nueces County Sheriff. There he made a reputation as a tough but fair lawman – and a fearless warrior against the drug trade. That brought him squarely back to law enforcement, his political trademark.

"A lot of people didn't like what the incumbent sheriff was doing," Ortiz said. "He wasn't having any success at wrapping up a major murder in the area. People started asking me to run for sheriff. I asked, 'How much does it pay?' When somebody said it was the same salary, I said, 'why should I run?' I was told not to be selfish," he smiled.

Intrigued by it, and having missed law enforcement while he served as county commissioner, once the idea was introduced, Ortiz got more and more excited by the prospect.

"But until now, I had never run countywide," Ortiz said. "Every race has a different dynamic – and a countywide race would include Corpus Christi, the biggest chunk of voters in the county, who did not know me. All they really knew was I was a Hispanic from Robstown. Some knew I was on the Commissioners Court, but that was it."

But winning the votes and the confidence of the sizable Anglo community would be a racial and political briar patch. Ortiz had shattered expectations before, but by now he had started a family and

33

had children.

Yet Ortiz slowly gravitated toward the sheriff's race, calling supporters and others to gauge their thinking on the race. Word began to spread that he was interested enough to be asking around.

But Ortiz had piqued the interest of the local kingmaker, Hayden Wilson Head. Hayden Head was the godfather of South Texas politics in the 1970s, a major political figure/fixer on the Corpus Christi scene.

"Hayden Head was just larger than life – he was also a pilot, he had a ranch in Mexico," said Frank Tompkins, a Corpus Christi realtor who now lives outside Austin. "He was a major mover and shaker around the state and internationally. Mr. Head wasn't really a Republican or a Democrat; he just pursued his interests."

"To do that, you had to be able to talk to people in both parties," said Tompkins, who was also Ortiz' long-time campaign manager. "His [Head's] influence was understated; he was real easy going, asked for things respectfully. If he didn't get what he wanted, he just asked somebody else. And didn't ask you for anything else."

Before there were political Action Committees (PACs) or super PACs, there was Hayden Head in South Texas.

"Mr. Head was a major player, not an elected official, but he was the essential guy to go-to in the political world," Ortiz said. "I was told to go talk to Hayden, so I did. We had a very long conversation about the state of law enforcement, the politics of a countywide race, and the possibility that Nueces County was ready to elect a Hispanic to the county's top law enforcement office."

"I was very impressed with him [Head]," Ortiz said. "He was candid that he was unhappy with law enforcement's handling of the prosecution of [stepson] Randy's murder. Hayden was a God-fearing man, a law-and-order guy, a businessman. He liked to get things done."

While Head was impressed with Ortiz, he had a couple of other dogs in the fight, Ortiz said. A new political movement, *La Raza Unida* [The People United] had emerged in Hispanic enclaves around Texas, including the Robstown area.

"Solomon always maintained he was a Democrat – long before *La Raza Unida* – even though he had sympathy with some of their ideas," Oscar Ortiz said. "But their tactics were just too confrontational. Some of my friends at college liked *La Raza*, wanted

Solomon to be part of the movement. But Solomon was always more about compromise than confrontation."

The establishment wasn't that worried about *La Raza Unida* as a political movement; its activists were agitating, and frequently moved to violence – either on their own or instigated by others.

But Head's other – more personal – motivation to help elect a new county sheriff was the murder of his stepson, Randy Farenthold.

Randy Farenthold – the multi-millionaire playboy stepson of gubernatorial candidate, Frances "Sissy" Farenthold, the grand dame of Texas Democratic politics – was found brutally murdered in the surf off Mustang Island in June, 1972.

Randy Farenthold's mother, Annie Blake Morgan, was married to Hayden Head.

The ballsy playboy was a gambler, and wildly popular as a stand-up guy among the crusty fishermen on the Gulf Coast. His gambling habits and subsequent debt was initially speculated as the impetus for his murder.

The gruesome killing nauseated the entire state. Farenthold was beaten, slashed, tied with wire, chained to a concrete block and dumped in the ocean.

Jim Peters, the famed Texas Ranger who investigated the case, found out Randy was a key witness in a coming federal fraud case involving a Corpus Christi contractor Bruce Bass (a known Mafia gambling enforcer), according to the book, *Jim Peters: Texas Ranger* by Lee Paul (Oct 1, 1997).

The trial was set to begin four months after Farenthold's murder.

Farenthold had reported threats on his life to local law enforcement and his Federal Bureau of Investigation (FBI) handlers, but tragically, nobody took those threats seriously. Without Farenthold's testimony, the fraud case against Bass was dropped.

There was still no indictment for the Farenthold murder, but hundreds of officers, investigators and law enforcement agencies ran over each other in the following years trying to determine the events around the murder, who pulled the strings, and who literally did the job.

In *Jim Peters: Texas Ranger*, author Lee Paul said Peters flipped "wise guy" Robert Walters (in jail near Houston) who said that Bruce Bass had asked him to set everything up for the hit. Walters said his brother, Donnie, helped him arrange the logistics for the murder.

Walters also told Ranger Jim Peters about another person involved in the hit with Bass, according to the book, but the man was never prosecuted. Several years later, the second man purportedly died from a heart attack.

By then it was 1975, and law enforcement was excruciatingly close to indicting Bruce Bass for the Farenthold murder. *Jim Peters: Texas Ranger* said then Bass was in a bad car wreck. As he lay close to death, police officers, so close to arresting him, got frantic. "If he dies," one said, "we'll never close the case."

But Bass recovered, pleaded no contest and was sentenced to 16 years in prison on June 20, 1977.

Bass won early release from prison, serving only six years, and then he was shot to death in Corpus Christi on June 6, 1984 ... 12 years to the day after Farenthold's body was found in the surf off Mustang Island.

As Ortiz was considering the sheriff's race in 1976, law enforcement had not yet rolled up all the conspirators, and Head was anxious for that long public family nightmare to be solved.

According to several people who remembered that time, Head believed that the current sheriff, Johnny Mitchell, had missed opportunities to run down the rest of the conspirators. As the election approached, Bruce Bass was arrested and was held in the Nueces County Jail.

In 2012, Senior United States District Judge Hayden Head, Jr. discounted the contention that either *La Raza Unida* or the Farenthold murder had anything to do with his father supporting Ortiz in the beginning.

"He [his father, Hayden Head] supported Solomon because he liked him," Judge Head said.

Hayden Head Sr.'s support was essential for Ortiz to win a county-wide race in1976. So far, he'd only won races centered on his base in Robstown – not the Corpus Christi area.

Ortiz was in the race ... and now on the outs with his wife.

"Mr. Head gave me money, and helped me raise money with the Anglo community," Ortiz said. "That meant that other Anglos could be convinced to either support me financially or endorse me. Or in some cases, at least not oppose me."

Head's support was gold for Ortiz's political success. He told Ortiz to go see Vernon Smiley – a Corpus Christi public relations expert. Smiley ran the press and marketing operations for top-level candidates in South Texas.

"I spent so much time writing my speech to announce candidacy," Ortiz smiled. "Vernon Smiley saw it, wadded up and threw it away. 'Speak from your heart,' he told me."

Head also arranged for a campaign manager for Ortiz, someone who could speak for him to the Anglo community, far across the divide from the Hispanic community. He needed somebody to give Ortiz a little credibility with the Anglo community.

"My friend, Mike Kendrick, was a young partner with Hayden Head," said realtor Frank Tompkins, who was about to become Ortiz' campaign manager. "One day, they [Kendrick and Head] took me to the Corpus Christi Town Club and asked me to support Solomon for sheriff – now ... I was just a young buck, scratching my way in the real estate market in Corpus Christi."

"I was not in a position to say no – I'm thinking, what do I do?" Tompkins remembered, laughing. "I didn't even know this guy. But I sure knew Hayden Head. Mr. Head was the kingmaker back then – both politically and business-wise. It was a little bit intimidating to be there with him in the first place."

"They told me this guy's been a constable and a county commissioner; their motivation was to replace Johnny Mitchell [Ortiz' predecessor as Sheriff]," Tompkins said. "They were very clear about that. Don't think I put it together in my head that it had anything to do with the Farenthold murder, but looking back on the timeline I expect that's exactly what it was."

"My friend Mike told me 'we need somebody in the Anglo community to help Ortiz win, and get Johnny Mitchell out'," Tompkins said. "We ended the meeting with me not sure what I was getting into, but agreeing to do this for Mr. Head. You just didn't say no to Mr. Head."

"I met Solomon the next day [following the Town Club meeting with Head]," Tompkins said. "Solomon is such a lovable guy, not bombastic, just all about figuring things out. That's why he stayed in office for so long. It was hard not to love Solomon. Same with Lencho. Both of them became a big part of my life."

Becoming the Hispanic political sensation in the area, Ortiz captured around 40% of the vote in a five-candidate race for the sheriff's office. Political watchers then dubbed Ortiz the 'golden boy'

– with a fearlessness that drew people to him.

"Lencho [Rendon] was an extraordinary narc; he was a legend in the South Texas Narcotics Task Force," Ortiz said of his then-Chief Deputy. "On his first assignment, I put Lencho undercover in our own jail. We had a suspect related to the Randy Farenthold murder, somebody we'd hoped could be an informant for other conspirators. It had been an incredibly high stakes investigation that had ended with a mafia figure convicted, but law enforcement knew we never fully wrapped up all the conspirators."

In a bizarre loop of history, Farenthold's son, Blake, was Ortiz' 2010 Republican opponent, in a year when circumstances conspired to keep the percentage of voters low enough to eject Ortiz from Congress by over 700 votes.

"Hayden Head was a Republican, and Randy Farenthold's stepfather," Keach said, remembering the political dynamic of the late 1970s. "Nobody was trying to close down the case [Farenthal's murder]. Nobody was brave enough to go after the bad guys, except Solomon. Hayden never forgot."

"Hayden Head was the guy who made Solomon's political career beyond constable a reality," remembered Lencho Rendon. "But Solomon wouldn't even take his call when he was in Congress. Solomon just didn't wanna be owned, and he sure didn't wanna say no. When Hayden called, he had to go through me first. Didn't matter how big or how little the kingmaker – Solomon just didn't wanna be owned."

Conversely, Rendon said, "Now if Joe [Nini] Perez or Benny Benavides or one of the Cheerleaders called, Solomon would take their call right away – he'd even leave a committee hearing to take a call from one of them. They couldn't own him – they were poor as church mice, but with hearts of gold. Solomon's people. That's who he fought for."

Just after he was elected Nueces County Sheriff, Ortiz attended a convention of county officials in Laredo, where he would meet a man who would stand with him in law enforcement and Congress for the next 40 years.

"It was after the 1976 election, but before I was sworn in as sheriff," said Ortiz. "I'd planned to go to the convention anyway, but was also recruiting staff for my sheriff's office. My friend, Elida Gonzalez, told me I should interview her cousin – his name was Solis

– he was the chief deputy in the Webb County Sheriff's office."

In Laredo, Ortiz said, everybody was excited to have a Hispanic sheriff in Corpus Christi, with a large percentage of Anglo voters. That was an enormous accomplishment at that time.

"Solis brought a big fella with him," Ortiz smiled. "His name was Lencho Rendon. I interviewed them both. I tried to hire them both, but both had taken jobs with other agencies. Solis called me early in December to say he'd accepted the job with the state. Then at the last minute, right before I was sworn in, Lencho called to ask if the job was still available – he'd changed his mind."

"When I met Solomon at a state conference, I was the personal bodyguard for Salvador del Toro Rosales, Mexico's Deputy Attorney General in charge of organized crime," Rendon smiled. "He was ballsy and brave – and unlike most Mexican judicial officials from the 1970s, he lived to be an old man."

"Del Toro was the speaker at the conference. My former chief deputy from the Laredo sheriff's office was the guy who introduced us to Solomon," Rendon said. "My first impression of him was that he was humble, a real 'people person,' and a straight shooter. We ate breakfast the next day and he talked about Nueces County, how much he cared about people there, and the multitude of drug problems in Corpus Christi."

"I was tired of running for my life in Mexico," Rendon, the former undercover agent for a joint DEA-Webb County Task Force, said. "I'd already taken a job with Bob Bullock in Austin, but I was so intrigued with Solomon … intrigued with starting with a new sheriff's office from the ground up."

"Every time I talked to somebody about him, they only had high praise" Rendon said. "To a person, they talked about his character, his fearlessness, his ease with people. All that convinced me to take the job with Solomon."

Rendon started as a deputy … rising rapidly to sergeant, then captain, and finally to chief deputy. Eventually, Jim Hickey was Ortiz' chief of administration and Rendon was his chief of operations.

"Solomon asked me before he took office as sheriff, if I'd come to work for him there," Borchard said. "Told him I didn't have any law enforcement experience, but he said I gotta fill a bunch of jobs, I need you to work in the office, doing administrative things."

Ortiz already knew what he would be going up against as sheriff, and he knew just one bad apple in his department would color everything that followed. He didn't just need deputies in the field covering his back; he needed every single member of his staff to be true blue.

"He depended on loyalty, needed people he could trust," Borchard said, describing the surreal nature of the first days in the Ortiz sheriff's department. "I went to pick him up to go to Corpus Christi. As we drove, police traffic on the radio kept giving a location, 'SPID' [South Padre Island Drive]. Neither one of us knew what that was. The street names had just changed, we knew it as 'Lexington'."

But it was one more thing that made the big city of Corpus Christi seem just a little more foreign to the old friends from Robstown.

Nueces County Justice of the Peace, Bobby Balderas, first met Ortiz when Ortiz was county commissioner, at the same time Balderas worked at courthouse in 1974. Balderas was one of the few officers Ortiz held over from the previous sheriff's department.

"Solomon interviewed everybody personally," said Balderas. "He cleaned house big time. He wanted to make sure we knew what he was doing and that he'd have our unconditional support. Solomon was the kinda guy who knew everybody by their first name anyway. If he was with a president of this or that, he'd stop and introduce you to him – no matter who you were, no matter who he was."

Richard Borchard illuminated another – subtle – racial undercurrent that made Ortiz a more palatable candidate for the Anglo community of Corpus Christi in the 1970s.

"Here's what really helped Solomon with the Anglo community in the 1960s," Borchard said. "The establishment did not want change, and another party showed up: *La Raza Unida* [The People United]. They got very radical. We fought them and won. The white community was very grateful. That went a long way to make the Anglo community comfortable with Solomon as a local leader. That helped a lot in the sheriff's race."

"When I was elected sheriff, the inmates were literally running the jail," Ortiz said. "They had 'tank bosses' that ran what went on inside the jail, dispensing favors and such to inmates."

"When I took office, the inmates in the jail rioted the next day," Ortiz said. "Had to teach them they didn't run the place anymore, so I responded with a pepper fogger machine. That got the word around pretty good. It was a new day in the Nueces County Jail."

There are very few times that the phrase: "There's a new sheriff in town," is literally appropriate. But Ortiz' election was one of them.

After working as a jailer for nine months, Ortiz put Balderas on patrol in one of what was then one of the hardest areas of the county: Robstown and enclaves west of Corpus Christi.

Two things were in play out there: the Bandidos drug gang's razing of the community, and *La Raza Unida*, which was not a violent movement, but which held rallies that sometimes turned violent and which added tremendously to the headache of the Ortiz Sheriff Department.

Ortiz needed to trust – absolutely – every single person in the Robstown sheriff's outpost. So he stationed his former Sunday School teacher, and staffer in his commissioner's office – Cheerleader Noemi Martinez – in the Robstown office of the county sheriff as administrative staff and working ID (fingerprinting) at the sheriff's office.

"I was still a rookie when he [Ortiz] started the 'Special Squad' – the drug task force," said Balderas. "I was young and cocky. They asked me to join them on the task force, one of several officers on it."

Balderas also offered institutional memory for his new boss, as the only holdover from Johnny Mitchell's Sheriff's Department.

Jim Kaelin, who met Ortiz as a county commissioner, had joined the Texas Department of Public Safety (DPS) after his college graduation. Eventually, he moved back to Robstown, after the stint with DPS.

"I wanted to be a businessman, opened a business on Main Street in Robstown," Kaelin said. "But I needed a salary while we developed the business. It was around 1981, and Solomon hired me as a deputy sheriff."

BANDIDOS

In San Antonio, circa 1966, a Marine veteran of the Vietnam War founded a motorcycle club known as the "Bandidos."

First a refuge for discontented veterans and other hard partying people on the fringe of society, the hard drinkers dabbled in small-time crime, quickly growing into a sophisticated criminal gang.

The raw brutality of the Bandidos grew with astonishing speed.

Soon their tentacles reached deep into all the bars, gambling, prostitution, massage parlors, and illegal gun smuggling interests in South Texas.

More tellingly, they were the 1970s version of the cartels that formalized in the late 20th century. The Bandidos assumed control of the Texas drug trade in South Texas.

By the late 1970s, the Bandidos had morphed into an organized crime syndicate responsible for those enterprises in South Texas, and were now the contract killers of choice in South Texas.

The real advantage the Bandidos had in those days was the generosity of the bribes they spread thick around the courthouses and police precincts of South Texas – with a very friendly reception in Nueces County. Sheriff Ortiz' jurisdiction.

The Bandidos didn't limit the bribes to law enforcement and judicial officials; they bought a little respectability in the business community by laundering money from the drug trade and other criminal enterprises through "respectable" businesses.

Business people nobody would ever suspect routinely raked in tens of thousands of dollars at the low end – hundreds of thousands of dollars at the high end – to deposit drug money in their accounts to launder it back to the Bandidos.

Texas Monthly [April 1, 2001] described the criminal gang this way: "If you weren't living here thirty or forty years ago, you might not have any idea who the Bandidos are. You probably have no inkling that they were once the terrors of Texas, so fearsome that when a rumor spread through a town that they were coming, people literally headed inside their homes and locked their doors."

"Just after Solomon was elected Sheriff, the Bandidos sent a guy over with a sack of money, hoping to get him from the beginning; they said they wanted to talk, to do business," Rendon said. "The Bandidos hoped Solomon would keep open their bars, massage parlors and gambling houses; a big chunk of the drug proceeds were channeled through those businesses."

"The top guy for the Bandidos – he ran gambling houses, bars, and such," Ortiz said. "When I was sheriff, he sent a Bandito to me; he said 'we can work together, do business.' I said 'What?' He was operating the massage parlors – god knows what else."

"He said I should assign a trusted deputy to be the 'bag man'," Ortiz said. "Then on whatever day, he told me 'you go to separate establishments to get money.' This had been the way they operated with the sheriff's office before. They wanted that arrangement to continue."

"I told him 'I want no part of this, there's a new sheriff in town'," Ortiz said. "Then I started raiding the massage parlors. There are legitimate massage parlors, but many back then were being used to launder money and for prostitution."

Ortiz said he never touched a dollar in bribes. "One of the few benefits of growing up poor," he smiled. "Can't be bought. Don't belong to anybody."

The Nueces County Sheriff's office was on the front line of the 1970s drug wars. Task forces between the FBI, the state, and counties offering more and better tools for law enforcement would come later.

Plus, Ortiz — and his talented captain of the narcotics division, Lencho Rendon — offered a cadre of informants, knowing the best way to get information was inside the room where drug deals were going down.

Rendon was already Ortiz' indispensable ally.

The sheer volume of money and bribes was endemic in South Texas. Ortiz was a lonely crusader; and it was a dangerous business. Fooling around with people's incomes and reputations was traumatic and dicey business.

Everybody Ortiz, and his sheriff's department, touched was angry and wanted revenge.

Ortiz' employees in the department were not immune to the bribes. It was rare, but just one officer turned by bribes was way too many for Ortiz.

Congressman Silvestre "Silver" Reyes (D-TX), of El Paso, met Ortiz in the early 1980s.

Ortiz and Reyes bonded first over law enforcement in Texas, then over mutual issues in the United States Congress.

Reyes first met Ortiz while Reyes was a young buck with the United States Border Patrol.

"I was in the regional Border Patrol Office in Dallas, Texas, when I first heard of Solomon Ortiz," said Reyes.

"We'd gotten intelligence on a big marijuana shipment the bad guys were moving by fast boat from Matamoros to North Padre Island, off Corpus Christi," Reyes remembered. "It was one of their new routes and it landed them north of the [Border Patrol] checkpoint in Kingsville."

Given the epidemic of corruption throughout law enforcement in Texas during that period, the Border Patrol had been repeatedly burned with intelligence sharing with local jurisdictions.

So before they shared sensitive information with local law enforcement, they vetted the locals to find out first if the local officers were trustworthy … or on the take.

"So we knew that the local sheriff was named Solomon Ortiz, and every white guy in the room looked at me and said, you're the guy," Reyes smiled. "You're Hispanic, speak the same language – go figure out where he's at."

"So I went to Corpus Christi under the radar and asked questions about Solomon – he seemed to be making the druggies' lives miserable," Reyes said. "He was a little bit of a folk hero to a lot of people there."

"Somebody I trusted down there told me to go talk to Lencho Rendon, said he'll tell you anything you need to know," Reyes said. "So I met Lencho first. He was easygoing and a great cop. They were decidedly under the gun from the drug runners, not on the take."

"He set up lunch for me with Solomon and we hit it right off," Reyes said. "Solomon offered to help us with the drug bust we were setting up for."

That initial operation by Ortiz, Rendon and Reyes netted a big bust. Reyes ensured that the Sheriff's Department got official credit in the form of forfeited assets from the drug ring they busted.

Forfeited assets include vehicles, real estate, cash and other valuables that put money back in local coffers.

The highly successful collaboration between Ortiz' Sheriff's Department and the Border Patrol – with Reyes as liaison – continued until Ortiz decided to run for Congress.

A deeply religious man since his childhood, Ortiz was moved to start a jail ministry, something that didn't exist before.

"Reverend Ernest F. Bennett was in charge," Ortiz explained. "I told him to get the ministers around the community to rotate having services in jail each Sunday, and to counsel inmates. Some of these guys were wholly ignored by the community, even by people of faith."

"It was a very Solomon idea," smiled Lencho Rendon. "It was

noncontroversial, and had the potential to change somebody's life."

"Many preachers got involved in the ministry," Ortiz said. "Many of the younger criminals went straight and even became ministers when they got out. Some wanted to somehow manipulate it to their ends; others wanted no part of it. But we weren't spending any taxpayer's money and reached out to everybody. It's what Jesus told us to do." [Matthew 25:31]

"There was this one mean guy, name was Frank Gonzalez," Ortiz laughed. "He was so touched by the power of God, when some inmates didn't want to pray, he'd try to beat them up. Not necessarily Gonzalez, but there were a lot of guys that changed their lives. We eventually even took a few inmates who behaved to area churches every now and then."

They took them in cuffs and leg irons, so the church visits were rare and unannounced.

"As a congressman, decades later, I was on the road to Brownsville and saw about a dozen bikes – they were Christian bikers," Ortiz smiled. "I don't remember if one of them found God at my jail, or if they knew a friend who did. But they knew my history – they prayed for me. At least one of them was a former Bandido."

But in the late 1970s, the Bandidos were dug in, killing people who got in their way, paying off officials in the police department and the courts. So much money was coming in, there was plenty to spread healthy bribes all around while still pulling in tons of money.

Their lawyers were part of their multitude of criminal conspiracies, said Rendon.

"Solomon ran for sheriff as a drug fighter," Rendon said. "He knew the cost of crime and the allure of the money resulting from the drug trade. The Bandidos were ruthless. Contract killing, no problem. Somebody in their way; if they can't be bought, kill them. Truthfully, most everybody could be bought off."

Ortiz grew up poor. He knew how to survive with no income. He'd been in the military. He preferred to go home at the end of the day, owing nobody. That was a very hard thing for the bad guys to penetrate.

Impossible, as it turned out.

5 – MONEY LAUNDERERS HIT BACK

"WE WERE HITTING drug dealers awfully hard, and upsetting some moneyed interests," Ortiz said. "It never ceased to amaze me the legitimate businessmen in the area who dragged in money hand over fist just to launder drug money. Some were getting an outright cut of drug sales. Others just laundered the money for a percentage of it."

"We had great success with undercover narcs [narcotics officers] buying drugs from bad guys," Ortiz said. "Once we had them, we'd flip them or negotiate down a plea to get the next guy up. Go up high enough and you pull the thread for financing and laundering of drug money. We were making lots of great arrests, everything was holding up in court. We were pissing off lots of people, fooling around with their livelihood."

Bobby Balderas said he was generally aware of the danger to his boss from the Bandidos, but unaware of the day-to-day dynamics of the inner office. "I was on the street. Part of our effort early on with the task force was trying to map out who was who among the Bandidos, and some of the more violent associates of *La Raza Unida*."

To edify, the Bandidos were a violent criminal enterprise; *La Raza Unida* was a political party working for change. They are not the same thing. *La Raza Unida* was a political problem for Democrats at the time.

Bandidos, and their organization, were Ortiz' target, a cancer throughout the body of South Texas … *La Raza Unida* was the bee

46

buzzing around the head.

"We were the guys that were gathering intel for the task force, we were stopping people for any little violation just to get IDs on who was who," Balderas said candidly. After which, he said, the task force could follow up on drivers' licenses and car or bike tags to see who was associated with whom ... and keep track of what drug transit points they showed up at.

"One night we had an informant giving up a big dealer," Ortiz said, as he detailed the operation that political opponents would leverage into indictments against three Ortiz' deputies in his Sheriff's Department, a low point in his service as a successful, ballsy sheriff.

"This dealer was a huge boss for drug trafficking in South Texas and we'd been trying for a long time to flip somebody or find an informant that could get us inside," he said.

"It happened very fast," Ortiz said. "Our informant found out the meet-up place was moved, and we had to deploy real fast. This is long before warrants could be issued in real time."

"The deputies frisked the informant – which we did to reinforce court cases; we could prove then that the informant wasn't carrying something in and faking a drug buy," Ortiz explained. "Then they warned him to be back out quickly."

"The narcs sat on the house for the buy with our informant, and called the office to get the warrant to move on the place," he said. "A deputy at the office applied for the warrant application, using the same language we generally used in applying for warrants."

On the fateful night of that drug bust, an undercover officer on the scene called to say the buy was successful; they needed a warrant to move on the house.

"The way we applied for warrants was an officer signed an application for the judge; there were a couple of phrases that the court required to have a high bar for warrants," Rendon explained.

"One of the things we'd say was 'I have personal knowledge of drugs on the scene.' Since I wasn't on scene, and I applied for the warrant saying I had personal knowledge of drugs on the scene, three deputies got indicted," said Rendon slowly. "It was bullshit, but there it was."

It was that series of events that Rendon's fellow officer, Captain Curtis Hildreth recited to the grand jury, saying the warrant been obtained fraudulently.

Captain Hilliard had been co-opted by the power structure, intent on protecting their significant individual stakes in the lucrative black market of concealing drug proceeds.

Given that the recipients of drug money profits included judicial officers, judges, lawyers, businessmen, and all levels of law enforcement, the system only worked for those that were part of it or bought into it.

Basically, the power structure did to Ortiz what the sheriff and his department were doing to the drug runners – they finally got an inside guy to flip for them.

Courts were not friendly to those who took on the local power structure.

Lawyers, judges and court officers stacked the deck very efficiently from beginning to end – indictments to verdicts – in an insidious slap at the very notion of justice.

Today, the Mexican cartel, the Zetas, drive around in marked vehicles so people will fear them, said Lencho Rendon. "They want people to know they are there. The Bandidos would do the same thing in the 1970s. They'd ride in groups of 10-12 motorcycles wearing the Bandito jackets. It was the same thing, to make people fear them."

Once a cop, always a cop. Rendon's DNA is wired to follow the dynamics of the drug trade – even in 2012. "Eighty percent of drugs we consume in the U.S. come from – or through – Mexico," Rendon said.

"The value of drug trade is three times more than legal commerce," said Rendon, now an international businessman. "Where are the cartels in U.S.? They get legitimized."

It was true then and it is true now. In 2012, the *San Antonio Express News* produced several news stories dissecting the now-legit-looking cartel money that flows through businesses throughout the San Antonio metro area.

"With millions of dollars coming through San Antonio from Mexico every year, it's easy for the *financieros* to co-mingle their drug proceeds with the flow of legitimate money," the *Express News* [April 16, 2012] said. "And it's big money. A top Justice Department official recently said the amount of money that drug traffickers launder in the U.S. approaches $100 billion a year."

"San Antonio has always been popular with the cartels as far as buying properties, houses," the *Express News* quoted Phil Jordan, former director of the Drug Enforcement Administration's El Paso Intelligence Center. That center is a multiagency hub for collecting and sharing information. "On this side of the border, they basically try to stick to the money end without touching the dope."

"The natural cycle of a criminal enterprise is that at some point it has to be legit," the *Express News* quoted Roger Enriquez, chair of the Criminal Justice Department at the University of Texas at San Antonio. "Not that anyone welcomes paying taxes, but there are advantages in that. You have folks that are operating car lots, restaurants, and are paying cash."

"To ensure that their money in the U.S. isn't quickly seized by law enforcement, the traffickers rely on front men who can safely invest it and remove the drug taint," the Express News said. "It's a lucrative enterprise," given the two to three percent profit, but it's a lot of profit, given the amount laundered, a law enforcement officer told the *Express News.*

Former law enforcement officers said money-laundering prosecutions alone are rare because they are difficult to prove and simply are not a priority for the federal government.

"They're long-term, very complex cases that require tenacious and dogged pursuit, and they don't produce quick results," the *Express News* quoted Alonzo Peña, former deputy director of U.S. Immigration and Customs Enforcement.

In the San Antonio-based Western District of Texas, Richard Durbin, head of the criminal division told the *Express News* that money-laundering charges are usually wrapped into indictments for other crimes, such as drug trafficking, but he said, "They're hard to find and difficult to prove."

Phil Jordan, former director of DEA's El Paso Intelligence Center, told the *Express News* [February 9, 2012] it can be hard to distinguish legitimate businessmen from those who launder money for Mexican drug traffickers and corrupt politicians.

"The modus operandi is they stay clear of any contacts with the dope dealers, with the cartel members, and behind the scenes they launder the money through legitimate businesses," the *Express News* quoted Jordan. "As a result, they join the Chamber of Commerce, and unsuspectingly to the real businessmen start rubbing elbows and they become friends to the point where they'll even contribute to politicians on this side of the border."

"In the U.S. today, punishment is more certain – you kill a cop, you are going to jail and most places they execute you after appeals," Rendon said. "In Mexico, they don't care." Brutality is still the coin of the realm for the drug trade out of Mexico … brutality that has frequently spilled over the border.

The Bandidos were the first organized drug cartel in South Texas, with the additional advantage of their heavy investment in law enforcement and the judicial system.

The system was stacked at every level.

"One of the things we were working to change when I was sheriff was the way we picked grand jurors," (the citizens that prosecutors must convince to indict people) Ortiz explained. "Courts were letting litigants pick their friends as grand jurors."

"So the powers that be were literally indicting anybody who got in their way with the dinkiest charges," Ortiz said. "Or they were opening big holes in cases, threatening jurors they didn't pick, to let defendants associated with the Bandidos go free after committing huge crimes."

Either way, Lady Justice wasn't wearing a blindfold in the South Texas of the 1970s – the bitch was looking out for the Bandidos and their vast, entrenched criminal enterprise.

In that environment, District Judge Vernon Harville – a city prosecutor for five years before being elected judge – easily tainted the grand jury in the matter of "the Solomon Three" in a frivolous prosecution … for using the same language law enforcement always used on a warrant for a drug bust in that era.

The target was Ortiz; the prosecution was using the indictments as a weapons to undermine him and his efforts to stymie the drug money in the judicial system.

The prosecuting attorney went after the three deputies first, hoping to build up to something bigger to indict Ortiz for, or hoping to flip one of the deputies to testify against Ortiz for something in a later trial.

Mind you, they had nothing. There was nothing … except that Ortiz was good at what he was doing – and that so many people's financial stake was under assault.

But then, that's why criminal enterprises that include the organs of the justice system are so very efficient.

Also, Ortiz knew something then that has never been revealed before: one of the grand jurors on that case was Ortiz' campaign chairman in Robstown, Alfredo Garcia.

"When he got the summons, he asked us if he should reveal that he was my campaign chairman," Ortiz laughed. "We told him he should just say he did not want to be on the jury. That's what he did. He said he didn't wanna be on the jury — and when asked why, he just said he did not want to serve on this jury."

"Maybe because he was so adamant about NOT serving, they picked him for the jury," Ortiz said. So, like the intelligence they gathered for drug busts, Ortiz and Rendon had a guy inside.

"We didn't talk to him until after the grand jury acted," Ortiz said. "We were careful about that. But that's how we knew that so many grand jurors inside the deliberations were angry the charge was brought in the first place."

"We all knew they hadn't done anything wrong," Balderas said. "Solomon and Lencho kept the concern about all that pretty tight — we knew it'd [the trial] be over quick. The officers and others in the department weren't following all that closely. I didn't read the paper."

The backdrop for this activity was another trial — this one a federal trial — in which another corrupt officer, from Laredo, Captain J.C. Davila had tried to bribe Rendon to change his testimony in an earlier drug case.

That trial ended in a hung jury, a win for the powerful drug financiers in South Texas. Davila was found guilty in a second trial.

In those days, judges themselves frequently chose friends to pick grand jurors who were friendly to whichever side the Bandidos — or the drug money — were on.

Indicting public officials for misconduct was a powerful weapon in the arsenal of drug runners and their many friends in law enforcement and the criminal justice system who relied on the bribe money.

Harville's grand jury indicted the three Ortiz deputies on the bust that night, for a fraudulent application for a warrant in a narcotics arrest.

Throwing every accusation in the book — plus the actual indictment — at the three deputies, the prosecution gave it everything they had, then stood behind the fig leaf.

News of the indictments landed loudly on the steps of law enforcement all over South Texas. The subliminal message: if the drug gangs couldn't buy you off, they had the means to put you in jail on trumped up charges.

Plus … there was always the unspoken revenge; they could also kill you.

"Oh, the day the indictments were handed down was during the sheriff's convention I was hosting in Corpus Christi. It was so humiliating – which was precisely the effect these guys wanted," Ortiz said. "They said to my face, and in headlines: 'you better shape up as sheriff'."

Those were dark days. "None of the Hispanic organizations came out to support me after the indictments came down," Ortiz remembered.

"Solomon screamed bloody murder when the indictments were handed down," Rendon smiled. "Through the press, Judge Harville told Solomon to back off. But Solomon don't do 'back off'."

Both Ortiz and Rendon understood that the indictments only illustrated their success in deconstructing the vast financial enterprise of the area drug trade.

They were about the only people in the Coastal Bend who saw the indictments as proof of the length the moneyed interests of the drug trade would go … just to stop Ortiz' drug busts, and protect the proceeds that Corpus Christi's "respectable" citizens were getting from it.

Rosa Lopez described the dangerous days of Ortiz' service as sheriff from the perspective of the Ortiz home, "We didn't know how much danger he was in; he protected the children and me from that."

"But one day he was pretty preoccupied, and Solomon sat down the kids to have a talk with them," Lopez said. "It surprised me, and it scared me. It certainly surprised and scared the children."

"He told the kids, 'one day I'm going to die, and you'll have to go on by yourself'," she remembered. "The kids were little kids, but old enough to understand things. They cried and cried; they were terribly upset."

Ortiz' drug fighting was cutting into to the bone.

"That dynamic really made Solomon's legend as a drug fighter, the little guy standing up to a corrupt system, with nothing but his gall and sense of right and wrong," Rendon said. "His ethnicity was an issue. Remember that was when Hispanics were just beginning to win local elections across the southwest, including Texas."

"DAs [district attorneys] and judges just really didn't know how to handle Solomon, the county's first Hispanic sheriff," Rendon smiled. "He didn't wanna be part of their 'just-us' system. He knew if he touched a dollar in a bribe, he was done. And he cherished the feeling of not being under anybody's control."

"Solomon was so loved... so respected," Rendon said. "I always knew that before the indictments. But after they were handed down, I saw that in a whole new light. He'd been in public office one way or the other for over a decade at that point and people knew him. Really knew him. Knew he'd keep his word. Knew he couldn't be bought. Knew he'd hurt himself doing the right thing."

A fundraising effort emerged to "Save the Solomon Three," to pay for defense lawyers for Ortiz' deputies. "People sold lemonade, BBQ, little foods – all to provide for the defense," Rendon said. "They were like a family wrapping the whole department up in their arms."

It was the "Ortiz Cheerleaders" centered in Robstown – again – who organized and moved quickly to make a difference. As always, Ronnie Flores and Benny Benavides stood shoulder-to-shoulder with them.

The people who supported Solomon at this critical juncture were an interesting cross-section of Corpus Christi, Rendon said.

Some were uncorrupted business owners, tired of competing against those enriched by the drug trade. But most were the Hispanic working class who'd started Ortiz' career as a constable, and who'd sustained him as he ran for higher office in Nueces County.

After a short trial, the verdict came back on the first of the three deputies charged: Deputy Ronnie Flores, the first of the "Solomon Three" to stand trial, was found not guilty after an hour of deliberations. The next day, charges were quietly dropped for the other two deputies.

Most significantly, the case came down to one line of a law that said if one police officer knows about the presence of drugs from another police officer, the officer applying for a warrant could indeed say that he had "personal knowledge" of drugs in the warrant application.

Dinky crap, so dinky that no grand jury should have billed an indictment … dinky crap later paraded before a jury – a jury embarrassed and confused about why charges were ever pursued, much less adjudicated.

After the deputies were acquitted, the community respect for Solomon as a drug warrior soared. People were so tired of the killings, and the drug money that soaked the local economy.

"This was … disconcerting; and probably spoke to the guilt this guy was carrying," Rendon said. "Curtis Hildreth, the officer that lied to the grand jury and started all this, had resigned after the jury cleared the first deputy to go to trial. He went back to Arizona, where he was from. It wasn't too long after that, we heard he'd killed his family and committed suicide."

Winning re-election for sheriff was not a lock, but with the indictments behind him, the election was Ortiz's to lose. Winning re-election by 60% buoyed his spirit and faith that voters in Nueces County agreed with how he was proceeding. In spite of the trial, his divorce and custody issues, voters stuck with him.

The indictments, and subsequent trials and violence, were both the high point and the low point for the Ortiz sheriff's department. The low point was the public humiliation of indictments on a dinky matter – a false dinky matter, as it turned out.

Everybody in politics knows an indictment nearly always spells the end of a political career. You can indict somebody for picking their nose – and eventually they would be found not guilty since it's not a crime.

But when headlines trumpet an indictment, that diminishes even entrenched political support; it emboldens an opponent to run; it dampens fundraising: and it sets up a primary defeat.

"I just didn't care at that point," Ortiz said. "If they killed me, my kids would get the insurance money. If I lost the primary, I still knew we'd done way more in far less time than all my predecessors – in terms of throttling back the drug economy. Only thing that scared the crap out of me was them getting my kids."

At that point, Ortiz put Yvette and Sollie in private school. "Didn't much like how that looked or sounded. We weren't 'fancy' people. I really couldn't afford it – between the alimony and our house. But I was scared for them. That gave them one more layer of security during the day when they were away from me."

Several law enforcement sources suspected that Bill Banner – the then-Corpus Christi chief of police – had a financial connection to the Banditos. Nobody had proof – there was never an indictment, no formal charge.

It was just rumored, several people said, given the department's conspicuous lack of pursuit of the Bandidos.

"The bad guys were very good, they reached up high into the Corpus Christi police department," Rendon said. "We were just very good at using informants, flipping witnesses. We got into places other cops couldn't get into."

"People trusted Solomon," Rendon said. "In him, they saw a lawman that wasn't afraid of the criminals, who wasn't tempted by the easy bribe money. In fact, we got more leads – had more people coming forward with information and as witnesses – after they couldn't get to Solomon in court."

"They [Corpus Christi power brokers] couldn't stand having Hispanics from this little Robstown, coming over and winning elections, taking over," Borchard smiled. "Just like when we were little bitty kids in church together, Solomon was the leader. He brought people together, they trusted him. He was able to beat back all the forces. Lord knows it wasn't easy, but he did it."

"Some of the judges over there at the courthouse were there for many years," Borchard said, recalling the animosity between the county's top law enforcement officer and the judicial officers in the area. "They were so mad that Solomon was elected – that he was being so successful, it was like they were saying: 'how dare you, sonny boy, go get back in your hole'."

"He didn't care, he just kept on winning," Borchard smiled. "He opened the door. He took a licking for doing all that – it was so much that it was hard to maintain the success. Nobody could touch us. It was a magical time. We had so much hope. Now you knew the Sheriff was somebody you could talk to. You couldn't do that before."

After the acquittal of Ortiz' deputy and the subsequent dropping of the indictments of the other two, the South Texas drug gangs, particularly the Bandidos, were painted further and further into a corner.

To some extent, they were even more isolated from the cadre of people they bribed in the station house and in the courthouse.

Having to utilize their connections in the courthouse, in a trial against a sheriff's deputy – and failed so spectacularly – they were a little isolated in the halls of justice.

Drug runners – and those who profited from their bribes – were in a new place. First, they were accustomed to buying off the local law enforcement, or at least getting to strategic places inside the department. Ortiz couldn't be bought.

Who wasn't on the take? Besides Solomon Ortiz, there were many area businesspeople … but few others. Judges in South Texas – then and now – run for election and must grovel for campaign contributions.

Local officials then were accustomed to Hispanics never questioning anything they did; Hispanics did not talk back to the white establishment. Until now.

Their gamble on prosecuting deputies in Ortiz' department failed loudly. The not guilty verdict for his deputies, and his re-election, meant Ortiz was still disrupting the drug trade, and their income from it.

The drug kingpins were at their last option. Nothing else worked, they were losing this wider war … for the first time.

In 1978, Assistant U.S. Attorney James Kerr was shot at in San Antonio, Texas. Kerr was a fearless prosecutor who was particularly harsh on drug dealers.

Judge John Howland Wood, Jr., United States District Court for the Western District of Texas was known for his uncompromising stand against the drug trade.

Judge Wood was assassinated by a contract killer and drug runner [Charles Harrelson, the estranged father of actor Woody Harrelson], in the backyard of his San Antonio home in 1979.

Nicknamed "Maximum John" for harsh sentences in drug cases, Judge Wood was a target of the Bandidos and the organized crime syndicate of South Texas, according to Rendon.

Wood's murder was the first assassination of a federal judge in the 20th century.

Ortiz and Rendon could never prove it in court, but they believed the assassin was connected to Curtis Hildreth, the corrupt police captain, through both the Bandidos and their lawyers, Rendon said.

The Bandidos were hurting by this point, Rendon said. They'd just exercised a nuclear option: assassinating a federal judge and U.S.

Attorney who displeased them, who hurt their financial empire.

Still, the drug operations were bottlenecked and more and more members of the crime organization were living behind bars, and the flow of drugs, money and weapons was disrupted enough to hurt them.

"The Bandidos had been rumbling about killing Solomon, and that didn't scare him either," Rendon said. "Mostly, we just thought they were full of crap, trying to intimidate him."

"But soon we were hearing from informants and wires that they were planning the execution – the assassination – of Sheriff Solomon Ortiz," Rendon said. "They were watching him to find the best time, and the price on his head soared."

The assassinations of both Judge Wood and U.S. Attorney Kerr always loomed largely in the background as Ortiz' department tried to prevent the assassination of their boss.

"Still, all that coulda still been intimidation, but at that point we were taking it so serious that we were keeping Solomon and the kids under surveillance 24-7," Rendon said. "We were worried that he was gonna get assassinated; he was more worried one of his kids could get kidnapped."

Ortiz and his deputies were pretty much on their own. They'd taken on the establishment and walked away; reputations slandered, yet back intact.

But nobody in the police department, the district attorney's office, Hispanic organizations, or the local political leadership was going out of their way to help Ortiz as he navigated avoiding an assassination or kidnapping inside his family.

They certainly weren't publicly cheering on the bad guys, but they weren't going to help the sheriff stay alive.

"Around the time of the assassination threats, we kicked up our stops to ID people, we were on high alert," Balderas said. "We were stepping on some big toes. When we made the first stop – it was for a DWI [driving while intoxicated] – the guy thought he'd get right off. The look on his face was priceless. We put bracelets on him, marched him away."

The Bandidos had declared war on the Sheriff's department generally and Solomon Ortiz in particular. Ortiz made the only move he could. He went on the offensive ... smartly ... after having mapped out the intersections, going deep into the cartel, flipping lieutenants, and grabbing bag men.

Nueces County Commissioner Oscar Ortiz remembered both the up side and down side of the Ortiz Sheriff Department. "Good for me, I was the sheriff's little brother, so nobody bothered me," he smiled.

"The danger he [Solomon] was in was a little lost on me till one night when I went to his house without telling him I was coming over," Oscar said. "I pulled in the driveway, and two sheriff's cars came up at me fast on each side. That's when I realized the threats on his life were serious, and ongoing."

But Ortiz had Rendon to watch his back; Rendon had come up in the DEA, informing on drug runners, and often staying just steps ahead of a bullet in his brain, as he outran and outsmarted the druggies.

"One day, as a deputy was bringing Solomon to the department, they saw a suspicious van that we'd seen before," Rendon said. "Solomon had a bad feeling about it. Since they were headed to the office already, we set up the take-down right there. There wasn't a big shootout; we just surprised the hell out of the Bandidos, found their scoped rifles, took them in."

"Solomon was a fearless sheriff, the people thought he was the kind who walked softly and carried a big stick," Rendon smiled. "Remember 'Walking Tall,' the 1970s movie about Buford Pusser, the tough Tennessee Sheriff? For a while, we were calling Solomon 'Bufordito' [little Buford]."

Surprising the Bandito assassins and closing off that assassination attempt so efficiently, on the heels of the not guilty verdict for the Ortiz deputies, really took the wind out of the sails of the Bandidos, Rendon said.

The Bandido's criminal enterprise and intimidation was spread over a wide swath of South Texas counties, all individual jurisdictions.

Ortiz took the moment when the Bandidos were off their game to take the battle to a larger field, with more reinforcements.

As a tool to aid law enforcement in the pursuit of the Bandidos and their criminal empire, Ortiz organized a five-county task force of sheriff's offices. Intra-county task forces were not on the law enforcement scene just yet, but Ortiz organized this task force through memoranda of understanding.

"If my task force was not the first in the state, it was among the first," Ortiz said. "They were a very good tool to combat the criminal enterprises around South Texas, particularly the Bandidos. They started off for purposes of hot pursuit [following criminals fleeing police in one county, and passing into another]. Then they grew up to include information-sharing. But they were very hard to set up."

"There were so many challenges," Ortiz said. "Liability was a huge issue; some counties didn't trust deputies from another county … which county would pay for damaged vehicles, or lawsuits that might come. But mostly, each department was afraid to share information, worried who could leak it."

But Ortiz's Sheriff's Department brought a powerful negotiating tool to the table: tremendous credibility, given their successes both at cutting deeply into the Bandidos' drug enterprise … and their success at getting through the briar patch of legal entanglements and crooked court officials so intent on stopping Ortiz' efforts.

"We had one of the very early task forces in Texas," Ortiz said intently. "They were already fighting a full-fledged drug war in Mexico. We were tied up so many ways, law enforcement could only go so far to get the bad guys. You wanna respect constitutional rights, but there were ways to work together, be more organized about our targets."

"Mostly we wanted to authorize pursuits beyond county lines, share information," Rendon said. "But this was the seed that made multi-jurisdictional task forces a powerful tool in law enforcement in the decade to come. At the time, it was absolutely visionary."

That was the point law enforcement formally recognized what Ortiz had known for a long time: the outlaw motorcycle gang was formally given the status of a "criminal organization." So money and resources began to flow into the hands of law enforcement agencies.

The night Ortiz was elected to a second term as sheriff, it was clear somebody was thinking about the possibilities of the next race, as early as 1980, Borchard said. "On Election Night, we were looking forward at a board where they were tallying votes. Late in the evening, somebody wrote across it: 'next, Congress'."

People could see, at least a little bit at a time, that Ortiz' department was chalking up success after success. The department was awfully adroit at knowing what and where the Bandidos were operating.

"The Sheriff's Department went anywhere," Balderas said. "Some people were jealous that we had such authority. Maybe even a little racist. The sheriff covered the county; other local law enforcement had their own corner of the woods."

"We had a couple of riots in Robstown, caused by *La Raza Unida*," Balderas said. "There was this big rally there. A fight broke out and we went to arrest the guys fighting. They hated us. We were the law, and they saw the law as the problem. Mind you, we were Hispanic, too, we just wore badges."

"Anyway, we waded into it to make the arrests, and everybody turned on us," Balderas recalled. "It was just me and my partner – and there were hundreds of them hollering at us. *"La Raza Unida* was just radical. We were all alone out there. People would see us coming and say, look who's here, it's 'Solomon boys." They didn't say it nice."

"We had to communicate by CB radio [outside the regular law enforcement radio communications], we couldn't even trust the constables in Robstown," Balderas said. "You could trust some of the city police [at that point], but the constables were monitoring our communications, so they could warn the bad guys we were coming."

"Our backups were us," Balderas said. "One Bandido, you could talk to; more than that, you got a fight. We grabbed up so many drugs, so many guns, so much money when we stopped for minor infractions. There are great people in the majority of Robstown, they needed help. We were hitting the drug guys hard … pulling in tons of guns and drugs during arrests, just on DWIs and traffic violations alone."

"But Solomon's big thing was the violent crimes," Balderas said. "There was a lot of heroin over there back then, too."

"Solomon put the job over politics," Balderas said. "Once we had a fugitive with a felony warrant out on him, and we heard he'd be at a funeral in Robstown. We met a bondsman at the funeral to bust him, and arrested him outside the funeral parlor."

"Well, the family was hot, went to Solomon saying it was wrong to defile a funeral to arrest somebody," Balderas said. "Solomon said, 'Hey, it's out of my hand, we had felony warrant. My officers were doing their job.' He always backed us up – we knew it."

By the time Ortiz ran for Congress, the Bandidos as a major

criminal enterprise were crippled beyond repair. They remained – and remain still – as a motorcycle gang of minor crime figures along the lines of Hell's Angels.

But Ortiz and his department achieved their most significant goal in removing the Bandido bribes from police and judicial officials. They made it much more risky for businessmen in the area to launder money. That was a huge victory. Plus, the sheer volume of drugs Ortiz got off the streets was staggering.

Despite the risk, local businesses would still launder drug money for the ease of keeping a piece of it.

"Believe me, you will never know – I cannot be surprised – at the types of people who will launder dirty money," Ortiz said. "Nobody can know."

"A woman who worked for me in my Corpus congressional office, her husband was arrested one day in the early 1990s for money laundering," he said quietly, sadly. "You just can't know. I don't know if they ever told Carmen about Robert's arrest; she was dying of cancer at the time."

6 – FIRST CAMPAIGN FOR CONGRESS

"BY THE TIME I ran for re-election as sheriff in 1980, we started hearing about a new Hispanic congressional district in South Texas," Ortiz said. "I loved public service and I loved being a lawman. That was my dream."

"What I didn't know – what wasn't part of my dream – was always looking over my shoulder for the Bandido assassin," Ortiz said. "Or the knife in the back from other cops, lawyers and judges."

"Figured the bad guys should be the ones looking over their shoulder," Ortiz said. "In my thinking, the cops and lawyers and judges ought to be working together AGAINST the bad guys. We all agreed the drug industry, the drug runners, the black market economy was all the bad guy."

"I guess I was a little restless, wondering if getting killed over this was gonna be worth it," Ortiz smiled. "Part of me said, heck yeah. The better part of me remembered I had kids. When you got kids, no decision's ever in a vacuum."

What to do if not the law?

"When I heard about a new Hispanic seat being drawn in the Texas legislature, that got me thinking about the members of Congress I met when I was an MP in the Army," Ortiz said. "They were so interesting, very diverse backgrounds, different expertise. More than one had encouraged me to run for public office."

He'd never given the advice another thought until his Robstown compadres [best friends] first proposed that he run for constable over a decade before.

"But I thought the work Congress did was fascinating," he marveled. "Public policy was going places in the 1980s. I started talking to other sheriffs in our original task force, to see if they'd support me if I got in the race. They were enthusiastic, which encouraged me."

Congressional redistricting – the once-a-decade practice of re-organizing the state population into congressional districts – is always divisive and difficult for state legislatures all over the nation.

It is complicated politically by the fact that most state legislatures are occupied by members who have one eye on a seat in Congress as the next rung up the political ladder.

Texas, however, with pockets of dense populations, in the midst of thousands of acres of sparsely populated lands, presents a giant redistricting adventure.

Add to the dynamic that as one of the most populous states, the stakes of congressional redistricting in Texas – every decade – represent an opportunity for one party or the other to win more seats in Congress.

Add also to the dynamic that political power in Texas is frequently divided; either between the legislature and the governor, or the two houses of the legislature.

That means reaching a resolution on any redistricting plan is always elusive.

Lastly, Texas is one of the states whose redistricting plan (until 2013 when the U.S. Supreme Court struck down the law) had to pass scrutiny with the U.S. Justice Department, by virtue of the Voting Rights Act (VRA).

The Voting Rights Act required that some of the southern states – with a rich history of screwing minorities in terms of political representation – have their redistricting map analyzed by the lawyers in the Justice Department's Civil Rights Division.

All these components mean that over the last four decades, the redistricting map in Texas has spent at least a little bit of time in courtrooms or before federal judicial panels.

The 1981 redistricting of Texas congressional boundaries was as rambunctious as promised. The legislature needed a special session to pass a congressional plan, finally finishing on August 10.

But the Department of Justice objected to two South Texas districts in the legislature's plan and the court said that those objections invalidated the entire plan.

The federal district court redrew districts in South Texas, creating a new seat along the Gulf Coast of South Texas, the 27th Congressional District, the stage that would launch Ortiz into the U.S. Congress.

The new district was anchored in Nueces County, south to the Mexican border – including the counties of Kleberg, Kenedy, Willacy and Cameron.

In terms of running for Congress, Borchard said few people supported that effort when they heard about it. "Everybody wanted him to stay where he was," Borchard said. "We wanted our leader to stay."

Despite the time constraints – or perhaps taking advantage of them – Ortiz jumped into the race for the 27th District, a new seat in the United States House of Representatives in Congress.

"When they drew the new Hispanic Congressional district – I met with Solomon, Lencho, and Mike [Rendon] in a hotel room," Frank Tompkins remembered. "Solomon asked me if I'd support him in the race for Congress. That caught me by surprise, I really didn't expect that. I didn't commit right then, wasn't sure what to do."

Unsure how to proceed, Tompkins returned to the kingmaker for advice. "So I called Mr. Head, who told me 'I can't support him [Ortiz] for Congress, he's not qualified for that'," Tompkins said. "A bunch of people filed to run for the Democratic nomination. In the next day or so, I called Mr. Head back and said, 'Hey, I can't leave 'em'."

"I respected Mr. Head very much, but he didn't call all the shots with me," Tompkins said. "My friend the Sheriff had asked me to help him run for Congress. I was a little ambivalent at first. But I decided if I was a supporter, I was a supporter all in … Mr. Head's guidance notwithstanding."

The Ortiz machine stretched itself out; now there was much more territory to cover. "We were all block walking, knocking on doors … the ladies were making tamales galore. We all believed in him – but we knew it was tough for him to win," Borchard said. "We knew he could win; but this was a multi-county, multi-candidate race, an enormous step. It was not a given. There was great uncertainty."

To run for Congress, Ortiz was required under county election law to first resign his office as sheriff, leaving him with the practical reality of not having an income. Rendon was in the same boat; both county officials had only the income from the job. But the race for Congress meant walking away from that.

In considering the race, and in running conversations with Rendon, the two men decided to launch a commercial enterprise – a security company – to provide income for them through the race … and, if it were profitable in the longer term, to continue providing an income for them … for whatever the next step would be.

Twenty five years later, Amtex, the security company they owned, would be a flash point of created controversy in the Corpus Christi area.

"I still remember when he called me to tell me he was going to run for the new South Texas congressional seat," said then-Border Patrol Agent Silvestre Reyes. "I said 'what in the world do you want to do that for? You're a respected lawman, one of the few Hispanic sheriffs in the state.' He was one of the good guys."

"After he won the election, we talked and I told him I'd miss him a lot, but I knew the people of South Texas were going to be better served because it was him," Reyes said.

The friends stayed in close touch after Ortiz left for Capitol Hill and Washington.

In that first campaign for Congress, "There were so many candidates, it was a lot of work," Rosa Lopez said. When she worked precincts, she took the children with her. "Sollie was a toddler."

"Every one of Solomon's races had been very hard, all uphill, all game-changing races, but the first race for Congress – that was certainly the hardest," Oscar said. "He was running against very educated, very experienced people. Early on I went to help out in the Brownsville office. I stayed at the house of a friend's aunt. We had absolutely no money."

Five candidates vied for the Democratic nomination for the new seat in Congress. They included: Ortiz; Jorge Rangel, a Harvard-educated lawyer and counsel to the local paper, the *Corpus Christi Caller Times*; and three former Texas State Representatives, Arnold Gonzalez – the advocate of creating the Hispanic district – Ruben Torres, and Joe Salem, the darling of labor unions.

"Solomon got zero support from the ivory tower types," Rendon said. "That was the first congressional race I was a part of. We started with the same coalition – the same cheerleaders who'd always had his back, with their unqualified support … the same business-working class coalition that deeply appreciated Solomon's anti-drug crusade."

"We were at a hotel victory party when the results came in," Borchard smiled at the 1982 memory. "Sure enough, we heard pretty early in the evening that Solomon made it to the runoff, we thought 'OK, now this will be easy.' The runoff was with Joe Salem."

"Labor never believed in him," Rendon said. "Joe Salem was their boy. In part one of the primary, Dr. Hector Garcia – all the Hispanic leaders – supported Joe. We got to a run off with Joe. Labor made all the difference. They made an outsized difference, actually. In the runoff, every single Hispanic leader endorsed Joe. Every damn one."

"They figured Joe had the legislative experience and was a good debater," Ortiz said. "But I still had the support of the rank and file in Nueces County, and the business community."

"Saturday was the election," said campaign manager Tompkins. "Joe Salem got less than 50%, and Solomon eked out around 15%, the next candidate in back, above the rest of the pack. Sunday morning, the next day, Mr. Head calls me, and he says 'I'm in [with Ortiz].' He didn't want Joe Salem. He didn't have any influence with him."

"Joe Salem was a tail gunner in the Air Force, I called him 'Tail Gunner Joe'," said Tompkins. "He was also a jeweler, but more importantly, he'd served in the Texas legislature from 1969 to 1977, so he actually had lawmaking experience, at least at the state level. The primary runoff was a pretty close race, but Joe had the momentum at that point."

The race was on. Ortiz had Head back on his side, but it was still an uphill climb. Tompkins described the surreal nature of tutoring a Mexican American on how to talk to the Anglo community.

"We started meeting in my office, almost every day," Tompkins said. "That was when John Nugent got involved. He was a great public relations guy. We're all in my office, practicing with Solomon how talk in a way the Anglo community might hear his message, worked on his diction."

"We had mock debates," Tompkins said. "He could have been insulted by it, but Solomon was a good pupil – this was about finding a way for the Anglo community to hear what he had to say, and finding a way for him to say it the best way for them to hear it."

"It didn't work," Ortiz deadpanned. In the end, we are who we are – and we sound like we sound – and that's something you can't, and shouldn't, change.

"[The campaign] was exciting work, but took a lot of thinking about how to do things, how things should get said," Tompkins remembered. "People needed to hear his message, and he needed to communicate it in a way that Anglos would get it. I mean, we were running against Joe Salem, and he'd been in the Texas legislature [1969 to 1977]. And Joe had gotten a quarter of the vote in the field of five; he was at least known as a legislator."

"I took Solomon to meet the Texas Realtors – they bought in," Tompkins said. "They really liked him right off the bat, and started giving him the kind of money he just had not had access to. That relationship, that source of money for his campaigns continued – I think – until he left Congress."

Ortiz finished first in the May 1 primary with 25.7%, barely edging out Salem with 25%. Now Ortiz and Salem were running head to head.

In the debates before the runoff in June, Ortiz simply came off as the nicer guy. They really wanted to humiliate him, Rendon said. "But he creamed this guy. He said, 'I'm not in your pocket, you ain't in mine. I'm not a Harvard lawyer; I'm the guy who works his ass off for you. I want to be your champion in Congress. I'll go after that work like I went after the drug trade here'."

The political dynamic: Ortiz and Salem were both from the Corpus Christi area. At least half the votes would come from the Rio Grande Valley. His entree to the Valley's heart was the uncompromising stand on drugs, anywhere and his connections to the local law enforcement there.

Last, and certainly not least, Ortiz was a Hispanic candidate in 1982; Salem was not. The large population of Hispanic voters in Cameron County and other Rio Grande Valley counties came in for Ortiz generously, offsetting the Anglo vote from Ortiz and Salem's home county.

In the end, the decision of Hispanic leaders to endorse Joe Salem – and of Head sitting out until the runoff – were more examples of how Ortiz owed nobody … not even the leadership in the Hispanic community.

Except ….

"Well, I'll always owe the cheerleaders," Ortiz smiled.

"Tony Bonilla [Corpus Christi attorney] was a brother-in-law of Arnold Gonzalez, one of my primary opponents," Ortiz said. "He'd promised me that if Arnold didn't make it into the primary, he would support me in the runoff." Ortiz smirked. "Then he went and supported Joe Salem."

"It was a new place," Borchard said. "We thought the runoff was gonna be easy, then all the Democratic heavyweights started endorsing Joe. We still knew it could be done, but it didn't seem such a slam dunk suddenly."

Then, during the televised debate, there was a candid moment that spoke volumes about both Ortiz and Joe Salem. At one point, Salem reared back in his chair as he made a point. He'd misjudged how far back to push, and lost his balance.

"As Joe fell back in his chair, Solomon caught him and righted the chair," Borchard said, laughing at the memory. "In the whole debate, that moment was what everybody remembered, on both sides. That re-energized us for the home stretch. The night of the runoff, there was even more enthusiasm ... to see the success, the victory at the federal level. It was just a richer, great feeling. And done with hardly any money. That couldn't happen today."

"We were all drinking Diet Cokes – just ecstatic, everybody was so joyful, so happy ... screaming, crying," Borchard remembered. "All these politically-innocent, hardworking people that worked hard to get this guy to this place, they were just so happy. It was a sweet and awesome euphoria. We didn't know better. We had such hope, but just had no idea we could attain that goal."

Ortiz won the Democratic primary run-off election with 56% of the vote.

Winning the Democratic Primary in May of 1982 gave Ortiz the edge in the coming November, given the historical political tilt of the new district's voters. Through Election Day 1982, Ortiz ran like crazy to accomplish several things.

First, he wanted no mistakes and figured people are more likely to vote for you if you work hard and don't rest on your laurels.

Second, he wanted to use the time to meet everybody he could in the Rio Grande Valley, the area of the district that bordered Mexico. He was from Corpus Christi, 125 miles north, and an entirely different social dynamic.

Last, he was following the tried and true political axiom: run scared or run unopposed.

While Brownsville/the border region and Corpus Christi share many things – including a large and vital Hispanic population – the feel of each place was (and remains) vastly different.

Population-wise, the Corpus Christi area has a larger Anglo population. While over 55% of the population in the Corpus Christi area is Hispanic, they are just under 40% of the voting population.

That's vital; in politics you aim your efforts at traditional voters … divided into core supporters, loyal opposition, and independent/swing voters.

The bottom line in campaigns is more math than ideas.

The border region of Brownsville and Cameron County was then nearly 90% Hispanic, and is culturally part of the border community of the United States and Mexico, with families strewn on both sides of the border, and both places tied together economically.

When Ortiz first ran for Congress in 1982, the border region was a slow-paced, charming place, rich with history … but thick with poverty and very little economic opportunity.

Industrial demographics of the southern part of the district included shrimping and Gulf fishing, tourism, water transport, agriculture and service industries.

The north part of the district/Corpus Christi area sported a large military complex, agriculture, oil rigging and petrochemicals … all industries that offered a living wage for working families and reflected a more dynamic economy in 1982.

His platform in the first campaign: jobs.

That remained his singular focus for the 28 years he would serve in the U.S. House of Representatives.

"Even as a little kid, I could draw the line between economic circumstances of my friends with the kind of job their parents had," Ortiz said. "South Texas was an area with traditionally high unemployment rates. There were two huge obstacles to figure our way through: increasing our focus on education, and getting the jobs here."

"Solomon's journey from a Mexican cotton picker to Congress was a very long road," Cheerleader Noemi Martinez smiled. "He went such a long way. I am so proud. The knock on him when he ran for Congress was he didn't know enough, didn't have the formal education for this. He didn't care; he just said I am running."

There was a window of opportunity, a new congressional district, and Ortiz was determined to try, even if he didn't win. A formal education was not a prerequisite for serving in Congress.

The General Election was much tougher than first glance might suggest. While the district tilted Democratic, there was no time for a full-on campaign. Redistricting, and the ensuring battle, meant an abbreviated primary and general campaign.

The Republican opponent was an old friend Jason Luby, the former-mayor of Corpus Christi. Luby had considerably better financial support, and deeper ties to municipal officials in the other counties.

Still, Ortiz handily won the general election, with 64% of the vote, becoming one of the early Hispanics in the United States House of Representatives in the U.S. Congress.

"It was an honor for Robstown to see him elected to Congress; people couldn't believe that he would have been that brave," Martinez said. "We were sure he wouldn't win the race over five counties. Everybody wanted to help; because for a small town, it meant everything."

"He was such an example. Today young people see themselves in him, know that if he can do it so can they," she said, parroting the line Ortiz delivered to schools for the rest of his career.

That may sound simple, but in the 1970s and even early 1980s, children in the impoverished Hispanic enclave had little to zero choices about their lives, and no idea how to improve their lives.

"Children can make something out of themselves… but they don't really know that until they have an example to follow," Martinez said. "We that have children, we know that there is always a way to do something that means a lot to you. But having an example of success for the children is something that means more than almost anything else."

"He was such a big example for a small town, to have somebody to go from Robstown to Congress," Martinez remembered fondly. "Still, in that first campaign for Congress, there were so many naysayers… we'd tell them to shut up, get busy and work for him."

7 – MR. ORTIZ GOES TO WASHINGTON

KEACH REMEMBERED HIS father, Carroll Keach, and the role the elder Keach played in Ortiz' early life. "When my dad grew up, they didn't have a whole lot," Keach said. "Nowhere near the painful poverty Solomon and his family endured – but he did feel a kindredship to him."

"The day Solomon was leaving for Washington for the first time, not long after the election, he heard Daddy was sick and at the hospital," Keach said, voice thick with emotion. "Solomon wouldn't leave for Washington until he'd seen Daddy to give him his respect, thank him for all he'd done for him and the Ortiz family. Daddy said – and I'll never forget this – Daddy said, "hey, you got my vote, now get your ass to Washington to get everybody else's vote."

"When Solomon went to Congress, the kids did not want to go to Washington," Rosa Lopez said. "Solomon called them every day. Every morning he called to check on them, then again after school. "When they wanted to go out, they still had to get permission from their dad."

The hardest moment for her, Lopez said, was when Solomon's mother died, and she had to give him the sad news in Washington.

Ortiz' mother, frail and sick for several years, was in a nursing home in the last years of her life, with her children at her side every day, usually around mealtime. Ortiz visited her every day he was in Corpus Christi.

"I was in D.C., going home the next day, when Rosa and Yvette called me to tell me mother had died," Ortiz' lip trembled at the memory. "She sacrificed so much for me."

There were other times that were hard, part of having a parent far away part of the time. "Sometimes Thanksgiving was hard," Lopez said. "That was when Solomon was with the troops. Other special days could be hard, like birthdays, since they were apart. It was hard for Solomon, Solito was in soccer, and his father didn't get to go to any games."

"But kids adapt," Lopez said, and Ortiz' children got used to his schedule. Parent-teacher conferences were by phone or on the weekend if need be, and the extended family (including Jerry Sawyer, from both the sheriff's office and his congressional office) attended life events, ball games and other moments that kids or teenagers need an adult there to embarrass them, remind them they are in a big family.

One of the first tasks of new members-elect is to hire Capitol Hill staff and find office space in advance of the formal convention of Congress in January.

Ortiz took Rendon with him, making his former chief deputy, longtime friend, and political confidant his new chief of staff, the top position in congressional offices. The two former cops navigated the new environment with the same detective skills they'd used in the sheriff's office and on the local South Texas political scene.

As former cops, they discovered, they won entree to the confidence of the Capitol Hill police force, who knew everything people did, heard things people said, and who knew every nook and cranny of the vast U.S. Capitol complex.

"We had no idea what we were gonna do, what we were supposed to do," said Ortiz. "We drove there and scoped out the place, made friends with cops."

Rookie members got the very last suites available, and it was tricky trying to figure which of the lousy suites was the best choice. So Ortiz asked a cop. It determined the suite in his first office lottery.

"We drove an old burnt orange car to D.C. so we'd have a car," Rendon smiled. "Of course everywhere we went – the Capitol, the White House – security was always looking at us twice, maybe three times. Here's these two Mexicans who don't look like they belong. It was a good thing we made friends with cops. Solomon mighta spent most of the first year just explaining who he was."

In early January, 1983, when Ortiz was sworn into Congress, he was hardly celebrating alone. It seemed like half of South Texas came to the nation's Capitol to cheer his election.

Hundreds of friends and supporters cried and cheered in the gallery of the House of Representatives as Ortiz swore an oath to preserve and protect the Constitution.

"Mariachi Ortiz" played on the Capitol grounds, putting a distinctive South Texas flavor on the celebration.

"When Solomon was sworn into Congress the first time, I was on the Capitol steps watching this huge party for Solomon on the Capitol plaza," remembered Frank Tompkins, marveling at the history he witnessed. "It was just a great day, seeing all these folks from Robstown there to celebrate with him, and the mariachis. I bet the Capitol hasn't seen a party like that since."

In a few weeks, Ortiz won a coveted seat on the House Armed Services Committee, only the second Hispanic to serve on that mighty committee.

"[Then-House Majority Leader, Texan] Jim Wright and [Texan] Charlie Wilson helped me get a spot on the Armed Services Committee," Ortiz said. "That was pivotal to expanding our bases in South Texas."

He was also assigned to the House Merchant Marine and Fisheries Committee (overseeing natural resources around the United States).

Ortiz had lobbied mightily to win slots on those two committees. The array of military bases in the Coastal Bend area and the historic tug of war over water (and other natural resources in the American West) made his committee assignments uniquely suited to South Texas.

When Ortiz was elected, the House of Representatives had already established a Select Committee on Narcotics Abuse and Control the decade before. Ortiz lobbied to be added to the select committee.

Both House Speaker Tip O'Neill and Committee Chairman Charlie Rangel (D-NY) wanted him on the committee, both for his heroic law enforcement credentials and his language skills. Speaker O'Neill put Ortiz on the select committee.

The select committee frequently traveled to Mexico, and Central and South America, to put their own eyes on the things Congress could do to try to combat the illegal international drug trade.

"I was the only one who spoke Spanish on the committee," Ortiz smiled. "Charlie [Chairman Rangel] told me that before I got there, they had to depend on the embassy to translate conversations, and frequently they felt like they weren't getting the whole story there."

There is only so much that one member can do to move events in a meaningful way – and nobody can do it quickly, or alone.

Staff-wise, Ortiz' first term was more tumultuous than need be. His instructions to Rendon: hire the very best staff there is.

He hired the top talent on the Hill, but in the end, the pros from Washington didn't particularly appreciate Ortiz' style or ideology, nor the conservative Hispanic district which elected him.

Ortiz was a centrist in what was still a relatively progressive House of Representatives, at a time (the 1980s) just before redistricting made districts even more hyper-partisan.

He was a working class kid who'd come up in law enforcement and local politics. He didn't hold the fancy law degree or business bonifides most members boast.

But his political skills and innate understanding of lawmaking were his strength.

Solomon has the best political gut of anybody he ever met, Rendon said. "You don't trust that, you lose."

Ortiz had a tough first year. The work was different from anything he'd ever done. The atmosphere was different from everything he knew.

"I did a lot of homework every night," Ortiz laughed. "The job was essentially judgment, but making good decisions meant talking to all the stakeholders, stepping back and looking at everything in context. It was an awesome responsibility and I wanted to make the best decisions possible."

"I hired people that knew the Hill, knew the legislative process, and knew the administrative side of the House of Representatives," Rendon said. "One of the top staffers was very liberal, others were conservative. The staff was fighting among themselves, based on their personal beliefs, not Solomon's."

"I was having staff meetings every morning," Rendon said. "It felt like they were moving away from Solomon's centrist position. The overall instruction Solomon gave his staff, for guidance on philosophical stuff, was to keep him in the middle. Again, he wanted to be in nobody's pocket."

Some of the talented staff Ortiz had hired literally tried to move Ortiz in a different political/ideological direction in his first term.

Putting a stamp on his office at the beginning of his second term, Ortiz fired nearly all the staff, hiring all new ones. He always hated dealing with staff matters.

"Solomon always believed success comes from the people around you," Rendon said. "Finding the right people is hard anywhere. On Capitol Hill, it's an even trickier challenge – so high profile. You're placing such great trust in very young people. I've always said the cheapest commodity in Washington is brains. There's so many smart people. Lawyers, Ph.Ds … all happy to volunteer. People work there for peanuts."

"I remember when Dr. Bob Bezdek came to volunteer with our office," Rendon said. Bezdek is a political science professor at Texas A&M-Corpus Christi. "Bob wanted real-world Capitol Hill experience to offer more insight to classes. Think he was there for a month, and he told me what he'd figured out: Capitol Hill has nothing to do with political science."

The new staff in Ortiz' second term included more Texans and more conservatives … and launched a dynamic that would remain the case until the end of Ortiz' career: his top office staff was not only talented, they would understand up front the essence of Solomon Ortiz and the district he represented. The staff was more like family.

Yet the new crew was hardly meek, they dug in to work very long hours.

Politics is much like the Mafia without the blood.

Members of a team in a congressional office – or a campaign – bicker with each other, perfect arguments, and do things that are remarkably important in the everyday lives of their fellow citizens. They do all this while practically sitting on top of each other in very close quarters.

They are bonded in ways others can never understand. Even when they disagree with each other, or even with the eventual decision of their boss – once there's a decision, everybody's behind it.

"In 1984, I came to D.C. to interview to be Chief of the Border Patrol's McAllen sector, which covered Solomon's district," said Ortiz' friend, Silver Reyes. "I got the job; and Solomon and Lencho were the first to call and congratulate me. So we had a new working relationship."

With Ortiz still clearly invested in law enforcement conditions on the border, and Reyes on the front lines, the Border Patrol Chief had a champion in Congress and the congressman had a trusted source with the inside scoop on bottom-line needs for border security.

By 1985, and the beginning of his second term, Ortiz' schedule was down pat: working on Capitol Hill Tuesday-Thursday, working all over the South Texas district from late Thursday until he had to catch a plane back to DC on Tuesday morning.

That schedule would pretty much describe his frantic back-and-forth between Texas and Washington for the 28 years he served in Congress.

In Texas, Ortiz split the four-day weekends between the Coastal Bend (Corpus Christi area) and the Rio Grande Valley of South Texas (Brownsville area).

In addition to the scheduled meetings in both ends of the district, Ortiz fielded "running meetings" on the road, in restaurants, at hotels, schools, and in stores.

Constituents approached Ortiz wherever they saw him with requests for casework (such as, "can you help with my grandmother's Social Security check?") … to South Texans weighing in with ideas or support/opposition to particular legislation.

For Ortiz, the 1980s was a building period; building alliances throughout South Texas and Washington, and building a congressional team that was frequently the envy of colleagues.

As a junior congressman, Ortiz had few opportunities to leave a mark on policy. Chairmen, political leaders in the House of Representatives, and more senior members were the ones who wrote the bills and made decisions on legislation.

From the beginning, Ortiz' mantra on constituent services was: do everything you can, then some. His junior status didn't matter in terms of constituent services. In the late 1980s, a sudden drought in South Texas brought frantic farmers to Ortiz' door; their cattle were dying from lack of hay.

Ortiz staffers worked through the weekend, securing emergency deliveries of hay to farmers affected by the drought. The following Monday, the staff members were summoned to the office of the long-time chairman of the House Agriculture Committee who was the representative for the congressional district west of Ortiz' coastal district in Texas.

The Chairman was a Hispanic pioneer in Congress himself, as the first Hispanic since 1917 to be the chairman of a standing committee in the U.S. House of Representatives.

The Chairman was angry that farmers in his district had not gotten the deliveries of hay that the farmers in Ortiz' district got, and reminded the staffers that HE was the chairman of the House Agriculture Committee.

They were upbraided, and told in no uncertain terms that junior members of Congress did not show up senior members … sending the message to Ortiz: "it's bad form to show off."

Ortiz roared at hearing the story of the Chairman's ire … and made the staffers promise never to let him become that way, more concerned with seniority and power than helping his people.

For several years in the 1990s, his teenage children refused to eat at restaurants with him because the steady stream of people greeting him, or getting in a quick request with his office, meant sharing the precious time with their Dad.

"When Solomon got home, he wanted home-cooked meals, but the kids always wanted to go to a restaurant," Lopez said. "By the time they were teens, they despised going out with him for all the people who demanded his time. It was their turn. They resented sometimes that they needed to share their father."

"As a public servant – Solomon's whole life was politics, but as a man, the children were his whole life," Lopez said. "I remember when Yvette had her tonsils out, Solomon never left her side. The most heartbreaking moment between them was when little Yvette told her parents she and Sollie would stay together."

"The children were always very united – a team," Lopez said. In the end, Lopez said, if you judge parents on their children, the Ortiz children turned out all right. Yvette is an educator with a young son (Little Oscar, named for his uncle the Commissioner); and Solomon, Jr., having served two terms in the Texas State House, is now a consultant and runs a nonprofit dedicated to educating minorities.

Back in Washington, Ortiz had discovered a secret to alliances on the House Armed Services Committee: international travel.

"My very first travel with the Armed Services Committee was with Pat Schroeder [D-CO] to see bases in Europe," Ortiz said. "People can only get to know each other just so much in Washington. We're just there a few days a week, and you only see each other in committee or for votes on the House floor."

77

"When we traveled for the committee, members really got know each other, really become friends," Ortiz explained. "Knowing a colleagues needs … their political dynamics, their families … brought us together as friends."

It also meant that, when they spoke later, Ortiz' words would weigh heavier, and matter more.

8 – NAVIGATING CAPITOL HILL

BY 1985, HE was already traveling every two-three months to win favor with the senior members of the Armed Services Committee.

Jimmy Miller is a fixture on Capitol Hill, a staffer who has seen it all. Miller worked in the U.S. House of Representatives for a third of a century, nearly entirely with the House Transportation Committee.

In 2011, he was the Director of Facilities and Travel for the U.S. House of Representatives' Committee on Transportation and Infrastructure, or as he puts it, "basically I am chief bottle washer."

Miller met Ortiz in the first year of his congressional service; the men remained fast friends ever since.

"Here's the thing about Solomon," Miller drawled. "He was reliable ... if he told you something, it was the gospel. That's the only way you can survive in this environment."

"Politics is always tough; alliances are always shifting," Miller said. "But if you are trustworthy among your colleagues – that's gold."

"Solomon was always just so politically savvy," Miller said. "The biggest fault of members today is they don't know who to trust. Here in this environment, you gotta be so savvy."

"You have to know both sides of an issue, of the politics," Miller said. "You have to evaluate – accurately – how something is going to affect you, your people, your interests ... and how it is going to affect your colleagues, their people, and their interests. Before you jump, think."

"Solomon knows how to do that," Miller said. "He can analyze a situation down to the local politics of a colleague, the response of interest groups, and the outcome of a vote. He's damn good at this."

It's been said that Ortiz graduated from the school of hard

knocks, with a Ph.D in people. Miller agreed with that.

"Tell you what else, he can keep a confidence," Miller said. "Solomon could keep it in the vault. You could tell him anything and it was secure forever. Nobody knows how to do that anymore."

Ortiz had a unique style of leadership. His methods were simple, Miller said.

"It was part natural talent and part his very pleasant approach that made his colleagues here gravitate to him," Miller said. "He has tremendous insight to people, what they secretly think, how they will react, what they need, and where the fundamental differences were."

"He could communicate so well," Miller said. "Solomon would know just what to say in a situation. He could be serious. He could be funny, lighthearted."

"He was great at articulating the issues, cutting to the chase better than anybody I've ever known," Miller said. "In all the years I knew Solomon, I never met anybody that disliked him. Ever. That's both people here on Capitol Hill, and down in Texas."

Clearly, Miller did not meet everybody in Texas, as Ortiz always had a number of detractors.

"Solomon came from such poor beginnings," Miller said. "That childhood helped him understand people, what makes them tick. He is loyal, he is generous. In politics, you must have loyalty."

Ortiz' service on the Merchant Marine and Fisheries Committee in the 1980s was much lower key than the Armed Services Committee. While the early debates in Armed Services were focused on international preparedness for the dreaded Soviet threat, debates in Merchant Marine were entirely regional.

The Armed Services Committee was one of the few non-partisan committees in Congress.

Merchant Marine debates and decisions were entirely about regional concerns regarding fishing regulations, coastal environmental concerns, and governance of water rights – all lifelines for the coastal district Ortiz represented.

Energy concerns were front and center as always, but in the 1980s, gas prices were generally low … with the gas wars and gas station lines of the late 1970s a distant (bad) memory.

Given that dynamic, energy companies were generally lower profile while Congress looked past them for government revenues as the government was running up what was then the largest debt and deficits in U.S. history.

As always, Ortiz despised any one person or group believing they had him "in their pocket." Voting on matters related to union rules or unions generally was always a difficult vote. Politically, the unions supported his opponent in the first race for Congress, then didn't support Ortiz later because he was inclined to vote in a "pro-business" way.

His early, loud support for business was intended to lay the path for more and better jobs in the South Texas district.

Yet unions were almost always on the other side of those votes.

But Ortiz was – at his core – a working man, albeit not one with a history of a unionized job in the right-to-work state of Texas. He always voted for higher minimum wages, just because he knew the poverty of families struggling to pay for the necessities of life.

Plus, Ortiz always voted with teachers' unions in pursuit of better education for young South Texans and with the union at the Corpus Christi Army Depot. So while he voted with business part of the time and labor part of the time; he remained – proudly – never in anybody's pocket.

The votes in the early-mid 1990s on NAFTA (North American Free Trade Agreement), GATT (General Agreement on Tariffs and Trade), and later, CAFTA (Central American Free Trade Agreement) – supported trade treaties that promised more jobs in South Texas.

Indeed, after NAFTA, the unemployment rate in the Brownsville/Rio Grande Valley area dropped from 17% to 7%.

Unpopular though they were with unions, the trade agreements certainly got South Texas closer what Ortiz wanted it to be: a place with enough jobs for his constituents.

After the turn of the century, union leaders reached out to Ortiz, joined hands, and formally supported him in each succeeding campaign.

While certainly a friend of the energy industry during his congressional career – given its prominence in South Texas – in his first two terms, Ortiz also won conservationist awards, a rare achievement for an energy industry supporter.

One of the conservationist awards was for stopping a waste management company from dumping trash in the Gulf of Mexico at a popular coral site.

For all the support Ortiz gave the energy industry, ironically, it didn't give Ortiz the same level of campaign money it gave other members who were as supportive of the industry.

In fact, for such a supportive Member of Congress – who served on a committee of great importance to them, Merchant Marine and Fisheries – the energy industry gave Ortiz a paltry amount of campaign contributions.

In the middle/late 20th Century, budgetary concerns in Congress were more regional than partisan. States and geographical areas allied their interests in pursuit of policies that would most benefit their region.

In the 1980s and early 1990s, the Texas delegation was singularly united on any matter that affected Texas at any level.

In fact, the entire delegation had an understanding. If one member needed to get language in a bill to benefit their district but didn't sit on the appropriate committee, whichever Texan did sit on the committee carried the water for them.

Once Ortiz promised Ralph Hall [then-D-TX] he would add an amendment Hall wanted in the Merchant Marine and Fisheries Committee's bill.

The committee members reached the end of the amendment process and Hall had still not gotten there to give Ortiz a copy of the amendment he needed included in the bill.

Members of the committee, antsy to be gone now that business was finished, sat patiently while Ortiz spoke, thanked everybody, and began to sort of ramble.

Thankfully, Hall tore into the committee room and rushed his amendment to Ortiz' hands and carried a copy to the clerk, as Ortiz began, "Mr. Chairman, I have one last amendment …."

Ortiz, wildly popular among his colleagues, was continually underestimated by them. His inclination in most circumstances was to avoid confrontation on matters with which he disagreed.

"You catch more flies with honey than with vinegar," he said, almost on a daily basis. His mother's wisdom to be nice, and Dr. Hector's wisdom not to burn bridges, informed nearly all his choices.

That inclination, Ortiz' easygoing personality, and his accent … all caused his colleagues to underestimate him since they did not know him well early on.

"It used to make me so mad; people used to treat like Solomon just a little bit like he was stupid," said Sheila McCready, a long time

Ortiz staffer and defense expert. "But that changed with the TED issue."

TEDs – turtle excluder devices – were large holes in the fishing nets required by the federal government to help turtles escape shrimping nets.

Holes big enough to allow turtles to escape also meant untold numbers of shrimp also escaped the catch. It was the death knoll for the Gulf shrimping industry.

Ortiz compared TEDs to a big hole in your pocket with lots of change in it.

As with all matters related to the Merchant Marine and Fisheries Committee, the question of TEDs pitted the shrimpers of the Gulf against the environmentalists around the country who did not represent shrimpers.

Despite his being on the committee, and strongly objecting to the TEDs language in it, the committee's bill went to the House floor in the late 1980s with a requirement that shrimping nets contain holes measuring several feet by several feet.

That would continue to decimate the shrimping industry already on the decline in South Texas and around the Gulf of Mexico.

Ortiz, in a desperate attempt to circumvent the damage that would be done by this new regulation, proposed an amendment to the bill to kill the new regulation on TEDs.

Despite the fact that Ortiz' amendment failed on the House floor, his colleagues were surprised. Most new guys in Congress – if they dared to offer amendments at all – submitted "throwaway" amendments, meant to satisfy a contributor.

Ortiz' amendment got the attention of more senior members. The near-success of his amendment surprised the committee and the House leadership. The new guy had done his homework, legislatively and politically on a national matter. Everybody was surprised that his amendment damn near passed.

After that, the respect for Ortiz' legislative ability soared among his House colleagues. But it remained his uncanny ability, personality, and unforgiving work ethic that won the favor of his colleagues in the decades Ortiz served in Congress.

9 – SOUTH TEXAS MILITARY BASES/BRAC

IN 1985, PRESIDENT Ronald Reagan and Congress were expanding the fleet, building a "600 ship navy" to project U.S. forces deeper and more consistently in the Soviet Union's face.

While the fleet strength never reached anywhere near that level, ship building did kick up and the Navy put out a call for communities along the Gulf of Mexico to compete for three new "homeports."

"Homeport" was the Navy shorthand for the naval stations arrayed along the coasts which served as the home port for a naval carrier group.

Military bases in towns across the nation are a certain and long-term economic boom for the communities in which they are located. Federal dollars are invested in the building of bases, then in maintenance, and good salaried jobs.

A whole new layer of stores and service industries sprout up to serve base activities. Federal dollars paid to troops are invested in the town's services, stores, real estate, and more.

Understanding ahead of time precisely the value of a federal investment like that is impossible, but generally accountants and comptrollers say a single federal dollar invested in a community is spent between 5-10 times over.

For instance, the government pays the military, which in turn buy supplies or services. A widget for an installation means a local supplier – which buy materials and pays employees – are the first couple of times the federal investment is spent.

The employees buy food and supplies for their families; the businesses from which they buy will reinvest in supplies, and pay their employees, and so on.

All to say, military bases in communities around the country are a mighty hot commodity.

When the word about the homeport competition spread to coastal communities in the Gulf of Mexico, every local official and chamber of commerce official in towns arrayed around the Gulf from Florida to Texas had a heady moment.

Every single community applied. When applications were winnowed down, the communities which were contenders included: Brownsville, Texas; Ingleside, Texas; Galveston, Texas; Gulfport, Mississippi; and Mobile, Alabama.

Unlike the other major-city contenders, Ingleside was a tiny hamlet on the bay across from Corpus Christi, Texas.

Nueces County – where Corpus Christi is located and which would see an uptick of economic development if the base were built there – threw all in with Ingleside in the fight to win a homeport for the region.

The Nueces County Commissioners Court and the Corpus Christi mayor showed the area's willingness to invest, as well, when they began a bond issue to tax citizens in their county to pay for amenities the base – in the next county over – needed.

"When Kika [de la Garza, D-TX] and I went to the Pentagon to lobby [Defense Secretary] Cap Weinberger on Ingleside, we met the nicest guy in his office," Ortiz said. "It was Colin Powell. He was already a general; he was Cap's top guy. I remember Cap asking us what we wanted. We told him we wanted the Gulf homeport at Ingleside. He said 'We want the MX missile'."

That was easy for Ortiz; he'd planned to vote for the MX missile anyway, but had feigned uncertainty to get the promise of infrastructure or funds for South Texas. That was a frequent ploy on his part in the churning waters of Capitol Hill.

Ortiz' MX missile vote guaranteed that one of the new naval bases would be at Ingleside, just outside Ortiz' congressional district.

The Chamber of Commerce began a public outreach effort to explain and quantify the investment and the promise of the return.

The economic and political community in the Coastal Bend of

South Texas was united in purpose in a way they usually were not.

The Chamber began an annual "CC to D.C." trek of public, chamber, and union officials, plus various businesspeople. Teams spent several days briefing members of Congress in pivotal places and on important committees.

Their pitch to the members, in the beginning, was this: we'll tax ourselves to invest $25 million in this; we'll get the State of Texas to match our investment; you can choose what parcel of land you want and we'll get the land donated. Other bases in the area were a complement to the plan.

It was an extraordinary effort, with no dissension. Texas Senator Phil Gramm (R) was the most helpful.

When Homeport locations were announced, Ingleside, Texas was a winner.

By 1988, South Texans and the Navy were breaking ground on the new facility.

Soon, Naval Station Ingleside would be the homeport for the training aircraft carrier, *USS Lexington, USS Wisconsin* and the accompanying battleship group.

By 1990, as the Cold War ended and U.S. forces drew down for the first time since the post-Vietnam era, the "600 ship navy" was an expensive, outdated pipe dream.

Soon, the Navy's force structure would shrink significantly and both the aircraft carrier, *USS Lexington*, and the *USS Wisconsin* battle groups were decommissioned.

That left the shiny new state-of-the-art naval station at Ingleside all dressed up with nobody to move in. Despite the considerable federal investment – and the $50 million local investment – Ingleside was left without a mission, even before the doors of the base opened.

As the writing on the wall became apparent in 1990 as to the disposition of Naval Station Ingleside and the carriers originally to be homeported there, Ortiz and his team went digging to find another mission for the base.

Ortiz was fighting on two fronts: keeping the building going at Ingleside in the midst of a moratorium on military construction, and finding a new mission for the base.

Ortiz and Gramm found one: mine warfare. The importance of the mine warfare mission was illustrated by the invasion of Kuwait by Iraq in August of 1990. Iraqi mines dotted the Persian Gulf as a first line of defense against any navy coming after them.

The U.S. Navy had determined the best way to be prepared for landing in the midst of mines in the waters was to have a center of excellence to study and train. But where to locate the new center?

The nation's east and west coast ports and coastal tourist communities were not far enough apart for a significant chunk of space for the Navy to practice.

Now Ortiz was fighting politically and legislatively on another front. Congress was determined to close outdated or unneeded bases, in part to save money and in part to reduce the nation's military footprint in the wake of the disintegration of the Soviet Union, the boogie man that just fell to the dustpan of history.

In 1990, Texan Dick Armey (R) found a path through the minefield of Congress in terms of closing military bases.

Congress passed his bill to empower the Defense Department to make a list of suggestions for base closure/realignment to an independent commission.

Base closure legislation and later actions soon were shortened to: "BRAC" – the Base Realignment and Closure Commission

The commission would conduct a careful review, visit communities, study other options, and give Congress a final report.

Congress was required to vote on the list within a certain amount of time after receiving it – and could only vote yes or no on the complete list. No amendments or changes were permitted.

So the only places Members of Congress could affect the outcome of the list was with the Defense Department, or with the Commission during their deliberations.

Pounding the table at his Armed Services Committee, then at supper with naval officials, day after day and night after night, Ortiz finally convinced his colleagues and the Navy to keep Naval Station Ingleside alive.

He did it with very little – or zero – help from others in the Texas delegation, especially the senators. They were all consumed with the health and well-being of bases elsewhere in Texas.

Occasionally, he did all this in spite of opposition from other Texas officeholders, who would have liked to have traded a South Texas base to get another Texas base off the list.

BRAC was a cruel process.

In May, 1991, the Secretary of the Navy announced plans to

homeport an array of mine hunters, and mine countermeasures ships, at Ingleside.

The moratorium now lifted, construction continued at Ingleside to support the Navy's new "Mine Warfare Center of Excellence."

Ships began arriving and Naval Station Ingleside became operational in mid-1992.

The timing was prophetic. The following year was the third Base Realignment and Closure Commission/BRAC round.

Military bases around the country have traditionally been extremely difficult to close or realign (realignment in military parlance means move missions from one base to another). Local members of Congress fight like a tiger defending a cub when it comes to keeping a local military base open.

Ortiz was no different, except he was at the table in Congress making decisions on military policy and he was already fast friends with all, or most, of the decision makers.

Ortiz had been working hand-in-glove with military officials for nearly a decade by 1991, the first year BRAC threatened bases in the South Texas area. None of the Coastal Bend bases were included for closure.

Every year the list of Base Closure Commissioners was announced, Ortiz looked at the list and said, "These are my friends. I know nearly all these guys."

When Ortiz spoke to his relationships with people, it was people whose "names he knew" (people he'd met), people he "knew" (casual friends), and "friends" (good friends). If it was somebody he knew but didn't want any part of, he'd smirk and stare right through whoever asked about them.

He would regale astonished staffers with how he knew this particular BRAC commissioner and that one.

He'd traveled with this one, served in Congress with another, worked with others from the Pentagon over the years.

Ingleside would have been an easy target to close with no mission for BRAC in 1991. Nearly all the new homeports were candidates for closure.

But armed with a mission – the importance of which had just been illustrated in the Persian Gulf, Ingleside was not listed by the Navy for closure.

Ortiz' lobbying, and near constant behind-the-scenes information sharing, had carried the day with the Navy and the Army. None of the bases in South Texas were listed for closure by the military.

But Naval Air Station/NAS Chase Field, in Beeville, Texas, 40 miles northwest of Corpus Christi, was on the Navy's closure list. Beeville was part of a triad of air stations in South Texas with NAS Kingsville and NAS Corpus Christi.

But the next phase of BRAC would always be the trickiest. Once the commission had the list, it was entirely theirs to alter in any way.

Those communities with bases on the BRAC list – and their members of Congress – would now introduce bases elsewhere to compare to the bases on the closure list.

That particular phase of the process dragged all four Coastal Bend area bases into the BRAC process. Naval Station Ingleside was compared to other new homeports on the list; both naval air stations at Corpus Christi and Kingsville were compared to other air stations slated to close; and Corpus Christi Army Depot was compared to other repair depots.

It was NAS Kingsville and NS Ingleside that were in the most peril in 1991.

But Ortiz and the community fought back using the Commission's own data to prove the superiority of the four Coastal Bend military bases.

The Corpus Christi and Kingsville Chambers of Commerce threw all in with Ortiz for the fight. Daily or weekly conference calls organized activities. Ortiz' leadership was hailed by all participants as inspired and heroic.

Even the local paper – which was never complimentary to Ortiz – gushed in editorials about his work to save area bases.

BRAC91 closed the Naval Air Station/NAS Chase Field, at Beeville, Texas. That was near, but not in, Ortiz' district. It was a loss for Ortiz, who had fought for Chase Field.

Base closure was now coming as quickly as elections, with just as much at stake.

Since BRAC91 plucked the low hanging fruit in terms of excess military bases, BRAC 1993 was a greater challenge.

For Ortiz, now BRAC was part of his daily life, even between BRAC rounds. If he wasn't getting money in the annual House Armed Services Committee to bone up weaknesses at area bases, he was planning and organizing for the next round.

The Coastal Bend business community – with over 25% of their local economy at stake – again threw all in with Ortiz.

When the Defense Department released their list of suggested closures to the Base Closure Commission in 1993, Ortiz' hard work had again paid off. None of the South Texas bases were suggested for closure.

But in 1993, the Commission did add Kingsville Naval Air Station to the list of bases to consider in contrast with naval air stations otherwise suggested for closure. But Ortiz' heavy lifting behind the scenes kept the other south Texas bases off the list of considerations.

When the Base Closure Commission sent commissioners to South Texas for a hearing about Kingsville and other area bases, Ortiz and the community welcomed them with a gigantic event at the Convention Center and a parade.

Ortiz' history – and his standing in Congress – made him the perfect person to unify and organize the South Texas community. The Anglo business community and the Hispanic working class rarely worked together on anything.

But Ortiz' history as a local county official, his ethnicity, and his outreach to the business community in the quest for jobs –offered everybody in the community something to cling to as Base Closure bore down on them.

BRAC93 – in the end – did not close the Naval Air Station/NAS Kingsville, or any other bases in South Texas.

Now Ortiz had a special challenge in front of him. Other communities had leveraged the weaknesses of the South Texas bases.

Each BRAC round had been excruciatingly painful. The coming round in 1995 was expected to be brutal. Few people believed all the bases in Ortiz' district would survive the 1995 round of closures.

So Ortiz switched tactics, moving from defense to offense.

No longer concentrating on preventing closure, Ortiz told his team to find missions already on the move from BRAC that could fit with bases in south Texas.

Now a senior member of the House Armed Services Committee, Ortiz and his team combed every conclusion from the 1991 and 1993 commissions for possible realignments from bases slated for closure.

As possibilities became apparent, Ortiz would add language to the annual Armed Services bill to make a south Texas base a more attractive option to move missions realigned from previous BRAC decisions.

"Sheila McCready [former military staffer for Ortiz] is absolutely brilliant," said Ortiz. "She has a great mind for strategy when it comes to military matters and to base closure. Sheila made it possible for me to do the things I did to keep our bases off the BRAC list, and to go on offense – and direct other missions to South Texas."

He would meet with Pentagon planners to plant the seed for moving this mission or that mission to south Texas.

"The beauty of this strategy was that it worked so effectively, and so consistently, over multiple BRACs," said Rendon. "Hard part was that very few people knew the strategy, all of whom knew to keep it on the QT. Any whiff of it going public would have derailed the tactic. But it was brilliant – and wildly successful."

When the Defense Department released their list of suggested closures to the Base Closure Commission in 1995, there was tremendous angst initially when the name Naval Air Station Corpus Christi was on the list, and was reportedly on the list for closure in the first minutes after the list was released.

Ortiz received the news with no concern. He knew what his staff would confirm for him in the next few minutes: the base was listed as a realignment, it was not slated for closure. It was listed as a receiver of missions.

NAS Corpus Christi was the designated bucket Ortiz was throwing realigned missions into.

Navy officials themselves suggested a realignment for NAS Corpus Christi, which Ortiz had lobbied for and organized.

NAS Corpus Christi would now host the multiple helicopter squadrons associated with the mine warfare mission at Ingleside, on the other side of the bay.

On one hand, it would bring more jobs to the area.

But more important strategically for the ongoing BRAC fight, it would heighten the interconnectivity of all four area bases.

That strengthened any individual weaknesses at any one of the bases, and seeded the understanding that the south Texas bases constituted an expansive complex.

BRAC95 did not close any south Texas bases in the complex-of-four.

In one of the supreme ironies of BRAC95, Ortiz won hundreds more jobs at South Texas bases.

Ortiz and South Texas were unusual in the community of bases considered by the BRAC Commission: they were the only ones in the country that picked up jobs in the massive defense industry shakeout.

The only ones that GAINED jobs.

Republicans who controlled Congress said President Bill Clinton politicized the BRAC process when he recommended replacing government ownership of two repair depots but leaving them in the same community.

The effort to save jobs in California, a traditional Democratic state, and in San Antonio, a traditional Democratic part of Texas, angered Congress and every other community slated to lose a base, and therefore jobs.

Depots are the huge repair places for tanks, helicopters, planes – all the big ass weapons in the U.S. arsenal.

BRAC95 recommended closing two maintenance depots: McClellan Air Logistics Center near Sacramento, CA, and Kelly Air Logistics Center in San Antonio, TX.

As an alternative to shutting the depots in two huge states, President Clinton proposed having private contractors take over maintenance work at the sites.

Republicans, shocked, shocked (!) that there was gambling at the casino, charged that Clinton could not be trusted to respect the "apolitical" BRAC process.

That was a great irony. BRAC was – always – entirely political.

Given Republicans said they could no longer trust Clinton to participate in the base closure process, they would not agree to schedule another round until 2001.

Events of 2001 pushed BRAC further down the road, to 2005. That decade of suspending BRAC was a break for the Coastal Bend community of military bases. Still, Ortiz planned for the eventual, next BRAC.

Ortiz and Gene Taylor (D-MS), and also a member of the Armed Services Committee) got a bill through the House of Representatives that would have moved BRAC05 to 2007.

It was an amazing accomplishment. There was also a perfect storm of events that moved the House to repudiate the White House and Department of Defense (DoD).

Many members were very angry that both wars in which the U.S.

was engaged were not being paid for. Plus the rapes, homicides and sexual torture at the U.S. military prison at Abu Ghraib sickened the world and embarrassed the proud reputation of the United States military.

All that – plus a need to stand up Homeland Security assets – made traditional BRAC supporters in Congress hesitate, for the first time in two decades, to support the base closure efforts.

But the Senate did not agree, so the base closure efforts moved forward as planned for 2005.

10 – THE SCREWING
OF SOUTH TEXAS

WHEN THE BRAC05 list was announced, it was a gut-punch to the now-expansive South Texas military complex. The Pentagon recommended closing Naval Station Ingleside, and re-aligning the Corpus Christi Army Depot and Naval Air Station Corpus Christi.

A full decade had passed since the last BRAC round, and the business community – particularly at the Port of Corpus Christi – seemed to have forgotten the stakes at hand.

Unlike 10 years before, when the entire community pulled evenly on the oars and engaged in the coming fight early and often. In 2005 the business community speculated behind closed doors that the closure could be a very good thing for the Port of Corpus Christi.

Closure at Ingleside would result in the property reverting to the Port of Corpus Christi, in which many of the area businesspeople focused their economic prospects.

They looked at the new infrastructure at Naval Station Ingleside, worth over two hundred and fifty million dollars, like a hungry man looks at food.

That asset, this timing … what a gift it could be to the richest people in the area.

It would not do for anybody in the community, business or otherwise, to mount a campaign supporting the closure. So Corpus Christi's business elite did what people do when they need something to fail; they just waited it out, feigning interest while sitting on their hands.

They delayed; they discouraged others from engaging full bore in the BRAC05 fight. At the very last minute, they strolled into the struggle to keep the base open when the larger south Texas community publicly realized and feared the loss of jobs associated with the loss of military assets. As they should have all along.

But the strategy of the area's business elite to undermine the effort had already yielded success. The "slow roll" tactic, or the delaying, left Ingleside vulnerable … with too little time to save the base. So far, the port's remarkable gamble was paying off, with little to no heavy lifting on their part.

The breadth of the realignments at the depot and NAS Corpus Christi were associated with the mine warfare mission at Ingleside, illustrating Ortiz' success at spreading around the assets associated with area missions.

The recommendation to yank up the carpet at Ingleside wasn't self-contained. It had an enormous effect on the other area bases — and would certainly shrink the job market for South Texans.

Ortiz knew from his position inside the Armed Services Committee that the Defense Department was to soon stand up a Center of Excellence for Homeland Defense and Security, which would bring another mission to the base, one as large as Mine Warfare.

He moved quickly to put the idea in front of commissioners and decision makers at DoD.

That effort ended unceremoniously after the BRAC commissioners reacted favorably to the idea when Ortiz floated it, and the commissioners at the Port of Corpus Christi panicked that their careful planning had not worked out as they'd hoped.

The Ingleside base was located in San Patricio County, across the bay of Corpus Christi.

"We worked with San Pat attorneys on a motion that would keep all the options open for the business community if a mission didn't develop by the time the base was scheduled to close," Ortiz said. "It preserved the base as a Navy asset until then."

It was a pretty audacious plan. Being on the inside, Ortiz knew DoD needed a place for their new homeland security mission, and South Texas was ideal.

Once again, Ortiz had figured a way through BRAC for his South Texas bases.

But in 2005, it was the local community's business leaders that undercut that effort. Immediately, they went to Texas Senator Kay Bailey Hutchison – and they contacted several commissioners – telling them that they did not want a new mission at Ingleside.

Publicly, they couched their opposition to Ortiz' plan as opposition to a "warm" base (a base that would remain open but without a mission) … even though they knew the coming homeland defense mission would stand up long before the mine warfare mission ended.

But their personal greed would prevail, at a tremendous cost to the local economy and local workers.

The local business and port decision makers – and Corpus Christi Mayor Loyd Neal – gave the BRAC commissioners all the reason they needed to close Naval Station Ingleside … by staying out of the fight until too late and allegedly getting word to individual commissioners that closing Ingleside would be fine with the community.

"My motion before the commissioners proposed the base would remain for two and a half more years, plenty of time for us to get a new mission together – AND preserve the commercial interests for the property, even if the mission fell through," said Ortiz. "It was the perfect marriage of business concerns for the property, and the economic concerns for the larger community."

"Senator Hutchison's staff assured me that she supported my motion to keep the base open," Ortiz said, describing the fast moving events at the marathon, days-long public BRAC hearing at a hotel in northern Virginia.

Final BRAC hearings were generally held at large hotels, so nobody had to go far to grab a nap, a shower, private meeting, or strategy session.

Staffs for Ortiz and Hutchison perfected the final language of the motion they would present.

The day before BRAC rendered a final decision on Naval Station Ingleside, Ortiz and his team played their final card.

"We told each commissioner the Texas delegation was united in support of my motion," Ortiz said. "We were so optimistic at that moment. Only one commissioner was mum on the idea. Every single other commissioner was intrigued by it."

"The Commission BRAC staff had already recommended that the

commissioners keep Ingleside open," Ortiz said, shaking his head, still amazed years later at the monumental mistake that was coming. "They were looking for the right way to do that. This was it. Everybody would have won."

It was noon. High noon, as it turned out, but Ortiz didn't know that yet.

Since the commissioners would discuss the future of Ingleside sometime that evening, Ortiz gave the BRAC staff the word that both Texas senators supported his amendment.

Ortiz took his team to lunch to continue the ongoing strategy session, talking about fallback positions to the vast number of possibilities.

On his way from back lunch, Ortiz saw a BRAC Commission staffer. What the staffer told him enraged him.

"The guy told me that Senator Hutchison had submitted very different language in a competing motion that could send this Center to any location in the Gulf, not to Ingleside – not even specifically to Texas," Ortiz said. "Her motion wasn't on behalf of Texas; it was on behalf of the business interests in the Coastal Bend – to undercut the BRAC commissioners' move to keep the base open."

Hutchison's move did two things: it undermined the momentum to keep Ingleside open; and it illustrated division, not unity, on the part of the Texas congressional delegation.

"She threw a great deal of confusion into the mix at a pivotal moment," Ortiz winced recalling the moment everything came undone. "I was blown away. You never really know who's on your side in a political battle, but in BRAC, no federal official ever opposes a base in their state. That's nuts."

But Hutchison did. Ortiz went hunting for Hutchison, who'd disappeared, along with her staff.

Ortiz was ... pissed. He ranted for a couple of minutes, coming to rest in front of a window – staring out. He made his last move.

Rather than stopping his efforts, he redoubled them, going back to each commissioner, reiterating that the motion originally had Hutchison's support, but noting that her support wasn't necessary for the commission to do the right thing by the Navy and the local community.

The local community writ large – including most business people, the area chamber of commerce, workers, families, etc. – supported

Ortiz' effort to keep the base open.

After going to all BRAC commissioners again, Ortiz still felt there was a majority-plus that would vote for his plan.

Gary Bushell, a local defense consultant and military supporter – who'd worked with Ortiz on every other BRAC round – was the voice bringing even worse news to Ortiz.

The downtown business community and several port commissioners had bullied San Patricio County Judge Terry Simpson into changing sides.

Naval Station Ingleside was located adjacent to Nueces County, but was literally located in San Patricio County, a smaller, poorer county.

Simpson had acquired a lawyer months earlier to look after San Patricio's interests specifically. Judge Simpson in Texas – and his lawyer in D.C. – were part of Ortiz' team working on language and strategy for Ortiz' plan on the Ingleside base.

"Before the commission brought up the Ingleside matter in the marathon hearing, we heard from Gary Bushell on behalf of San Patricio Judge Terry Simpson, telling us Judge Simpson asked us to stand down," Ortiz said, shaking his head.

Bushell said Simpson did "not seek any language or action that delays the Port of Corpus Christi to take control of the Naval Station Ingleside property."

That final knife in the effort to keep Ingleside open was the death blow. Without the support of the top elected official in the county where Ingleside was physically located, the gig was up. The Port of Corpus Christi and downtown business community won the political-economic battle.

Ortiz' efforts were now sufficiently undermined.

"I wanted to keep NSI [Ingleside] open to ensure Homeland Defense in the Western Gulf of Mexico," Ortiz said. "We were undermined at several junctures. The state political leaders did not attend the all-important site visits in the summer of 2005, telegraphing the BRAC commissioners that NSI was not important to them."

"The only time Governor [Rick] Perry [R-TX] came through for our community with a state financial package – only five weeks before the commission acted – was when the opportunity came to move NAS Oceana [an air station in Virginia] assets to Kingsville,"

Ortiz said. "They just acted as if they didn't care about Ingleside. Ah, they weren't acting."

"My biggest concern all along was homeland defense … and our ability to secure the gulf, the Strategic Military Sealift Port here in Corpus Christi, and area refineries," Ortiz said. "From a purely military point of view, I was deeply concerned about al Qaeda cells loose inside the U.S. and elsewhere."

"BRAC commissioners told me they understood the need for homeland defense in the Gulf, and wanted to include that language in their report," Ortiz said, still shaking his head. "But once the business community pulled the San Pat judge out of our effort, it appeared that the local [San Patricio] political leadership also wanted Ingleside closed."

"My conscious was clear then – and now," Ortiz said. "I am at peace that we did our best to save the base. After BRAC, not a single Navy ship was left in the Gulf. God forbid … an attack in the Gulf would cripple our nation and our petrochemical industry."

"As it was, just a week after the BRAC commission voted with the Corpus Christi business community to close NSI, Hurricane Katrina illustrated the urgent need for a military presence in the Gulf coast," Ortiz noted. "Katrina blew away our Gulf oil platforms and kicked one of the legs out from under the national oil supply."

"It was ships from Ingleside that responded first to the tragedy on behalf of the federal government. The other port that would send a response was at Pascagoula [MS]. But their assets were in the hurricane's path," he said. "Most were damaged or scattered. East coast ships steamed there as quickly as they could, but stocking and steaming days meant they were a week away."

"It still absolutely breaks my heart that the local community got so completely screwed in all this," Ortiz scowled. "We could have been screwed a little worse. First, local taxes could have gone up to pay for the Port to take possession of the property."

"That would have been particularly insidious for us, given that the Nueces County taxpayers had helped pay for the base in the first place," he said. "We were their first investors."

"So I got the Congress to forgive the $250 million it would have cost for the port to repossess NSI. On that," Ortiz shrugged, "Senator Hutchison worked with me, since – on that matter – it was what the local business community wanted. A free, modern port structure."

"We also could have been a little more screwed in terms of how the closure, redevelopment, post-redevelopment job training, education, and such were structured," Ortiz lamented. "As it was, I was not willing to direct all the federal money – available to communities around the country affected by BRAC – to the Port of Corpus Christi alone," as the Port wanted.

"Candidly, I was still pissed at the lengths they went to in order to assure the base was closed while they alone would be able to profit off the property at the base while South Texans lost jobs, and many small businesses lost a big part of their consumer base," he said, in a way that screamed he still remains irritated.

"But back then, many of the port commissioners, the business community – even the local paper – demanded that the port be the sole recipient of all federal funding, and lead the redevelopment efforts as they saw fit," Ortiz said, eyes narrowed. "I been in politics long enough to know that the business community takes care of themselves first."

"This was just too important a thing to leave to unelected, self-interested businesspeople and port commissioners, with no training in job training or transition," Ortiz explained. "The only way to fairly administer the massive, community-wide redevelopment was to have it governed by the local elected officials from the counties and cities most affected by the Ingleside closure."

"You know, it's possible the port and the Corpus Christi business community could have pulled off a successful redevelopment, but they haven't," Ortiz said.

"Their strategic vision didn't include the global economic meltdown at the precise moment we needed desperately to find a new entity to make Ingleside its hub of operations," Ortiz said. "Right when we needed to grow big, in a new direction, the economy melted down."

"My philosophy has always been: 'if it ain't broke, don't fix it'," Ortiz smiled. "Naval Station Ingleside did not need to be closed. Up until the moment the commission voted, it was possible they would side with the wider South Texas community ... and homeland defense needs."

"But the local business community won," he said. "They wanted to do more and make more money from the property. It was a strategic, stupid gamble with the economic futures of so many in the coastal bend of Texas."

"They lost on that spectacular gamble," Ortiz said evenly. "When that gamble foundered, so did the economic opportunities for tens of thousands of our neighbors."

11 – DEPOT WARRIOR

RENEGADE HOUSE MEMBER Walter Jones, (R-NC), spoke glowingly of the Democrat he described as "a very special person."

A conservative Republican, Walter Jones followed his father (Walter Jones, Sr., D-NC) to the House of Representatives.

Ortiz served on the Merchant Marine and Fisheries Committee when the senior Jones chaired it in the 1980s and 1990s – so Ortiz knew both father and son.

As a freshman Representative in 1995, the young Walter Jones landed on the House Armed Services Committee, where Ortiz had been serving for over a decade. That – plus Ortiz' connection with his father – laid the foundation for a friendship that began immediately.

"We served together on the Armed Services Committee," said Jones, in his rich Carolina brogue. "Solomon was a rare man in Congress. He wanted to get things done, and so did I. We became good friends."

Jones talked about the rarity of a friendship across party lines, in the mid-1990s, just after House Speaker Newt Gingrich (R-GA) had successfully infused the GOP spin machine with the narrative that Democrats weren't just wrong, they were evil.

But there were a small number of members of Congress who wanted to proceed to cooperation – not whiney confrontation over made up issues.

Ortiz was rare, Jones said, because, "Solomon wanted to find common ground with our colleagues … and he would do anything for our military. He is a guy who prefers agreement, not disagreement."

Simple as that description is, members of Congress preferring to solve problems were a tiny minority.

"Very early in my congressional career, we worked together on the Depot Caucus," Jones said. The House of Representatives had – and still has – self-prescribed working groups that are ad hoc and not part of the committee structure.

The Depot Caucus is one of the larger, more significant working groups. Depots are the huge repair places for tanks, helicopters, planes – all the huge weapons of transport and war in the U.S. arsenal.

A number of people not well versed in how the United States maintains, stores, and repairs these large weapons advocated in the mid-1990s that the military could "outsource" those activities … or "contract out" the cost for that work.

Maintaining and repairing large vehicles costs a great deal of money – from the specialty spare parts needed on site to repair sophisticated technology … to the high end labor with the expertise in these repairs … to the gigantic facilities needed to house all those elements.

While less than half of the maintenance of the armed forces can be done cheaper in the private sector (grounds keeping, food preparation, etc.) – the most important part, or "core work," of the depot system – is the vehicle maintenance and repair, and attendant real estate needs.

Congress actually formalized a split of what it called "depot-level" work: 40% could be done by private contractors … but 60% (including everything deemed "core" work) was to be conducted in military depots.

That was known throughout the Congress and the Pentagon as the "60-40" language, or the "Ortiz" language.

The Ortiz language stemmed the ability of private contractors to appropriate the weapon maintenance work from the public depots around the country.

The political climate in the mid-1990s provided the first real chance private contractors had to break into the government depot market, and they saw an ideal chance to "compete" with the government for the same work at a lower price.

But their logic was laughable.

They claimed they could do the work cheaper if the government gave them the property and paid the bills for the property. But then that's hardly doing the same work cheaper, since the plans of private contractors depended on the government to provide the overhead.

Many people could do the work cheaper if the government provides the overhead.

The political motivation of congressional supporters of private contracting for the military's large weapons, centered on the civilian unions that were part of the specialized depot labor pools.

That was where private contractors found common cause with the Republican leaders in Congress – nearly all unions tended to support Democrats, and vice-versa.

Ortiz' (successful) argument in keeping the maintenance of the big weapons was two-fold: it was most certainly not cheaper to privatize the major depot work; and the labor pool made all the difference when it came to successful depot maintenance.

The actual cost of depot maintenance was laid bare in a GAO (General Accounting Office – the investigators for Congress) report requested by Ortiz. The GAO report emphatically reaffirmed that private contractors could NOT do the same work cheaper.

The Persian Gulf conflict of the early 1990s offered insight into the people who conducted maintenance and repair on the battlefield.

"Many workers at CCAD – and most other depots – are veterans," Ortiz said. "So they know how battlefield operations work. When the Army needed helicopter repairs on the battlefield in 1991, there were a few private contractors from the companies that built the helicopters, but most were CCAD employees."

"Once the bullets started flying, the private contractors fled," Ortiz said, shaking his head. "Leaving the civilian CCAD workers laughing their asses off, to carry the entire workload."

There was no clearer example of why the military wanted the maintenance of the helicopters, planes and tanks – that carried U.S. troops into battle – conducted by civilians who understood the importance of every single repair … and who would stand with troops in the field as long as necessary.

"Working with Solomon on depots solidified our friendship," said Rep. Jones. "He was a leader in making sure depots did not get privatized. He taught me quite a bit, particularly on depots, but also on the Armed Services Committee."

12 – DEFICIT REDUCTION

THE EARLY 1990s was a time of tremendous success for Ortiz and the 27th Congressional District.

The military complex around the northern part of Ortiz' district was a great economic engine, as were international water ports at both ends of the district.

International trade agreements moved labor markets closer to Mexico, and the movement of goods from Mexico meant that the southern part of Ortiz' district – the Rio Grande Valley – was benefiting tremendously from the associated traffic now moving through that corridor.

In 1993, President Bill Clinton was pushing the first comprehensive budget deficit reduction bill, the foundation of the effort that expanded the U.S. economy in the 1990s to historical levels.

As with any effort to put the nation's finances in order, deficit reduction is extraordinarily painful. People who earned more than $250,000 annually would see an income tax increase under the Clinton plan that passed; and businesses would see "user fees" – aka corporate taxes – to offset the cost of federal services. This included the energy industry.

The budget bill was incredibly unpopular. Republicans, who'd held the White House for a dozen years, organized themselves into a potent opposition. They represented the bill as a tax increase for all Americans.

The lie was relatively easy for them to perpetuate.

Their voters were already angry that Clinton had bested George H.W. Bush in the 1992 election, and were easily convinced that any attempt by Clinton and the Democrats to balance the federal budget would do them great harm.

Republicans were already trying to stack the political debate – as early as 1988 – with the bombastic and popular Rush Limbaugh reaching socially-conservative voters and indoctrinating them with false information and wild distortions.

By 1993, that meant Democrats in Congress found themselves fighting battles on three fronts: actually passing the legislation, explaining what was really in it, and then battling the lies already part of their voters' basic understanding of the deficit reduction bill.

The political dynamic in Congress as a result of the remarkable disinformation campaign meant members – including Ortiz – were facing voters who were certain their taxes would go up, even when that was patently untrue.

One of the industries the Clinton deficit reduction plan would tax was the energy industry, a major player in both Ortiz' South Texas district and elsewhere around Texas.

Voting in favor of the deficit reduction plan would be a risky proposition for a member from an oil state. Ortiz was conflicted about the vote.

"I must have cast tens of thousands of votes on the House floor – but there are a few I remember like it was a few hours ago," Ortiz said. "Going to war in the Persian Gulf in 1991, the deficit reduction vote in '93, the 9-11 response and war on al Qaeda in 2001, postponing BRAC in 2004, and maybe a few others are so vivid."

The only one of those votes that was non-military in nature was the deficit reduction vote. The high profile nature of it, and the electoral fallout that was sure to accompany it, traumatized Ortiz.

"Lord knows it was time to pay the bills," Ortiz snorted. "But then – like today – the conversation is run by the people who make over a quarter million dollars a year. And the lie they perpetuate is this: everybody's getting their taxes raised."

"That was frustrating," he said. "The only people who were calling me were the pissed off people that Limbaugh and his ilk fooled into believing that everybody's taxes were getting raised."

"In the end, I had faith that the dishonesty about whose taxes were going up would be dispelled when people actually did their taxes in the following year," Ortiz grimaced. "I don't know why I thought that."

What stiffened his spine on the vote was a summary of the number of people in each of the five counties in his district by income category.

That stark math illustrated precisely how many people in Ortiz' congressional district would see a tax increase: 0.0083% of them.

Far less than one one-thousandth of Ortiz district would see tax increases.

"But in the end, it didn't matter what the facts were, it didn't account for the number of people who got so fooled by the talk show crap," Ortiz said candidly. "People filled out their taxes, only mad that they were paying taxes; and never put together that their federal taxes either went down or remained the same."

It was easier to be in a mob that didn't care about the truth, than to seek the truth, to be curious, to be informed.

"Political debate has always been tough; candidates distinguish themselves from each other at the margins, we exaggerate the opponent's weaknesses," Ortiz said. "But this was a whole new level of fooling people."

"I've got lots of friends that are Republicans, friends here in Texas who were supporters, even friends who weren't politically supportive," Ortiz said. "I had lots of friends in Congress who were Republicans. This is not about Republicans and Democrats."

"This was about facts and made up crap," Ortiz said. "1994 was a bad year for the republic in terms of our political debate. Half the country believed the lies the Republicans were serving up about what we'd done; the Republicans were tutored by Newt Gingrich to describe opponents as immoral and illegitimate. They had a whole list of poll-tested words calling us the devil."

Despite the political hurricane blowing through the country, Ortiz still won re-election by nearly 60%. Blessed with a weak opponent who had no money, Ortiz survived the wrath of angry constituents in the 1994 mid-term election. But he was elected with a depleted margin of victory.

The *National Journal* said following that election, "Ortiz was one of the few Democrats who did not have to sit down in horror on election night," when it was clear the Republicans had claimed the majority in the House of Representatives.

It was a rare place for any member of Congress, but Ortiz was a long-time confidant of dozens of Republicans in the House and the

Senate.

"The country definitely lost a lot in the 1994 election, but for us, it wasn't so bad in terms of navigating the legislative process," Ortiz explained. "I mean, the committee chairmen and senior members were good friends of mine. I looked for places to maneuver – and still got money for South Texas education, defense, and economic development."

"The Republican leadership in Congress began a focused, consistent series of investigations into the Clinton Administration with the singular goal of finding something to hook impeachment on," Ortiz said.

Three years later, they finally hooked onto something perfect for their nefarious political needs. Testifying before a civil court, Clinton lied about fellatio with intern Monica Lewinsky.

The oral sex part was icky – and demoralizing for Democrats and Independents – and wasn't against the law. But it did make for marvelous political theatre.

What they could not win at the ballot box, they tried desperately to overturn through impeachment.

"Those were very unsettling times," Ortiz sighed. "Every week I weighed not seeking re-election. We weren't legislating anymore; one side was destroying the other for sport. But I just couldn't – wouldn't – quit just because opponents made it uncomfortable and more difficult. It's supposed to be hard."

Each time he had the internal debate about not seeking re-election, Ortiz said, it ended with the certainty that he was doing the right thing for the people he was representing, and he put it out of his mind.

Indeed the Democrats did bleed over the votes they cast to pay the nation's bills. They lost the majority in Congress. Marjorie Margolie (D-PA) was a freshman member of the House then; when she cast the last, deciding vote on deficit reduction, the dye was cast for her political future. She lost the next election.

But history proved them exactly right in the move to pay off the deficit and the debt the nation had accrued in the 1980s and early 1990s.

The new Republican majority spent the following years proclaiming the austerity measures and added revenue in the economy were both merely flukes. The deficit reduction bill, they claimed falsely, was unnecessary to the economic development in the United States. The deficit would have reduced itself magically. Right.

By 1996, Rupert Murdoch's Fox cable network launched a unique type of reality show they called a "news" channel, that big-footed into the midst of the conservative political food fight, opposing Clinton and the Democrats at every turn and being the centerpiece of what Hillary Clinton famously called the "vast right wing conspiracy."

The conspiracy the then-First Lady described was wealthy interests using conservative radio and the Fox Cable "news" channel to label traditional news media as an enemy of "real" Americans for promoting liberalism (which conservatives associated with balanced information, gun bans, gay rights, minority rights, abortion, taxes and government).

Liberals for decades were successfully described by opponents as "tax and spend." Democrats have never been as single minded about simple message discipline; but for years, they unsuccessfully tried to hang the moniker of "borrow and spend" on Republicans.

Yet the people who needed to hear that simply weren't listening. They heard only what the Fox cable channel hurled out … echoed by the conservative radio hosts inspired by Rush Limbaugh.

13 – SAD TALE OF BORDER SECURITY

THE SECURITY FIRESTORM that followed 9-11 burned through the traditional mindsets of the national security complex, and the times demanded new, smarter thinking.

The United States policy makers did not rise to that challenge.

Their remarkable focus on tax cuts, banking reform (favoring the nation's biggest banks and landing a body blow to the world economy later in the decade), and privatizing aspects of the government to reward generous (mostly Republican) contributors … all conspired to add to the enormity of the U.S. debt – and deeply damaged U.S. national security in the early years after 9-11.

Ortiz was at the center of the conversation on two central security issues: military readiness and border security.

Given he was a former lawman – and represented a border district in South Texas – Ortiz was intimately familiar with border security along the Mexican border.

On September 10, 2001, border security was conducted among several agencies – each a fiefdom unto themselves – in a sort of patchwork along the 2,000 mile U.S.-Mexico border.

Undocumented job seekers from Mexico and Central America regularly illegally crossed the notoriously porous U.S.-Mexico border.

But Ortiz was blown away by the story he began to hear repeatedly from Border Patrol agents and other law enforcement agents along the border in the years after 9-11.

For a very long time, the regular practice for the Border Patrol was to release the large number of non-Mexican illegal immigrants, caught by our Border Patrol, into the general population of the United States.

"The most frightening part of this was the border cops were certain they are letting bad guys go in this process," Ortiz said, his voice rising, clearly still animated by the boneheaded U.S. policy. "Now understand this was not about legal immigration, or illegal immigrants we weren't catching. This is entirely about illegal immigrants our government caught, then released."

The notoriously stupid policy was called "catch and release" – and prior to 2001, it was an avenue into the country understood by very few people.

Here's how it worked: when the Border Patrol caught an illegal immigrant, they processed them. Mexicans went right back over the border. Mexico must take Mexican citizens back.

But when they weren't Mexican, they were classified as "OTM" ("other than Mexican").

"As with everything in the government, it all came down to money," Ortiz said grimly. "Border and immigration officials didn't have the funding to house all the OTMs we were catching ... so, they released the non-Mexican immigrants they caught ... into the general population of the country."

"The truly stupid thing we did was give them a letter compelling them to return for a deportation hearing sometime in the future," Ortiz smirked. "Right. Then they dropped them off at bus depots, to travel to other points in the U.S."

"We knew they'd been doing this for a long time, but we couldn't get the administration engaged to end it – because it would cost so much money," Ortiz said. "Once we started digging, Customs officers said over 95% do not return for their deportation hearing – and I thought that number was low."

"They would not say how many were released or were then at large within the United States," Ortiz said. "What law enforcement told me was mortifying. They said, 'We feel like we are letting terrorists loose inside the U.S.'"

Those were the high-stress times after the 9-11 attacks, when everyday was September 12.

"Cops told me, for instance, they'd caught hundreds of illegals without papers, who didn't speak Spanish, and who appear to be Arabic or African – from their appearance, dress and language sounds."

"These OTMs would cross and seek out a Border Patrol officer to surrender to in order to get the letter for travel purposes," Ortiz continued.

"They'd make up a name and country, so they wouldn't show up on a watch list – and a magistrate gave them the letter to return for a deportation date," Ortiz said.

Then these illegal immigrants, whom the U.S. border authorities had arrested, and now released, were free to go anywhere in the United States they wished.

Certainly nearly all these immigrants were hooking up with family or friends or jobs, for the same reason immigrants always come here, to live free, make money, and improve their lives.

It was the small percent who were exploiting this policy to do us harm that Ortiz and his colleagues worried about.

"These front line cops were terrified … and they were tough guys," Ortiz said. "They are terrified they were letting al Qaeda in and handing them a pass … scared if they said anything, they'd lose their job … and scared of sitting in front of the next 9-11 Commission testifying: 'yes, we knew they were al Qaeda … yes, we let them in.'"

"Nobody had wanted to mention it because just to say it out loud would get them fired," Ortiz said evenly. "These were cops with kids in college and a mortgage. They were forced to choose between their job and their family's security – and sounding the alarm about this security breach."

Front line officers told Ortiz that so many OTMs from special interest countries (Arabic nations in which al Qaeda were known to operate) were coming through every day, that the Border Patrol was overwhelmed.

Part of what motivated law enforcement to come forward was the brouhaha over whether or not the nation should have a comprehensive analysis of what happened before and during the al Qaeda attacks on 9-11.

Many in Congress, the media, and advocacy groups around the country, advocated a special, nonpartisan commission – in part to learn precisely what happened, and in part to fix areas in which the government fell down on the job.

Part of the Administration's (and Congress') motive in pushing the decision on the Iraq war in advance of the 2002 elections was to deflect both the fact that they'd let Osama bin Laden escape in the mountains of Tora Bora, and the loud demands for the non-partisan commission to understand exactly what happened.

In late 2002, after the midterm elections, during which the hostility to establishing this commission was a bigger issue than the Republicans had imagined, Congress was finally embarrassed into passing the legislation setting up the commission.

President George W. Bush, dragged kicking and screaming to support the bill, finally signed it into law. Bush had legitimate political concerns with what he was doing.

In effect, he was giving a nonpartisan group of citizens a warrant to talk to anybody and review anything associated with the attacks.

Under the very best of circumstances, any administration's response to a surprise terrorist attack would include any number of missteps – that's part of it.

The 2004 presidential election loomed large at this point. Bush and his allies feared a report that would find fault with anything they had done and put Bush on the defensive in the 2004 campaign, a campaign that was promising to be as excruciatingly close as the disputed election of 2000.

But the Bush Administration had plenty of moves to undermine any real examination of their actions or lack thereof, motivations surrounding what they did to prevent the attacks, and their response on 9-11.

The second war – this one in Iraq – launched in March of 2003.

By the spring of 2003, the 9-11 Commission was off to a slow start, operating on the fly with insufficient funding to help it meet the target day for the final report in late May 2004. The first hearings began on March 31, in New York City

Americans – and the world – began to hear the pained, and painful, testimony of officials whose work in advance of the attacks, and in response to the attacks, was not ideal.

Much of the testimony was deceptive.

The Commission's senior counsel, John Farmer, Jr., told the *St. Louis Post-Dispatch* in 2009 that the Commission "discovered that ... what government and military officials had told Congress, the Commission, the media, and the public about who knew what when – was almost entirely, and inexplicably, untrue."

"At some level of the government, at some point in time ... there was a decision not to tell the truth about what happened," Farmer continued. "The (NORAD) tapes told a radically different story from what had been told to us and the public."

That Farmer waited until Bush was gone from office reflects the political pressure to keep actual information about the deception out of the public realm – because the cover up would make Bush susceptible to impeachment, although that was unlikely given his party controlled Congress and had almost religiously followed the White House's instructions over the years.

In Farmer's book, *"The Ground Truth: The Untold Story of America Under Attack on 9/11"* (published September 2009), he quotes the chairman of the 9-11 Commission, former New Jersey Republican Governor Thomas Kean sharing his conclusion.

"We to this day don't know why NORAD told us what they told us, it was just so far from the truth," Kean told Farmer for his book about the commission's journey.

But it was the powerful testimony before the commission alone, beginning in the spring of 2003, that inspired Border Patrol officers to risk their careers, their family's livelihoods, and their future liberty to get word to the commission and Congress about the very real, current national security crisis on the southern border.

If the administration had known who was talking to Ortiz (in early 2004) – and soon others in Congress – they would have been fired immediately and charged with treason.

It was just that important for the powers-that-be to keep these matters under wraps.

Ortiz, ever the Mr. Bipartisan, worked with his Texas colleague Henry Bonilla (R-TX). Ortiz and Bonilla co-chaired the Border Caucus, an ad hoc organization of House members who represented border districts.

Neither one wanted to embarrass the administration, endanger the careers of law enforcement officers talking to them, or throw another scare at a very twitchy population. But both wanted answers – and they would take them behind closed doors. They never got any, even privately.

Repeatedly rebuffed by the agencies with jurisdiction over this mess, Ortiz and Bonilla raised the stakes by taking their concerns directly to the President during the late summer before the 2004 election.

Sufficiently ignored and frustrated, they raised the stakes again and went public.

They made the clarion call in a letter to the president in early August 2004, asking him and Department of Homeland Security (DHS) Secretary Tom Ridge a series of questions Ortiz and Bonilla believed were at the heart of quantifying how many OTMs were at large inside the country, and how to find them.

"Yet nobody wanted to quantify the amount of OTMs at large in the general population, and nobody wanted to talk about it," Ortiz said. "I started taking members down to Texas to talk to front line law enforcement guys."

Then DHS tried to bar any of their employees from talking with Ortiz, Bonilla, ANYBODY else. That ham-handed attempt was unsuccessful. More than one patriot disregarded those directions.

Except for Bonilla, most House Republicans had zero interest in bringing this to the forefront just months before an election.

Congressman Jim Turner, the top Democrat on the House Homeland Security Committee released a report on homeland security failures, including the release of OTMs into the general population of the United States.

"Every single administration official – every one – ignored us, stonewalled us, or just acted like we were wildly panicking for no reason," Ortiz sneered. "We were so pissed. Our border agents were finding coins, newspapers, clothes that were unique to countries of interest to us – places where we knew al Qaeda was operating."

Despite going public with the information, with no direct sources to quote by name, media outlets were disinclined to follow up on initial stories. They had a chatty congressman making extraordinary claims. And they had no more.

Once or twice, Ortiz persuaded an agent to talk to a reporter, with his office on the line, and without using the agent's name. Still, that gave stories nowhere to go, nobody to quote.

But at the end of 2004, the new Homeland Security Department made a big mistake – and lent great credence to what Ortiz was saying. In a year-end report highlighting their successes in fighting terrorism, they included a blurb about the capture of a South African possibly connected to the bombing of a U.S. Consulate office.

"On July 19, 2004, Border Patrol agents conducting routine

immigration inspections at McAllen Miller International Airport in McAllen, Texas noticed discrepancies with a South African passport belonging to a passenger," the DHS press release read.

"Further research indicated that the passenger was wanted for questioning for involvement in the bombing of a U.S. Consulate office," it continued. "…agents interviewed the individual. Removal proceedings were initiated for this individual."

Almost immediately, the press release was pulled, corrected, and re-released without reference to the South African at the McAllen Airport.

Ortiz later learned from officers making the arrest that the South African, a woman, was carrying wet clothes and did not arrive at the airport by plane.

Almost immediately, a U.S. Attorney (who worked for the Bush Justice Department) in Houston, called Ortiz to beg him not to talk about it. While the U.S. Attorney was cagey with information, he alluded that they flipped her and set her loose to go after the next guy up in the terrorist cell.

While that verified Ortiz' contention that terrorists were crossing the South Texas border, he went quiet on the particulars of the South African arrest.

The 9-11 Commission issued its final report on July 22, 2004, and both presidential campaigns extolled excerpts of the report that segued with their message, and essentially said they were still studying most of the recommendations.

What the administration and the Republicans in Congress could not anticipate was the overwhelming, popular response to the commission's hearings, and painful fairness.

Neither presidential campaign knew what to do with the information Ortiz was giving them. President Bush settled on ignoring him.

Senator John Kerry, the Democratic candidate, determined the issue was too difficult to understand and might cost him support among the Hispanic communities of Arizona, Nevada, New Mexico and California – all of which he would need to prevail in the general election.

The commission's report – compelling and well written – became a best seller on Amazon.com.

Suddenly, politicians began campaigning on adopting the

commission's recommendations in their entirety after the elections.

In December 2004, the Congress enacted the Intelligence Reform Act, which codified the commission report's recommendations into law.

A key component of it was to beef up border security measures with specific funding to radically increase the presence of all the agencies that dealt with border control.

The commission noted that their recommendations were the very least the government needed to do to begin fixing border security lapses.

Specifically the law required 10,000 additional Border Patrol agents, 4,000 additional immigration agents and 40,000 additional detention beds, at minimum, to begin addressing the border security issues the nation had ignored for so long.

But bowing to the dual realities of a burgeoning deficit borne of tax cuts and unpaid bills since March of 2001, the commission recommended stretching it out over five years.

That gave Ortiz and border security experts hard numbers to fund and follow to put their hands around the OTM issue, and the myriad of other security concerns there.

So every single year until 2011, the law required funding for 2,000 additional Border Patrol agents, 800 additional immigration agents, and 8,000 additional detention beds.

The mounting debt infected every decision that crossed the deck of the ship of state. Bush and the Republicans – trying to fit in the annual bribe aka "tax cut" despite the crush of the deficit – simply didn't fund the border security components they'd just passed into law.

The first presidential budget out, instead of funding the 2,000 Border Patrol agents by the 9-11 commission law, Bush funded only 210 – 1,790 below what the commission said was the least we should do.

Despite the fit Ortiz pitched to guilt the Congress into living up to the law they had just passed, the final appropriations bill delivered only 1,000 Border Patrol agents, half of what the commission said was the very least they should do.

The same bill funded far, far fewer immigration agents and beds to hold OTMs.

By the next year at the end of the funding process, Congress had funded 1,500 fewer Border Patrol agents than the 9-11 Commission demanded, and 8,250 fewer detention beds than the 9-11 Commission demanded.

And so it went. Congress was pretending to do something, but never spending the money to make it so.

14 – IRAQ WAR AND THE FIGHT TO FIX A BROKEN MILITARY

MILITARY "READINESS" DESCRIBES the condition of the military force before, during, and after deployment. To be ready, the force must be able to accomplish the mission it is trained to do – with the right people, equipment, and sufficient time to train on that equipment.

How ready we were yesterday foretells how well we fight today; how ready we are to fight today determines how well we fight tomorrow.

Readiness is the central concern for U.S. military policy makers; it is how we collectively judge our military might.

In the week after 9-11, Deputy National Security Advisor Richard Clarke was shocked that President George Bush gave his national security team instructions to hook Iraq into 9-11, which became an albatross around the neck of Bush – and the nation – in the decade to come.

Just nine months after sending U.S. troops to Afghanistan to battle al Qaeda – and months after Bush lost bin Laden in his bunker in the Tora Bora Mountains – the administration desperately needed something else on which to focus the attention of the United States.

That would be Iraq. It was unfinished business of the president's father, George H.W. Bush in 1991. Hussein made an attempt on Bush-the-father's life in Kuwait in 1993.

But publicly, those were not good enough reasons to go into Iraq.

So the administration either made stuff up, or – as Ortiz believed

– Bush just naively took things Iraqi ex-patriots made up at face value, to lead the nation to believe Iraq had – and was developing – weapons of mass destruction, and that al Qaeda was operating there before the U.S. invaded.

Neither of those things were true.

Well, the al Qaeda part would eventually became true when bin Laden's forces massed in Iraq AFTER THE U.S. INVASION to train against, and fight, the Americans in the field.

Before the invasion, Iraq was one of the few nations in which the United Nations kept a nation's military under their thumb – with the U.S. and Great Britain providing the bulk of the air power.

But a "no-fly" zone does not cover most things happening on the ground, so manipulating a large part of the U.S. population to believe that Iraq had secret weapons to turn against us worked with extraordinary – but alarming – precision.

While nearly every nation on the planet stood with the United States in the months after 9-11, the United States' insistence that a war was necessary in Iraq drove them away.

The U.S. stood alone. Then with Great Britain, but without NATO.

Later the United States formed a "coalition of the willing" which included a dozen to 40 troops from a variety of nations, for which the U.S. paid a pretty penny to enjoy the illusion that the U.S. first strike and occupation of Iraq was the result a multinational coalition.

Great Britain was the only actual military ally for the U.S. in Iraq.

Bush – with Secretary of State Colin Powell and others in the administration – successfully manipulated just over half the nation into believing that the danger was so astounding that it justified the United States becoming a first-strike nation.

Since half the nation and the Congress were unconvinced – indeed unilaterally opposed to a second war in Iraq – Bush used that, making a second war a matter of (false) patriotism, dividing the country even in the midst of an already-ongoing war.

It was a shameful gutting of national spirit precisely when the nation could ill afford it.

So completely did the Bush Administration and his political organization fool the nation, that in a poll – prior to invading Iraq – 70% of Americans believed Iraq was responsible for the 9-11 attacks.

Like so much they manipulated the American people over, that was incredibly wrong.

The attacks were – in fact – planned by a Saudi, an Egyptian, and a Pakistani. Their names and nationalities were widely known in the hours after the 9-11 attack. It was no mystery.

The 9-11 hijackers themselves were almost entirely Saudis, plus a few other Middle Easterners – zero Iraqis. Zero.

Once it was apparent that no weapons could be found, the purpose for the second war in Iraq evolved into bringing democracy or nation-building, otherwise a prospect that galled Republicans.

Iraqi scientist Rafid Ahmed Alwan al-Janabi (codename: "Curveball") was the primary source for the Bush Administration of the bullshit upon which we committed our blood and treasure in Iraq.

NO WEAPONS OF MASS DESTRUCTION

In February 2011, Mr. al-Janabi ("Curveball") candidly told the *Guardian of London* that he lied to the Central Intelligence Agency (CIA) about biological weapons in order to get the U.S. to attack and remove Hussein from power.

Al-Janabi professed to be very surprised that his large tale of massive weapons was the foundation of the U.S. justification for war.

But during 2002 – long before the U.S. Congress was seriously considering authorizing another war – the amount of ordnance British and American aircraft dropped in the no-fly zones of Iraq increased by almost 300% compared to earlier years.

By August of 2002, the no-fly zone strikes became "a full air offensive," according to sources that talked to the *Guardian*.

The *Times of London* later quoted General Tommy Franks, the U.S. allied commander, saying that the bombing was designed to "degrade" the Iraqi air defenses in advance of the coming invasion.

In October 2002, the U.S. Congress finally debated the Iraq war resolution.

Ortiz did not vote on passage; the date of the vote moved around a half dozen times or more and Ortiz had scheduled and re-scheduled a medical procedure around the vote.

Finally, he scheduled the surgery on his throat to repair his vocal chords the last time. He went to the House floor to speak in favor of the resolution authorizing force, but he remained deeply conflicted given the dearth of proof on the question of WMD in Iraq.

His support for passing the resolution was based on two things: overwhelming support for the second war in South Texas, and his desire to give the administration the "benefit of the doubt" when it came to trusting that they had the goods on Iraqi WMD.

"The president's guys went through all the evidence with us – and they didn't have it," Ortiz said.

It was compelling, but felt thin, Ortiz said. That was the most common backroom chatter among the House members before the vote. That was overlaid with the political concerns of the Republicans who needed this vote, so they could use this issue against Democrats in the 2002 midterm election.

"But they also told us, they had more they just couldn't share," Ortiz said. "That made everybody feel like a tool. It came down to giving the president the benefit of the doubt in the midst of a war."

Ortiz gave the commander in chief the benefit of the doubt. He regrets that decision.

SUPPORT OF THE WAR

"Of course I regret supporting the Iraq war – we were lied to and based our decision on what they told us," Ortiz said. "I believed the president. I believed he would not intentionally go to war on so little information. I was wrong."

"But once soldiers are deployed, that's it," Ortiz said. "You support the guys – whatever they need."

Therein was the brilliance of the strategy of President Bush's political guru (Karl Rove) in bringing the vote before the elections. Once the troops were deployed, any naysayers on the Iraq policy would be said to be "against the troops."

That bullshit works every single time.

"The worst thing the administration did – besides mislead the nation and the Congress on the huge question of launching a second war – was to insist that we vote on the question just prior to the 2002 election," Ortiz said. "That was awful, for the country, for the military, for our NATO alliance … for history."

About the time Ortiz went under the knife, the House of Representatives passed the Iraqi war resolution, 297-133.

A decade later, the U.S. military has almost entirely left Iraq, in the wake of losing over 4,400 U.S. soldiers, with 32,000 wounded in action, (at least) 100,000 civilian deaths, and the aftermath of an ongoing savage sectarian war.

By late 2003, the massive movement of troops and equipment was beginning to panic those in Congress who dealt most often with U.S. military policy.

The force, geared up for action in Afghanistan, then diverted to Iraq, was running low on equipment and other resources – and deployments were happening so fast that troops weren't training sufficiently.

"Our reliance on the National Guard is a good thing," Ortiz said. "They are part of the active force when the big Army is overextended. But we ran through their equipment and deployed too many Guardsmen."

It was a moment in time that Congress was dealing with multiple new domestic security issues. Deploying so many Guard assets meant insufficient Guardsmen and equipment to respond to another massive 9-11-type attack.

Here's the kicker – any Member of Congress who talked about the widening gap in resources would be charged with a crime, to be forever remembered as a traitor. In order to talk publicly about the diminished military, Members of Congress had to be prepared for all the political/legal baggage that comes that that level of a crime.

So for months, Members of Congress who wanted to speak up, hand-delivered personal letters to the president or members of his administration that were immediately classified top secret.

The Members' collective anxiety built and spread beyond the Armed Services Committee.

They were in an untenable position. They knew what was going on. By now the force in the field was cannibalizing equipment to repair other equipment, in the absence of new equipment.

The U.S. had eaten through forward-stationed materiel and equipment positioned at critical places around the planet.

The question finally came to the fore when a soldier, in Iraq, in an audience hearing Secretary Donald Rumsfeld speak, asked the secretary about the acute equipment shortage and talked about how that affected military operations.

The most astounding part of that exchange was when the question was asked of Secretary Rumsfeld, and the soldier took him to task, the applause of several hundred troops listening was loud and sustained. And long. That was remarkably rare.

At the outset of the readiness crisis, circa late 2003, Ortiz instructed his Readiness Subcommittee staff to find a legal way to make the facts known about the seriousness of the matter.

That was an impossible task, given the tight control the administration had over any matter that could portray them unfavorably – even if it cost the lives of soldiers in the field.

By early 2004, Paul Arcangeli, Ortiz' brilliant Readiness Subcommittee expert and former Army bomb disposal expert, made a breakthrough. He suggested that Ortiz request that the General Accounting Office (GAO) conduct a series of investigations – and public reports – to evaluate the U.S. readiness stance.

GAO is the government's top accounting firm. They work for Congress and their investigators also hold top clearances for their work.

Painstakingly thorough, GAO reports are not a bang-bang effort. They never promise when a report will be final, and the typical turnaround is at least a year.

They also bear purposefully bland names. The first Ortiz-requested reports were named: "Biennial suggestions for Congressional oversight" and "Improved Oversight and Increased Coordination Needed to Ensure Viability of the Army's Prepositioning Strategy."

Later reports bore more succinct titles, then finally a more dramatic one: "Equipment shortfalls at critical levels."

Suddenly, lots of people in Congress were interested in military readiness. Ortiz sent Arcangeli to individually brief members of Congress, who were only partly aware of the deep damage done to the military, even as they were conducting two wars.

By then it was early 2006, and still the problem was causing consternation in the field, policy councils in Washington, and the backrooms of the Pentagon.

When it came to legislating, Ortiz was old school; you pass legislation and you pay the bills – what the bills actually cost, not what you need them to be mathematically, so the cost of "tax cuts" can be justified.

MILITARY BUDGET WARS

In April 2006, Ortiz was furious when the Republican budget came out and freakishly ignored the monumental needs of the moment. Worse, it pretended we lived in a happy, peaceful world.

Members of Congress were astonished.

At the time, Ortiz said, "Despite the conduct of two wars, the Republican budget cuts real security – cutting homeland security by $6 billion and slashing veterans' health care by $6 billion over five years... and offers us up a truly false assumption: that the cost of the wars in Afghanistan and Iraq in October 1 of this year will be zero."

"Zero. Nobody believes that," Ortiz thundered on the House floor. "We are tired of funding the Pentagon and both wars through a series of supplementals. We have a budget and appropriations process to fund the national priorities."

He pointed to another absolutely unrealistic assumption in the 2006 Republican budget: there would be no need for new veterans needing services in 2007 and the following years. They needed to keep those soaring costs "off budget" to make the math work so they could keep giving "tax cuts." In actuality, those "tax cuts" were money (bribes) borrowed from China.

"Causalities are coming home at the fastest rate since Vietnam – the total number of injured and killed in Iraq and Afghanistan each month was roughly equal to a battalion (800) – and we have never been able to meet fully the demand for health services for the men and women who have worn our uniform," Ortiz said in 2006.

"Every year – every year – the majority in this Congress pulls the wool over the eyes of the American people on the true cost of the wars to pretend there is enough money for tax cuts for those who are sacrificing the least for this nation in our time of war," Ortiz said angrily in 2006.

In 2006 the political message machine of the Bush White House and the Congress worked like this: anybody who found fault with the budget "didn't understand the larger complexities of the entire budget" or just got labeled "unpatriotic."

"It was essentially the Pentagon and White House working in secret, not letting Congress or the American people know how much they were spending on military operations," Ortiz said, still irritated, even years later.

"The Pentagon depended on emergency supplemental funding bills, where it's very hard to keep track of the money," Ortiz said. "We wanted them to give us a real estimate of cost and put it in their budget so our committee – and the Congress – could know precisely what the money was for and so we could follow it."

Absolutely nobody seemed to care that the military crisis was growing exponentially, and every policy entity – except the Armed Services Committee Democrats – gleefully ignored it publicly.

"Part of our dynamic – everybody around me was saying 'go public – nobody here cares that you don't want to politicize it'," Ortiz said. "But I was serious about my commitment to the military, to the guys, to our mission."

"The Bush Administration politicized our military in a very dangerous way," Ortiz said intently. "That is the worst thing you can do to the troops … for the security of the nation. Citizens from all walks of life join the military; it defends the Constitution and all of us."

"But to make the military a functionary of one political party or another makes us equal to any of the dictators of the world that turn on their populations," Ortiz said. "That's when nations descend into chaos."

Politicizing the military – at any level or on any matter – was unheard of since Vietnam and before the U.S. descent into the additional war in Iraq. But Ortiz, and many of the other "old school" guys, were deeply offended by that. But to say so publicly would mean their motives would have been slurred.

"It was surreal," Ortiz said of the time. "Republicans on the committee – except Walter Jones – were mute in public, but were cheering us on in the anterooms. Walter was already publicly – very publicly – chastising the administration for the Iraq War."

As the U.S. approached the fifth anniversary of 9-11, concern about the crisis was widespread in Congress.

In early summer, 2006, the GAO reports ordered by Ortiz, to offer context and general information about the readiness shortfalls, were finally released.

"We put the GAO reports to good use," Ortiz said. "While saying it ourselves would bring charges of treason – quoting the GAO saying it was altogether different. And GAO is even-handed, nonpartisan, so they have credibility."

Finally Ortiz could publicly describe the crisis to the American people by quoting the GAO reports. But he would not go there alone.

In July 2006, Ortiz and the Armed Services top Democrat, Ike

Skelton, wrote an extensive editorial, laying out the nature of the crisis.

Like the OTM issue, the readiness shortfalls were so extreme – and the evidence difficult to follow, or followup on – that reporters had trouble quantifying the problem.

The White House and the Pentagon denied any such shortfall existed. As expected, they chastised Ortiz, Skelton and any other member that spoke of it, questioning their patriotism and demeaning their extraordinary effort to tell the story.

"The combat stress in Iraq fell most heavily on the Army and Marine Corps," Ortiz explained. "Nearly all of the Army units – including those in the National Guard that weren't deployed then – could not complete their assigned wartime missions if they'd been called up."

"The troops knew it," Ortiz said. "More than half the troops who responded to a Zogby poll in November 2005, said U.S. armed forces were not ready to fight another war or were unsure if the U.S. was prepared to go to war."

The House Armed Services Committee held hearings about these matters weekly, constantly mystified at the testimony, which was woefully incomplete.

Plus, the Bush administration classified so many aspects of readiness indicators that the Iraqis, Afghans, and foreign fighters in both wars knew more about the holes in our military readiness than the American people, "the people who foot the bill for our military, and for whom our military fights," Ortiz said.

"Couple of things were going on with the Army's ground equipment in Iraq and Afghanistan," Ortiz explained. "First, we were losing wheeled vehicles at a much higher rate than we'd expected. Plus increased usage and the huge weight from extra armor wore out equipment in Iraq up to nine times the regular rate."

"The equipment situation was even worse for the National Guard," Ortiz said. "Most of their equipment was in Iraq and Afghanistan instead of in National Guard armories in the U.S."

"Equipment shortages – along with the historic under-funding of the Guard, the reorganization of Guard brigades, and the U.S. border mission – left Guard units in the States with just 34% of their equipment."

"That meant, until we repaired the damage, we were vulnerable here at home in the event of a hurricane, fire, another natural disaster, or – in the worst case – an attack on the U.S.," Ortiz said.

Around that time, a National Guard Colonel went to the National Guard Armory in Brownsville to inspect the equipment. There was none there.

"By 2005, the Army missed its recruiting goal by more than 8%, or almost 6,700 soldiers," Ortiz said. "We had to keep Army end strength up by offering expensive signing bonuses to currently serving soldiers and a 'backdoor draft' [demanding troops remain in the service after their tours were complete and extending combat deployment of units in Iraq] just to retain our current force."

GAO also found increasing numbers of alleged and substantiated cases of wrong-doing by recruiters as they sought to convince people to serve under more difficult conditions.

"Part of the problem – a very painful part – was that so very few military veterans served in Congress," Ortiz said. "That hobbled our ability at many levels – both before and after 9-11 – to make and explain military policy to congressional colleagues."

"This just broke my heart," Ortiz said emotionally. "Our soldiers – and their families – were the only ones carrying the burden for those wars. Nobody else could be bothered, even to pay for them. Supporters of the military often put yellow ribbons on their cars and flags on their lapels. And no more."

Ortiz' love of the military has always been deep, personal and sincere. Throughout his congressional career, he pulled heavily from the rich trove of personal experience he had as a low level Army Specialist and MP.

His special love of U.S. troops took him overseas repeatedly to U.S. bases, and into various military theaters to visit troops. He took them favorite foods, and spent hours talking about sports, news and gossip from home.

One of the sweetest things Ortiz did for troops he visited was to call their parents, wives – or whatever older female relative would be most interested in hearing about them.

Ortiz would ask troops from Texas to write down their name, the relative's name to call, and the phone number. He would arrive back in Washington, his wallet thick with the tiny papers of phone numbers and names.

The calls themselves did not last long. He would call the relative (usually a mother), introduce himself as a Member of Congress just back from seeing troops, and wanted to tell her he'd seen her soldier, how good he or she looked, and that the soldier sent his or her love back to their family.

Of course, the calls were always short. Whomever he called was genuinely surprised, taken aback, then emotional (usually crying) by the time Ortiz ended his message. Always grateful, families choked out a thank you and Ortiz went to the next call.

"Solomon was such a great friend of the military," said Jimmy Miller, Ortiz' old Capitol Hill friend. "He enlisted in the military as a kid and always said if it weren't for the military, he wouldn't have gotten where he did. That love of the military stayed with him forever."

"In October 1983, Solomon heard I was staffing a trip to Lebanon," Miller said. "Terrorists had just blown up our Marine barracks there and we wanted to get there quickly. We wound up losing over 300 guys there. Members wanted to get there very fast."

The barracks bombing on October 23, 1983, in Beirut, Lebanon, happened at the height of the Lebanese Civil War, when two truck bombs struck separate buildings housing United States and French military forces – members of the Multinational Force in Lebanon – killing 299 American and French servicemen.

Islamic Jihad claimed responsibility for the bombing.

"Solomon buttonholed me on the House floor and said, 'I wanna go with you; there's a bunch of Marines there from Texas'," Miller said. "Actually about 70% of the Marines there were from Texas."

The legendary Mississippian, former National Guard General Sonny Montgomery led the delegation.

ALL ABOUT THE BOYS IN UNIFORM

"When our plane landed in Germany at Ramstein [U.S. military base], Solomon said 'let's go see the boys'," Miller said. "We were just a few miles from Landstuhl Regional Medical Center, where we always bring wounded from that part of the world."

"As we went into the hospital, they were literally still bringing in wounded kids from Lebanon," Miller said quietly. "Remember, we got out and headed over there very fast, and the medics bringing in the kids from Lebanon had triaged them there, stabilized them for the flight to Ramstein. So we were arriving at the hospital at the same time."

"That affected Solomon very much. It affected me very much," Miller said. "These kids were literally dying at our feet."

"Solomon and I were together, talking to a young African-American Marine, who was in such physical trauma," Miller remembered, eyes closed. "He was having so much trouble breathing. We were talking with him, telling him to hang on."

"We were patting his arm, telling him everything was going to be OK," Miller said. "I think Solomon was praying for him. Then everything was quiet. The nurse came in, and told us he had just died."

Miller paused at the memory. "That stuff stays with you."

Ortiz winced at another memory. He'd insisted that they go to the morgue. The loss was overpowering.

"We went on to Lebanon, landed at Beirut under fire," Miller said. "No kidding, we could see missiles firing as we went in. We could hear them as we were landing, see them landing nearby. The pilot had us jump off the plane, and took off without refueling or stopping."

"The place was in full-fledged civil war," Miller explained. "I'd stopped at the exchange at Andrews [Air Force base] before we left and got all of us fatigues to wear, so we wouldn't stand out among the troops, invite sniper fire at us. Anytime we were outside buildings, we were walking behind six foot high halls of sandbags to avoid sniper fire."

"But Solomon was so great with the troops; he so genuinely loved the military," Miller said. "He was great with these Marines. We went into the mess and he hollered, 'Anybody here from Texas?' Hell, they nearly all were."

"Sonny Montgomery [the crusty Democrat from Mississippi who led the delegation] was talking to this young Marine who was standing a post on the perimeter," Ortiz remembered. "Sonny points at the Marine's rifle and says, 'Got ammo?' Marine said, 'No sir.'"

"Later when we met with commanders, we asked why in the world we had Marines standing post, with no firepower," Ortiz said, shaking his head. "The guy said, 'We don't want an international incident.'"

"What the hell do you think this is?" Ortiz remembers Sonny Montgomery chastising the commanders.

"I met this young Marine from San Benito [Texas – in Ortiz' congressional district] who'd survived the attack," Ortiz said. "That was a hard conversation. We greeted each other like family. That's the way it was – a couple of folks from South Texas in some desolate spot on the Earth."

"His name was Alfonso Hernandez and he told me: 'I don't think I will get out of here alive.' I wasn't sure he would either, but we talked in a huddle for a long time," Ortiz continued. "We prayed at the end. The delegation waited a long time on us. Nobody cared."

"These Marines all went over to talk to him, crowded around him," Miller smiled. "He ate with them, told them stories from back home, asked them to talk about their families, their lives. They stayed there for hours."

Just like he had such an easy way with his colleagues and others in Washington, his easy style was what drew the troops around him to talk.

One of Ortiz' cherished photos is one of he and Alfonso Hernandez (the Marine from San Benito) who did survive that engagement, and then went on to serve in many more.

Flying in or out of a war zone is tricky business.

"To get out of Beirut, we knew what time the plane was to be there, and we had to meet the plane on the tarmac, hustle on, taxi back out," Miller explained. "It was night, and we could hear our plane before we could see it. It landed and then turned lights on."

"The tension was real high and the plane rolled over to us, still we heard rockets and gunfire," Miller said. "It stopped long enough for us to hustle on board, and went back to take off immediately, no lights."

"The ground fire was still popping off all around us," Miller said. "We were silent on board. When we finally got out of the airspace, everybody was clapping and cheering."

"That was a very emotional trip, a very emotional three to four days," Miller said. "Solomon was very circumspect, seeing those Marines dying – Marines from Texas – was very emotional for him."

"We went from there to Athens Greece," Miller said. "We were still in fatigues when we arrived at the hotel, where American tourists cheered us as U.S. troops. It was so late and we were so tired, we didn't correct that. We thought it was funny really that a group of aging men were mistaken for troops."

"Next day, they saw us in civilian clothes at supper and sent us over a pitcher of beer to thank us for our service," Ortiz said. "We invited them over to drink it with us, and said we were honored they'd think we were servicemen. But we were only congressmen."

"Solomon always asked commanders in the field to meet Texans," said former Pennsylvania Republican – and longtime Ortiz friend – Curt Weldon. "He would greet them like a father, talk about Texas, give them advice, get contact info and call their families when he got back. They responded to him like he was an old friend, even if he was just meeting them. But then Solomon was that way with anybody he met."

Congressman Walter Jones' stance on the Iraq War was confounding to Republicans and uplifting to Democrats who had opposed a second war in Iraq, while the U.S. was fighting al Qaeda in Afghanistan.

Jones initially supported opening a second front in Iraq, but he quickly became the leading Republican in the House of Representatives opposing continued involvement in Iraq.

By 2005, he said he was wrong to support the second front in Iraq, believing that there had been little reason to go to war.

He condemned the administration for sharing selective intelligence to manipulate Congress, and called on President George W. Bush to apologize for misleading Congress to win a vote on authorizing the additional war in Iraq.

Jones said if he'd been given the same intelligence the President saw, "I wouldn't have voted for that resolution [on Iraq war]."

While Jones' stand on the Iraq made him wildly popular outside Congress – and with Democrats in Congress – the Republican leadership made him persona non grata.

"After the Democrats took control of the House in 2007, Solomon was the [Armed Services Committee's] Readiness [subcommittee] Chairman," Jones said. "I was in line to be the [subcommittee's] Ranking Republican."

But it wasn't meant to be. The Republican leadership can trump seniority in Congress when it comes to awarding committee leadership positions.

Rep. Duncan Hunter (R-CA) was both the top Republican on the Armed Services Committee, and a member of the Republican leadership committee that affirmed or denied seniority for leadership positions.

Jones recalled the moment his colleagues' collective retribution for his outspokenness on Iraq trumped his seniority of public service.

Duncan Hunter delivered the bad news. "Duncan came to me and said, 'I just can't support you for that'," Jones said, relating a moment that still clearly bites. "Solomon was so disappointed for me. He couldn't get over the injustice in that."

"Injustice is the nicest way to describe it," Ortiz said emphatically. "Walter was the next in line – seniority matters in Congress. But when they put party over country, that's what happens. He got screwed. Bad."

"But he was a good soldier – Walter just kept on going," Ortiz said. "He was pissed, of course – but he was perfectly OK with being punished for telling the truth to power. In the end, it brought him tremendous credibility on military matters. Because he was right. And brave."

"Solomon was inspiration to all Americans," Reyes said. "He was an Army veteran; he was all about helping the armed services. Being a veteran, he personally related to the sacrifices of military families."

"We ask the military to do the hard, dirty work for all of us in the world, and me and Solomon both believe that the least we can do is make their lives as easy as possible," Reyes said. "He was always taking care of military families … training, equipment, housing, family services – all the things that can make a big difference in military life."

Ortiz' biggest priority was military readiness, Reyes said. "He and I talked lots about the history of the U.S. Army, combed through mistakes we made in Korea and Vietnam … always looking to find ways to make the lives of our troops and their families easier and better."

"Solomon was great listener for troops," Reyes smiled. "He is so genuine, so great at personal relationships. He always followed up. He wanted results, not just hot air. His South Texas constituents appreciated his efforts, that single-minded search for results."

"When we traveled, wherever we went, we always talked to the troops," Reyes said. "His philosophy was this: generals can always walk into our offices – let's focus on the guys whenever we get the chance."

"You really get the perspective of how things are going from the guy at the bottom of the totem pole, he told me," Reyes said.

That philosophy manifested itself was when Congress was making policy. Ortiz focused military leaders and policy makers on practical matters, expectations of command and control (when multiple countries or jurisdictions were involved), and rules of engagement.

"When the U.S. was in engagements with other countries, Solomon questioned everything, took military officials through dozens of scenarios … really got to the heart of the matter," Reyes said.

In one meeting between Ortiz and military officials from the Pentagon and the Texas National Guard in the years after 9-11, the discussion was the deployment of state National Guards to patrol the border.

Every question Ortiz asked begged several more questions; nobody could answer to his satisfaction the logistics of command and control between the federal and states forces.

Frustrated, Ortiz sat back in his chair, looking pained … finally saying pointedly, "Guys, this is exactly the wrong time to make our troops have to figure out who's in charge of them."

As the military officials tried to placate him, he cut them off. "Let me ask you this. One of our Guardsmen gets picked up for drunk and disorderly. Who comes to bail them out?"

When the officials he was meeting with hemmed and hawed about that question – again without a specific answer – Ortiz smiled and told them he wanted to see them the next day and to get a direct answer to his questions.

Seeing them out, he told the general, "Figure it out – this is the conversation we want to have in my office. I don't want you to have to go through that in front of a hearing room."

In a very Solomon Ortiz way, he injected the common sense engrained in him since his own service in the early 1960s.

15 – BEING NICE, WINNING FRIENDS

ONE DAY IN the mid-1990s, after the Republicans captured the House of Representatives, Ortiz left his office to give a speech on the House floor in support of an amendment offered by his good friend, Silvestre Reyes (D-TX). Reyes was amending an appropriations bill that had stripped out money for a Texas priority.

Reyes' amendment was to add the money back in the bill.

When Ortiz got to the House floor, he saw his old friend, Joe Skeen [R-NM], the chairman of a House Appropriations subcommittee, running the bill for the majority.

"Let me see if we can get this in the bill without putting it to a vote," Ortiz told Reyes. Then Ortiz crossed the aisle to talk to Skeen.

This wasn't even a big amendment, Ortiz explained to Skeen, but it was of huge importance to Texas border communities. Was it possible for the Chairman to accept the amendment and work things out in conference (House-Senate negotiations)?

"Skeen was from a border state and understood the significance of that," Ortiz said. Plus, the two men had travelled together and their offices were next door to one another in the Rayburn building.

"Solomon, if it were anybody else, the answer would be no," Skeen told Ortiz. "But for you my friend, we will accept the amendment."

A staffer, hearing Ortiz back in the office but without having heard his speech on the amendment, approached him asking, "What happened on the amendment?"

Ortiz told her and she marveled, "How do you do that?"

While Ortiz' reputation in Congress was as a workhorse, he also had a reputation as quite the jokester.

One day Ortiz picked Charlie Stenholm, his Democratic colleague from Texas, on whom to play a little bit of a practical joke. Stenholm, the all-business, top Democrat on the House Agriculture Committee, was an expert on all matters related to farming and agriculture.

"Hey Charlie," Ortiz said, in the midst of a series of votes on the House Floor. "Where does virgin wool come from?"

Stenholm, in his trademark style, began to explain the process of making virgin wool, as Ortiz nodded and appeared to be interested in the explanation.

When Stenholm finished, Ortiz deadpanned, "Oh, I just thought you got it from ugly sheep."

Stenholm looked mortified for a millisecond, and then sat down laughing in a seat on the House Floor. "You got me," he finally got out. He was still laughing about it later in the week when reminded of it in the elevator.

Congressman Charlie Gonzalez (D-TX) represents the legacy of Hispanics in Congress. His "old man" was the legendary Henry B. Gonzalez, who was one of the first Hispanic members elected to the House of Representatives.

But Charlie Gonzalez, a lawyer and a judge in San Antonio before his congressional career, didn't come from privilege, but from public service in the Texas justice system.

"Tell you what, Solomon was a creature of habit," Gonzalez smiled. "There were restaurants I expect he helped keep open – like Mr. K's downtown and Hunans on the Hill."

"Solomon saw humor in everything," Gonzalez laughed at the memory. "He was never mean about it, just funny, always taking tension out of situations. He followed the maxim: take your work seriously, but never take yourself seriously."

Known throughout Congress as a wicked jokester, Reyes said his best prank ever was on his good friend and mentor.

It was September, in the late 1990s, during the Hispanic Caucus annual celebration. The Hispanic Members of Congress and several other elected officials gathered at the Naval Observatory in northwest Washington, the official residence of the Vice President of the United States.

Vice President Al Gore, who served with Ortiz in the House of Representatives (Gore represented a district in Tennessee before leaving for the Senate), was an old friend of Ortiz.

Ortiz, famously single on the Washington scene, was having quite the time seated between two pretty young women, neither of whom was his date.

Reyes was hit with the inspiration to embarrass his old friend in the company of the Vice President of the United States, many Members of Congress and other political heavyweights.

Reyes talked to Vice President Gore's top guy, Moe Vela. "Hey, you should tell the Vice President he oughta congratulate Solomon on getting married – he's here with his new wife tonight," Reyes cackled at the memory.

With no idea that he was now the straight man for Congressman Reyes, the Vice President stepped right in it.

Positioned so he could see Ortiz' face while Vice President Gore spoke, Reyes heard Gore congratulate his old friend on the occasion of his wedding.

Ortiz' smiling face froze in horror, then went pale, mouth open.

"He seemed to shrink into his chair," Reyes hooted, animated. "He was so happy, talking to this one, then to this one," Reyes mimicked someone flirting with the person on his right, then on his left.

The real art of this prank? "I was the only one in on it," Reyes hit his knee, laughing his ass off.

"Everybody was clapping and cheering that he got married, not really sure which woman it was. I saw him say something to both women … he was all pale – then he was bright red. And I laughed and laughed, and watched people nearby slap him on the back."

Proof, of course, that men never grow up. If Hollywood is "high school with money" … Washington is "high school with power."

Ortiz winced at the memory. "Gawd I hate to think about that; I was so pissed," Ortiz said. "My stomach got hot, I couldn't quite breathe right. I'm trying to decide what to tell the ladies beside me. Wondering why the hell Al would say that."

"Silver is a … rascal – that's all I'll call my friend for now," Ortiz smiled, but still spitting at the memory. "I hate that it happened, and

I've hated it every time Silver's enjoyed the hell out of it when he's told the story."

The incident was also related in a *Washington Post* profile on Reyes when he ascended to the chairmanship of the House Intelligence Committee in 2007.

"You know, I love Silver, I always will. And it was funny – from every other perspective," Ortiz confided. "But the thought of it still gives me the shudders."

"It was the best prank ever," Reyes said. "And Solomon's been trying to get even ever since."

"This institution would be much better served with more people like Solomon Ortiz," said Rep. Jones. "He always smiled, always had a kind word. He wanted to make a difference."

"My relationship with Solomon was just very special," Jones said. "Whether we were working on depot issues or fisheries issues, he always wanted to help. There's just a goodness in him. We miss that here."

"I have such admiration for him, for the quality of man he is," Jones said. "Solomon didn't let this place change him. He just did a good job."

Solomon's back and forth to Washington every week really didn't affect the children, Rosa Lopez said. "He talked to them many times a day; he was always aware of the kids' tests, activities, and ball games.

The vast and extended Ortiz family (Oscar, the cousins, Jerry Sawyer) held the children close, and tried to compensate to make up for the days Ortiz was on the east coast.

"If Sollie came in a little late, I was calling his father so they could talk about it," Lopez smiled. "Even when Sollie was in college, and wanted to go out, he had to ask his father. Even when Solomon was out of the country, I still made him call his dad."

In some ways, being the constant female figure in the children's lives was a little uncomfortable for her, Lopez said. They loved their mother, Irma, who was Lopez' cousin.

Even years later, when Solomon, Jr. won the chairmanship of the county Democratic party, one of Lopez' friends said, "Your little boy won," which still made her uneasy.

Far safer than serving as sheriff, "We knew some of what Solomon was doing in Congress was dangerous," Lopez said. "We worried about him on all his trips … particularly when he went to outlaw countries. On 9/11 – I was out walking and didn't know it had happened until Solomon called to say he was fine."

16 – DIPLOMATIC JOURNEY

CONGRESSMAN CURT WELDON, a Pennsylvania Republican, has known Ortiz for well over 20 years, both though similar committee posts, and through a common desire to show the world the faces of real Americans.

Both men often lamented that when they traveled with their committees outside the U.S., even leaders in other nations had misconceptions of who the American people were, what was important to them, and how Americans view the world.

Weldon and Ortiz' friendship began in 1987, just after Weldon was elected and assigned to the House Armed Services Committee with Ortiz.

"Solomon was the nicest guy and was the easiest Member of Congress to work with," Weldon said. "Not just the easiest Democrat to work with, easiest member altogether. You could always count on his word. You could depend on him to do the right thing over politics. He didn't mind doing something hard or unpopular when it was the right thing."

"But we got really close in the early 1990s on a Merchant Marine and Fisheries subcommittee on oceans," Weldon said, remembering the origin of one of the famous bipartisan relationships in Congress. "Solomon was the chairman and I was the ranking Republican. Our first trip to Russia together was for the subcommittee."

Those were interesting and heady days for Members of Congress who simply wanted to go out in the world and make a difference.

On a whole other level in the previous decade, Texas Congressman Charlie Wilson had almost singlehandedly figured out how to diminish the Soviet military to end the great rivalry of the late 20th Century, immortalized in the Tom Hanks movie *Charlie Wilson's War*.

Ortiz and Weldon wanted to make a difference too, via simpler methods.

"We were always looking to do humanitarian work out in the world," Weldon said, describing their dual passion for making the world a better place."

"Solomon was the epitome of the American success story, coming from abject poverty – the child of immigrants," Weldon said. "From there to Congress. I was from a poor white family in rural Pennsylvania. The face of Americans the world usually sees are the stuffed shirts from the diplomatic corps, the president, and the misbehaving Hollywood types."

"Solomon and me wanted to show the world different faces," Weldon explained. "Most of America looks like us. We aren't all rich or graduated from Harvard. We scrapped through life. The world can relate to that. They don't see that picture of us; they don't talk to people like us."

Ortiz and Weldon were constant traveling companions, eventually becoming known as the Amigos. When Silvestre Reyes joined them in Congress, that trio called themselves the "Three Amigos." Rarely did any one of them travel out of the country without the others.

It was a road show that worked. The Three Amigos raced around the planet to meet as many people in other countries as possible, to develop as many sources of information as possible, and to make as many friends as they could in abbreviated time frames.

"Our premise for the international travel we did was to work through parliamentary working groups … members of our Congress meeting and taking to members of their legislative body," Weldon said. "The goal was to meet the future leaders of that country. All told, we had 12 parliamentary projects: Russia's Duma, the legislatures of the Ukraine, Uzbekistan … a lot of Central Asian/Eastern European countries, all developing democracies."

"State Department diplomats are assigned to a particular country for three years, tops," Weldon explained. "Members of Congress usually served for a decade or two. We thought – for that reason – that it was so important for Congress, as a co-equal branch of government, to get to know the people at the top levels of government in other countries. Chances were, in several cases, we'd be meeting the next president or other top official."

"Our goal in Congress was to get other members to find an interest in at least one other country," Weldon continued. "We really wanted Congress to be a larger player on the international scene. Congress advises the administration on foreign policy, we fund all of it. When Congress approaches that task with good information, the country and the world are better served."

"Solomon was a great internationalist," Weldon smiled. "He was a natural. He and I together were yin and yang. Silver [Silvestre Reyes (D-TX)] joined us in the mid-1990s, and the three of us became best friends. I trusted them over anybody else in Congress."

"I was so happy when Silver ran for Congress," Ortiz said. "He's a great public servant – and he's funny as hell. I knew we could have some fun at some very boring meetings."

Curt Weldon, Ortiz, and Silvestre Reyes – the "Three Amigos" – were famous for behind-the-scenes diplomacy in capitols around the world.

"Solomon and I were different – and sometimes had similar sensibilities," Weldon said. "He was a cop in an earlier life; I was a fireman," Weldon said. "We were both from poor families. We were both municipal officials before we came to Congress. I was a Republican. He was a Democrat. We both loved the military – and all of us only wanted to represent a side of our country on the world stage."

"We never ever pretended to negotiate and never undermined the sitting administration, of either party," Weldon said. "We had different talents, but that made us a really good team."

"Once, we flew to Siberia to see a nuclear reactor," Reyes said. "The plane ride took forever, and then we took a bus for four or five hours to get to an isolated city there that depended entirely on the reactor for power."

"We were hosted by the mayor and town council – they wanted us to know they wanted to comply with the treaties, but had no other power source," Reyes said. It was a very cold place to have a solitary source of heat.

September 11, 2001, was an outsized moment for the United States – and Ortiz' – journey in Washington. The event dramatically changed everything that followed.

One of the great ironies of that day: when the plane hit the Pentagon, Ortiz was at a press conference in the Radio Television gallery in the U.S. Capitol on the third floor – with Weldon and Reyes. The billing for the press conference was: "*Is America Prepared for Future Military Threats?*"

"The press conference was postponed," Ortiz deadpanned. "One of the most interesting foreign policy dynamics on 9-11, and the days that followed, was the sudden, new moment with Russia."

Ortiz and Weldon had traveled to Russia almost a decade earlier and had dozens of government and non-governmental sources to tap for information. Two weeks after 9-11, the "Three Amigos" and eight other members of Congress left Andrews Air Force base for their own personal brand of intense congressional diplomacy.

"Remember, at the turn of the century, Russia was being a little belligerent – in a bid to win favor in the world," Ortiz said. "They certainly stayed in our face. But, on 9-11, Russia had a previously scheduled military exercise. We asked them to stand down – and they did. They did it in solidarity with us. That was a new moment."

"One of the goals of our mission was to go hold hands with nations in the vicinity of Afghanistan and help with the foundation for a 'floating alliance' of nations with whom we weren't particularly close," Ortiz said. "That was the precisely the sort of alliance we needed in fighting a war with no borders and inside no particular nation."

"Everybody was being as creative as we could," Ortiz said. "What we in Congress were doing was what the diplomats were doing. It was just a very unified moment. We spent a lot of time conveying to our friends that we understood bin Laden gave Islam a bad name; that Islam was not at issue. We had trouble convincing other countries that Americans understood that. Truthfully, many Americans didn't understand that. Still don't."

"We hoped this would be a new awakening on our part, realizing that what happens in other countries in the world can certainly affect the United States," Ortiz said. "Our security depends on it. Still."

"In Moscow [Russia], we met with members of the Duma, Russia's legislature and talked about ways we could work – Congress to Duma – in pursuit of al Qaeda," Ortiz said, smiling at the enormity of the moment.

"In the end, we offered language for a resolution that we passed in

Congress – and in the Duma – to oppose terror campaigns and to establish a bi-national commission to study and fight terrorism," Ortiz said. "That may seem small, but it was a huge international moment. The U.S. Congress – and the Russian legislature – working together on anything would be huge."

"But this wasn't a small thing; it was former enemies working together to fight terrorism … terrorism that had gone international, threatening all of us," Ortiz said. "That old saying in the Middle East was repeated fairly often: 'the enemy of my enemy is my friend'."

"The irony of some members of this coalition was lost on none of us," Ortiz said. "Russia was the largest part of the USSR, our enemy for the better part of the latter 20th Century. We all put our previous relationship in the past and pledged to work together to solve the first great challenge of the 21st century."

"We met with dozens of Russian administration officials, other leaders, and security officials familiar with both the Soviet war in Afghanistan and terrorist activity then in Russia," Ortiz said. "We talked to a security advisor to former Russian President Boris Yeltsin, a veteran of the Soviet war in Afghanistan."

"The fact that a Member of Congress had organized the Soviet demise in Afghanistan 15 years before was noted, but not mentioned again," Ortiz smiled, referring to fellow Texan Charlie Wilson's legislative genius in arming the Afghani rebels and crippling the mighty Soviet military in the late 1980s.

"Yeltsin's guy was incredibly helpful to us on possible military strategy and ways to combat terrorism," Ortiz said.

In Italy, the delegation met with the banished former King of Afghanistan, King Mohammad Zahir Shah, to discuss ways to utilize the Northern Alliance in Afghanistan and to create a larger opposition coalition to fight the ruling Taliban government there.

"The king was still in close touch with the leaders of the Northern Alliance, a confederation of the tribes in northern Afghanistan which had repelled the Soviets in the 1980s, and which continued to oppose the Taliban there," he said.

"The Northern Alliance representatives in Italy with the exiled king gave us very specific requests for assistance, particularly humanitarian assistance, to pass on to the administration," Ortiz said. "They were so grateful that we understood this was not a religious war, that Islam was not the enemy, only those who pervert it."

Next, the delegation hit Turkey, an important NATO ally in the coming war. Turkey had been providing humanitarian assistance (financial aid for water infrastructure, schools, etc.) in Northern Afghanistan for decades.

"Turkey has long been an U.S. friend; and that was putting them in a dicey position. Remember, it's Turkey, Iran, Afghanistan," Ortiz said, gesturing at an invisible map in front of him, placing Turkey on the left, Afghanistan on the right, with Iran in the middle. "They were the closest NATO ally to our battlefield. And their geography was needed to provide the bulwark of our military supplies and troop transport."

"Germany is our major foothold enroute, but the closest to the front was Turkey," he said. "Now, Turkey takes a lot of crap in the Muslim world for being our friend. At the time, they were one of two Muslim democracies, and we try very hard to help any democracy sustain their system of government."

By 2001, Ortiz had been through Turkey dozens of times, with hundreds of friends in his wake.

"Mostly, we were there to stand in solidarity with them, see what they needed to know we had their back," Ortiz recalled. "The Turks were quite happy to help us take justice to bin Laden. As Muslims, bin Laden embarrassed them. They also told us the most important thing the U.S. could do was continue to insist our fight was utterly with bin Laden and the global terrorist networks, not Islam, not Muslims."

"But they had conservative elements they needed to quell, given the high profile nature of launching U.S. planes to make war on a Muslim nation," Ortiz remembered. "One of the ways we thanked them was forgiving a $5 billion debt to the U.S. You know, at the time, we had every expectation we would be paying the bill for that. We had no way of knowing that the Congressional leaders would start – and then keep – punting our bills down the road, to the point our national debt in 2014 is obscene."

Ortiz has a silly side he rarely tried to keep in check, ever, even on the international stage.

"Another trip, we were in Greece, at a Crete military installation for security briefing," Miller remembered. "Solomon and I went on a walk on the beach. We met two girls from Greenland there. Solomon introduced us like this: "Meet Jimmy from America, and

I'm Frank."

"That night at reception in hospitality suite," Miller laughed, "One of the delegation members, a dignified Maryland congresswoman, was sitting by the phone when it rang. "She kept saying, 'Who are you looking for? Jimmy from America?' Solomon and I were laughing our asses off. He never stopped calling me that."

"The last trip we went on in 2010, Solomon was still telling the stories, was still the life of the party," Miller said. "So many trips with him, everybody liked him so much. He'd regale colleagues, diplomats, people on the street, everybody with stories of politics and Texas."

Nobody was immune from Ortiz' teasing on international trips. He even teased the wives along on delegation trips. "Once we were in the Middle East, saw girls in burkas," Miller said. "Solomon started talking about how pretty one was."

One of the wives chastised him, also teasing, Miller said. "'You can't see enough to know what she looks like, silly.' Later that night – I think it was Jimmy Duncan's wife – went to Solomon's room with a veil and dark towel over her, acting like she was a local and asking him to open the door."

"Course, he got all chicken shit and wouldn't open up the door then," Miller laughed. "We got a huge laugh about that."

"He draws you in – in a genuine way – he makes you feel good," Miller said. "He never made fun or belittled. He is just a great jokester. It was like if you had Solomon around, you feel better about things; he'd make you feel good about yourself."

"That's really invaluable on international trips," Miller said. "He has a knack for making people feel at ease. These uptight, formal meetings would always turn around after Solomon spoke. If the mood needed some comic relief, he provided it. If it took hard perspective, he provided it. He always got the conversation going in a better, easier way."

"During a trip in the spring of 2011 [the first Congress after Ortiz' defeat] – we came out of a meeting that wasn't very productive," Miller said. "The Chairman says, "Where's Solomon? We needed somebody to break the ice."

"It is hard to describe Solomon's impact on the world," Miller said. "His genius – and it was genius – was in being genuine. He didn't know how to be anybody fancy, didn't want to be anybody fancy. He was an American walking on the world stage, connecting to people one-to-one."

"He never forgot anybody he met, whether it was in Texas or Washington or capital cities around the world," said Miller. "Here's an example – from early 2000s. Maybe 2001. We had a delegation of members in Europe and when we were in Turkey we wanted to meet with Onur Oyman, an important government official who was famously secular. We wanted them to get our message that Islam was not what we were after."

"But the official – who was a former Turkish ambassador to several European countries – didn't have time to meet with us," Miller said. "They were going to send a representative, but we really needed to talk to the guy."

"Suddenly, Solomon asked, 'Hey, isn't he the same Onur Oyman that used to be their ambassador someplace in Europe?'" Miller remembered. "It was, and the U.S. embassy sent another message to him, this one from Solomon personally, asking to see him."

"This time, Oyman told the U.S. embassy he'd love to see Solomon, please bring him over," said Miller. "The entire delegation went along and Solomon and Oyman greeted each other warmly, as old friends. Solomon said, 'can my friends stay here with us for a visit?'"

"They'd met in Turkey before, so he knew Solomon was smart about international relationships. They spoke Spanish for a while. Solomon, being so genuine and so charming, Oyman remembered him fondly," Miller said. "That blew everybody in the delegation away. How does this really nice guy just call up a country's opposition leader and be seen immediately? He was Solomon. That's how he rolls."

"I miss him," Miller mused. "I miss how exceptionally nice he is. If everybody could be just a little bit of the man Solomon is, we'd be a far better place here [on Capitol Hill]."

17 – "AXIS OF EVIL,"
SUBSEQUENT DIPLOMACY

MONTHS AFTER THE September 11 attacks, then-U.S. President George W. Bush laid the foundation for his military/foreign policy vision that included the United States as an aggressor, first-strike nation taking on an "axis of evil."

In the president's mind, the "axis of evil" was comprised of nations with unfriendly governments that he accused of exporting terrorism and seeking weapons of mass destruction. Bush labeled Iran, Iraq and North Korea as his "Axis of evil."

Certainly even then the U.S. government knew of Iran's intentions to undermine U.S. efforts in Afghanistan, provide grudging refuge for al Qaeda in Iran's eastern frontier, and its determination to build nuclear weapons – under the guise of nuclear power.

The U.S. government also certainly knew about North Korea's nuclear intentions, its progress, and its successes (but mostly failures) in missile tests.

Iraq was still sufficiently under our thumb, given the strictly-enforced no fly zone. Nearly everybody suspected Saddam Hussein was holding some level of weapons of mass destruction, such as the nerve gas he had readily used on Kurds in the north. But even that – and everything beyond that – were unproven allegations.

The nuclear gains in North Korea and Iran were proven over and over again.

In his State of the Union Address on January 29, 2002, Bush was in a precarious political position. The U.S. effort in Afghanistan had lost Osama bin Laden in the Afghani mountains of Tora Bora, along the northeast border with Pakistan.

Military experts at the Pentagon and in the field had begged for more troops for the Afghanistan onslaught, but the military mission in Afghanistan was held to a tiny force. They were instructed to rely on CIA paramilitary troops already there, Afghan militia – and technology.

The loss of bin Laden could have been a political gut punch for Bush's military leadership. But the emotional national response after 9-11 – plus Bush's political gamble that Americans wary of further domestic attacks wouldn't hold it against him – gave him a pass on losing bin Laden so early in the game.

So the "axis of evil" slogan was born. It would also telegraph the president's intentions to come in Iraq.

Shortly after that, John Bolton, an Undersecretary of State, added another three nations to the U.S. hit list: Cuba, Libya, and Syria. This second verse was titled: "Beyond the Axis of Evil."

Cuba was included strictly for political consumption in Florida, the state that held up the disputed 2000 election. Libya, the U.S. government knew then, had nuclear intentions and was progressing forward in nuclear power.

Plus, Muammar Gaddafi, the head of the Libyan government, had ordered the bombing of Pan Am Flight 103 in 1982; two thirds of those killed in that attack were Americans onboard the flight. Gaddafi also ran terrorism raids in Europe, once targeting a nightclub of Americans.

For that and much more, Gaddafi and his country were deservedly long-time pariahs among the developed nations of the world.

Syria was getting chesty in Israeli matters and generally becoming more belligerent in the Middle East.

Senior military and foreign policy experts in Congress – including Ortiz – collectively drew back their heads in surprise at a doctrine that listed countries the U.S. would be making war on. Or trying to make war on. Or using the threat of war to leverage concessions or information from those countries.

Or something more nefarious. But nobody really knew … not even the hacks at the White House who were making it up on the fly, mostly to advance the Bush 2004 campaign.

"Everybody in Congress wanted to do anything to keep the country safe from another attack," Ortiz said. "But a whole bunch of us – Republicans and Democrats, mostly senior members – thought producing a list of nations we were coming after was unproductive. We were not a first-strike nation. Or we weren't yet."

"From our perspective on the Armed Services Committee," Ortiz said, "It was as much about how to array the force to do all the things we usually did – the Far East, Europe, NATO obligations and such – but from the back seat. The Afghanistan/al Qaeda mission was the whole front seat."

"I still remember disagreeing with the president on the number of troops he sent right off the bat to Afghanistan," Ortiz said, head shaking. "I was a soldier, worked in law enforcement. You go into a situation like that with overwhelming force. We didn't do that."

But through those eyes – and in back rooms among themselves – wary Members of Congress looked at Bush's doctrine, doing the math and bemoaning both the massive, immediate draft they'd need to institute in order to bulk up the military fast to cover conflicts spread so far and wide … and the taxes they'd need to raise to pay for it all.

Once they got past the math of the staggering cost – and the dynamic of a mandatory draft, the first since Vietnam – foreign policy experts in Congress were most worried that the United States was no longer a nation that used the military only when we were attacked.

The U.S. was now using a first strike to threaten several countries the government didn't like. In some cases – the U.S. had been trying to get inspectors in to judge their use of nuclear power, and their progress in moving from using nuclear energy for merely power ... to using it for nuclear weapons.

"Before 9-11, our national security policy and foreign policy was to join military alliances and act in defense of the United States, or in defense of a NATO or UN objective, as we chose," Ortiz said. "But the Bush Doctrine meant that – on our own – we would pursue wars in a half dozen other countries – that had not attacked us."

"That was crazy," said Ortiz. "Crazy. Behind closed doors, members were talking, planning, and weighing in against the doctrine of do-what-I-want-or-I'll-kick-in-your-door. Before this, our big stick was our economic stability and trade policies, backed up by an army."

There was little to nothing Members of Congress could do to affect any of this, but they kept looking for an opportunity in diplomacy if one existed. They found two giant, and vital, nations in which to use their own brand of diplomacy: Libya and North Korea.

"I'll tell you what scared us the most at the outset of the war in Afghanistan," Ortiz said candidly. "Our essential ally right next to the battlefield was Pakistan, a nation plagued as the aggressor against India, the world's largest democracy. But more importantly, we knew as far back as the 1990s that their nuclear expert, Dr. Abdul Khan, was selling that technology to whoever paid. It was to all the wrong countries."

The 1971 Pakistani-Indian war cost Pakistan roughly 56,000 square miles of territory. Plus the nation lost millions of its citizens to the newly-created state of Bangladesh.

Humiliated, the Pakistani leaders and scientists – particularly Dr. Abdul Qadeer Khan, a German educated engineer – vowed to pay any price to join the club of nations with nuclear weapons.

The early investment for this effort in Pakistan was from oil-rich Arab states, particularly Saudi Arabia and Libya. Crafty as well as brilliant, Khan accelerated the Pakistani program with stolen nuclear technology blueprints from a Dutch research firm. By the mid-1980s, the Pakistanis had their nuclear weapon.

Khan, an unquestioned nuclear expert, soon realized the weapons he was creating had more than just a military function for Pakistan. Other nations would pay top dollar for the technology.

What is unclear is whether the governments of Pakistan were Khan's confederates in his nuclear proliferation; but some things about Kahn's nuclear transfers are public.

The United States government, certain that Pakistan was exchanging nuclear weapons technology for ballistic missile technology, raised hell with them.

In March 2001 (six months prior to 9-11), Pakistani President Pervez Musharraf promoted Khan to "Science Advisor to the President," supposedly to keep Khan's hands out of the daily management of the weapons program.

Given the desperate need for Pakistan's cooperation in the Afghanistan war, U.S. officials tapped down their earlier demands that Khan must face international justice for the nuclear proliferation.

By February 1, 2004, the Pakistan government reported that Khan had confessed to providing Iran, Libya, and North Korea with designs and centrifuge technology to aid in nuclear weapons programs.

Khan had admitted – privately to Pakistani officials – to transferring centrifuge technology and information to Iran between 1989 and 1991 ... to North Korea and Libya between 1991 and 1997 (although U.S. officials at the time knew that the transfers to Libya continued until 2003) ... and various weapons technologies to North Korea until 2000.

On February 3, 2004, the *Washington Post* reported that Khan had implicated President Musharraf and a number of senior military officials in his global proliferation scheme "according to a friend of Khan's and a senior Pakistani investigator."

On February 4, 2004, Khan appeared on Pakistani national television and confessed to running the massive global nuclear proliferation ring. He also said the government had no knowledge of his activities, seemingly changing his story from the previous day.

Hours later, on February 5, 2004, the day after Khan declared his guilt on TV and insulated the government from association with his nuclear proliferation quest, President Musharraf pardoned him.

Khan remained under "house arrest;" a house arrest that was rarely inconvenient for Khan. By 2009, the high court of Pakistan rendered him a full and free citizen of Pakistan. He remained free in 2014.

18 – TRYING TO TAME LIBYA

BY LATE 2003, a decade of disastrous economic policies in Libya, Libyan leader Col. Muammar Qaddafi's squandering of Libya's rich oil resources, and ever-deepening international isolation … all crushed the nation's economy beyond repair.

"The White House really didn't want us to go to Libya," said Curt Weldon. "Solomon and I were going on an Afghanistan-Iraq swing and wanted to stop in Libya. The administration said no, and we got to the point where they agreed we could take a U.S. military plane one country over and fly commercial into Libya."

"To make it fit, we couldn't take commercial transport, so I arranged for a Russian airline to take us into Libya," Weldon smiled. "Those were our arrangements."

"Given what was going on in Pakistan with Kahn under the microscope – and Qaddafi's source of weapons and nuclear technology cut off, he was in a new and desperate place," Ortiz said. "Even if he wanted to keep going with his nuclear weapons program, he would have a harder time finding a source and couldn't afford it even if he did."

Consequently, Qaddafi was a quasi-changed man. Desperate for western investment, he was now willing to give up his quest for nuclear weapons in exchange for that investment. It was the only move he had to make.

"He was doing what he wanted to do, in one of the few times it was what we wanted him to do, too," Ortiz said. "Qaddafi was pretty astute in terms of international policy matters. He couldn't wait till after Kahn was hung out to dry. He had to get in front of that to capitalize on it."

In January 2004, the *New York Times* laid out the evolution of the Qaddafi conversion. "In a private conversation [in December, 2003] with foreign diplomats and intelligence officers, Colonel Qaddafi confided that he would begin a campaign to persuade other nations, starting with Iran, to give up any ambition to acquire nuclear weapons."

"According to one person who was present, the colonel said such arms 'do nothing to enhance security' and retard development," the *New York Times* reported. "As for the timing of the colonel's proclamation, it may have been motivated primarily by a desire to use Libya's final payout of the $2.7 billion in Lockerbie compensation as leverage to win eased American sanctions, say Western officials who have been involved in the negotiations."

The *New York Times* continued, "'He realized that Libya was on a path of international isolation and internal stagnation after 30 years of concentrated economic wrecking,' said one European diplomat. 'But there is no question that the Lockerbie settlement has set the time frame for his actions. He had to make the announcement on weapons if he was to test how George Bush would respond.'"

"The other big reason for Libya's change of mind was this: their oil industry desperately needed our expertise," Ortiz said. "Experts told us Libyan oil production had declined gradually from a peak of 3.3 million barrels a day in the late 1970s to about 1.4 million barrels a day by 2003."

"Without oil money, Libya looked like other desperately poor African nations," Ortiz said. "Their schools, hospitals and infrastructure had deteriorated, and western pilots said their national airline was dangerous to fly."

Just before the turn of the century, Libyans were finally saturated with satellite TV and the Internet. That unblinking eye, both on their own country and on the outside world, shocked many Libyans as they saw the backward conditions they lived in.

"This didn't happen overnight," Ortiz said. "In March of 2003, Colonel Qaddafi sent his intelligence chief, Musa Kussa, to approach the British with an offer to trade Libya's secret weapons programs for a new era of relations."

"Those of us aware of the approach were excited, but cautious," Ortiz said. "Curt and I were dying to get there. Negotiations went on for months. In October 2003, American and British intelligence grabbed a ship headed to Libya carrying nuclear centrifuge technology from Khan's Pakistani nuclear scientists."

"Suddenly, it looked like Qaddafi was only using the negotiations with the Brits to throw the U.S. off while he was trying to finish building a nuclear weapon," Ortiz said.

But in December 2003, Qaddafi made his declaration public – just two months before his nuclear weapons supply would be cut off. From this time forward, Qaddafi pledged, Libya would join a peaceful community of nations.

He swore off the quest for weapons of mass destruction. In exchange, he wanted Libya to be a focus of western development, particularly in the oil sector.

In January of 2004, Weldon, Ortiz, Reyes, and a half dozen other members of Congress, had planned a swing through Iraq, Afghanistan and other "stans" where U.S. troops were stationed.

Never really convinced that Qaddafi was being honest, the members of Congress were relatively confident that Qaddafi was reaching out because he needed the western investment.

U.S. trade is generally a much better persuader of people than wars.

"If we could be helpful in solidifying his decision; that would be very good," Ortiz said. "Also, we wanted a look inside there, hoped to gather intelligence. Last, but very importantly, oil guys in Texas had been hoping to develop oil fields in Libya someday."

No official American delegation had been to Libya in 38 years. That changed on January 26, 2004, as the congressional delegation arrived in Tripoli.

"Remember, the administration made us plan for commercial air travel into Libya," Weldon said. "After we were on the way, the administration changed their mind, got intelligence from inside Libya that they wanted to see us … so the White House guy called me to say, 'fly U.S. mil air [military airplane] all the way in'."

The word of that change never got to the Libyans.

"Libyan air control didn't have word of a huge U.S. military plane," Weldon remembered. "As we were approaching Tripoli, the staff guy on the trip came back to tell me that Libyan Air Command was asking the pilots for our authorization number and the name of the person who gave us the authority to enter the country."

"My congressional district was the seventh district of

Pennsylvania," Weldon said. "So I said, 'Tell 'em our authorization is PA-007, and we have permission from Col. Muammar Qaddafi.' Guess that worked, we weren't asked again."

But getting to the meeting with Qaddafi was a harder – exceptionally unnerving – exercise in the dark African night.

"To see Qaddafi, we had to travel by car from Tripoli to his compound, pretty far away," Ortiz said. "We drove and drove and finally stopped. But the stop was only to take all our electronic equipment, phones, cameras, everything. Then we transferred to an SUV and kept on driving for another hour or so."

"Finally we see lights heading toward us," Weldon said. "After they gotten our electronic devices, and we changed vehicles, we went off-road, literally across the sand... going even deeper into the desert for another hour or so."

"I thought we might never be seen again, as we sped across the desert," Reyes remembered. "It was black dark. They separated us from each other; we were all in different vehicles. I had a driver, I was in the front seat, and a guy with an AK47 was sitting behind me."

Ortiz candidly admitted everybody in the delegation was trying to quiet the inner suspicions that they were about to be shot in the dark and desolate Libyan desert. "But the next time we stopped, we saw Qaddafi," he said. "It was just a long drive."

"When we saw lights again, it was Qaddafi's tent compound," Weldon said. "Qaddafi, clad in a beach shirt, was waiting for us, and embraced us. We met with him for three hours. Again, in this way, we showed – at that time a former enemy – that Americans are human; diplomats just can't do that. Our goal: show our enemies or former enemies real American faces, to tell them we are ordinary people who don't want war."

During the three-hour marathon meeting covering an array of topics, Qaddafi tried to up his price for ending his nuclear program. In addition to western investment, Qaddafi added a demand for a White House meeting as part of the price for his ending his attempts to constitute a nuclear weapon.

"That was unexpected," Ortiz said. "But he was serious. So we had to appear accommodating to his face. When we were out of their airspace later, we laughed pretty hard. We took the information to the White House of course. But we judged it as a hopeful add-on while members of Congress were there."

"He got the money," Ortiz said. "That's what is most important to the petty dictators. He probably wouldn't scuttle the whole deal insisting on a White House meeting. But then, he was petty. So you never knew."

"We saw the Libyan nuclear reactor, not that we could judge its stage of completion or conditions before we arrived – but it was an interesting moment," Ortiz said. "We also paid a surprise visit to a market to see everyday Libyans – and the people knew we were Americans. They were very friendly, very warm."

"The way we looked at it was this: you don't make peace with your friends, you make peace with your enemies," said Ortiz. "Libya was long our enemy, and by 2011, they were again. But events just a few years ago put them on a new path – and we were willing to judge their behavior from that moment forward."

The aggressive – personal – diplomacy by members of Congress, and other Americans since, likely sowed the early seeds of discontent that led to Libyans joining the Arab Spring of 2011.

"It was very important to us, as members of the U.S. Congress, to go as many places as we could, even countries recently our enemies, to make sure other nations saw other American faces and knew we were not an enemy."

After their historic visit, the same Congressional delegation returned to Libya a month later, at the invitation of the General People's Congress, the Libyan parliament. As they left Washington on that second trip, the U.S. began the process of lifting many of the economic sanctions so long in effect.

"We knew that long journeys of friendship and peace begin with a single step, and that those efforts needed to be tended," Ortiz said. "When our legislature reaches out to other legislatures, it's a more direct way to communicate with other countries, an avenue our diplomats just don't have."

"We spoke at the [Libyan] Parliament's formal opening," Ortiz said. "I talked about the days after 9-11 when we took important steps to re-assert a new relationship with Russia … and our legislatures stood together – the U.S. Congress and the Russian Duma – to denounce terrorism, for the first time. I likened that unique moment in history to this one with Libya."

That worked relatively well until the Arab Spring of 2011, which was largely peaceful until Qaddafi mowed down peaceful protesters. That ended his brief experiment as a participating member in the community of nations.

In 2011, he died a gruesome death at the hands of his countrymen, whose lives he had so devastated.

"In all the dangerous countries we went to, we told them that Americans want to trade ... that Americans believe economic prosperity eliminates radicalism and anger in political dissent ... and that Americans believe peace ALWAYS beats war," Ortiz said. "Be great if we could pick the leaders for other nations, but that's not how it works."

19 – WEIRD LITTLE WORLD
OF NORTH KOREA

ONE YEAR AFTER the foray into Libya, in January 2005, the "Three Amigos" – and another three members of Congress – went to North Korea, whose bellicose actions repeatedly stunned the civilized world; and whose nuclear program seemed to progressing, despite the purported loss of guidance from Pakistan's Khan.

They continued to test long range missile delivery systems, and reportedly, to enrich uranium.

"Everything we know about North Korea is suspect," said Ortiz, describing the most secretive, backward nuclear power on the earth. "They are a world unto themselves – completely cut off, ever since the Korean conflict of the mid-20th century."

Just flying into North Korean airspace was a major diplomatic coup. "The administration – again – did not want us to go," Ortiz said of the high level maneuvering to arrange transportation and entry to North Korea.

"Curt [Weldon] was – still is – fearless," Ortiz said admiringly. "The president, the State Department – nobody wanted us to go. But Curt was in their face – respectfully. It was classic Curt Weldon. That guy got something in his teeth and he would not let go."

"I loved serving with Curt in Congress – but I often thought his talents were wasted in Congress," Ortiz mused. "He is absolutely brilliant. Brilliant with people; hyper-dedicated to a peaceful world. Curt should have been Secretary of State. When we were in Congress he really was fearless. Not afraid of the leaders of his party in the White House, and not afraid of dictators."

Weldon, who had been trying to get a delegation to North Korea for years, never let it go. Finally, he got permission from the insular North Korean government. That was easier, as it turned out, than permission from the U.S. government.

Eventually, on January 10, 2005, the delegation left Andrews Air Force base with six members of Congress, and State Department translator, Tong Kim. Kim was President Bush's interpreter and a State Department veteran of 17 meetings with the North Koreans.

"Just to sort of kick us in the pants on the way out, the administration put us in a small plane – and it's a very long way to Asia from the east coast," Ortiz scowled. It took a long time to fly to the Pacific Rim, stopping to refuel every few hours.

The delegation changed planes in Seoul, boarding a private plane to make the last leg of the ride into forbidden territory.

"Entering North Korean airspace was just eerie," Ortiz recalled.

It got much worse very fast.

"Suddenly, a Soviet-era MIG [fighter plane] came up beside us, and the pilots called back urgently for the translator," Ortiz remembered.

"As we flew over the DMZ, our MIG escorts painted the plane [with radar to target the plane] as we flew into North Korea," Silvestre ["Amigo"] Reyes remembered.

The next tension-filled minutes passed as Tong Kim talked to the pilots and related the delegation's permission so the pilots could check.

That crisis passed; the MIGs remained as escorts all the way to Pyongyang, the North Korean capital.

"As we disembarked at the airport, all these security guys came rushing up, made us get back on the plane," Ortiz smiled, shaking his head. "It was around the SARS outbreaks. They brought doctors in to swab our mouths to make sure we weren't bringing SARS into the country."

The MIGs, and holding the delegation upon arrival, could have both been as much about intimidating the American delegation … or North Korean delusions … or even something else. But every member of the delegation was aware that the North Korean leader was just nuts.

The North Koreans might decide they would be better served by shooting the delegation out of the sky and claim they deterred an invasion. They might snatch the delegation for ransom, or imprison them for a fake crime, for a larger platform to convey their psychosis to the world.

All the things the North Koreans might do, the members had already thought them through, decided to go anyway. The gamble for better insight to the North Koreans was worth it. Most members of Congress are mighty hard to intimidate, generally.

But the Three Amigos simply couldn't be intimidated. They'd been everywhere in the world. They'd talked with dictators and other boogeymen ... and after each visit, those renegade nations and leaders were a little easier for the State Department to talk to.

Even if there were a gun to their head, they were more likely to joke about it, keep an even keel, and talk their way out of it.

But the ham-handed intimidation was un-artful, not actually serious, and only at the beginning of their excursion into North Korea.

"The ministry representatives that met us at the airport were incredibly nice, very formal ... but incredibly uptight," Ortiz remembered. "They were intrigued that we were so determined to come to their country. But they are genetically disposed to be distrustful, to see things that are not there."

"Still, we were an American delegation in North Korea," Ortiz sighed. "We were in a place our spies were having trouble getting into ... a place diplomats hadn't been in for a while." The North Koreans had been refusing for years to negotiate with the nations of Asia.

"Our primary mission there was to try nudging the North Koreans back to the negotiating table," Ortiz said. "The North Koreans wanted to negotiate with the U.S. alone, but we – and every other Asian nation on the Pacific Rim – wanted the negotiating to include six countries, including us."

"We also wanted to pick up any intelligence we could and wanted to put a face on the United States for the North Koreans," Ortiz explained. "When you know people, when you meet them personally, you have a relationship with them. And that makes our country seem less threatening. Or at least we hoped."

The congressional dynamic, Ortiz explained, was to humanize the United States for the North Koreans.

By day, the delegation ran from meeting to meeting, talking about what normalized relations with North Korea might look like. Weldon and Ortiz wanted the North Koreans to know what life might be like should they want to enter the community of nations.

"We talked about agriculture, education, defense and security, economic foundations, energy, the environment and health care," Ortiz said. "We spent a lot of time on how our system of government worked and talked about our judicial and legal systems, local governments, and Congress."

"It was hard for them to understand our constitutional system of checks and balances; it's the opposite of how they do it," he said. "They were amazed that Congress is co-equal branch of government; that Congress is the branch of government that pays the bills and declares war."

"I explained to them that half of us were from the opposition party in Congress, but that on the nonproliferation issue, the goal of the two parties is the same," Ortiz said. "I also told them that we believed that by simply talking about all this, we could find solutions together."

"Curt told them about congressional initiatives we'd taken with Russia, Ukraine and Libya that could be available to them if they gave up the nuclear weapons program and joined the civilized world community," Ortiz said.

"Over and over again, I explained that we were not there to negotiate issues with the North Koreans, and that none of us represented President [George W.] Bush," said Curt Weldon. "Rather, we were just there to talk to them about our congressional oversight responsibility and to put a human face on America, with the ultimate goal of avoiding war."

Both sides were very open and candid. At one point, the delegation had a marathon, ten-hour visit with the Vice Minister; and an hour and a half meeting with the nominal North Korean head of state, the president of the Supreme Peoples' Assembly.

The North Koreans escorted the delegation around to the local sites that they believed would convey that Pyongyang was a modern national capitol. But, since North Koreans had no clue about what a modern capitol city looked like, the delegation put on quite a show to appear impressed.

"We come in the spirit of friendship and cooperation," Weldon told one of the top generals. "We've been working for the past two years to achieve a resolution to the nuclear standoff that exists."

But it was the afterhours socializing that netted the delegation's biggest intelligence coup; and where they made the biggest impression on their hosts.

"We were at a big Pyongyang hotel, drinking rice wine with our hosts and the negotiators," Weldon said. "Solomon, me and Silver [Silvestre Reyes] were talking politics and world events and deliberately argued in front of them. They were blaming the ills inside the U.S. on Republicans; I was blaming it all on the liberal Democrats."

"We were debating – see – showing the differences of opinion between us on policy stuff," Weldon explained. "We were showing them democracy. Illustrating how people with different ideas work together. Showing them the essence of a free democracy. In the end, that is always going to be our most valuable export."

"We started talking about our families back in the United States," Ortiz said. "We were pulling out our wallets and showing each other the pictures of our grandchildren, our children. It was a very human moment. All of us could see the others' faces in the faces of our families. That was the first time our escorts let down their guard."

Then the serious drinking started.

"I've never been a big drinker," Ortiz smiled. "But I have been with lots of people who do drink, and their inhibitions almost always show through. We had a secret weapon. Curt Weldon can drink most people under the table.

"I was pouring my drinks into the plant beside me," Ortiz said. "The other Americans were pretending to be drinking far more than they actually were. The floor behind us was pretty wet. All by design."

"When I was a lawman in Texas, the best technique to get something out of an informant was: get 'em drunk, let 'em spill," he said. But only Weldon and all the North Koreans were matching each other drink for drink.

Somebody toasted plutonium. They drank, slammed the glasses back on the table and laughed like teenagers.

Suddenly, one of the North Koreans squealed and exclaimed: "We have enriched enough plutonium to make six nuclear weapons."

At the translation, all six Americans snapped their heads towards the official.

"WHAT?" they said in unison.

The translation was accurate; one of their North Korean escorts had just revealed how much plutonium they had enriched to weapons-grade strength, a difficult part in making the fuel for nuclear weapons.

"Maybe the slip was intentional," Ortiz conceded. "Maybe they wanted to plant that they had more weapons grade plutonium than they did. But I don't think that's what it was. They'd been bragging about their weapons program, how advanced they were. I think it was spontaneous."

U.S. intelligence at the time was publicly speculating that the North Koreans had enriched enough plutonium for six to eight weapons.

"Midway through supper, Kim, the translator, asked to see me alone and we go to the men's room," Weldon remembered. "He told me the most amazing thing: 'I have been with these people 17 times; this is the only time I have ever seen them laugh.' That – for me – was gold."

The next day, the hosts were even more candid.

"One of them told us that they knew they had no chance in a toe-to-toe fight with us," Ortiz said. "All they had, he said, was one shot at us: a nuke aimed at our nearly 30,000 troops in South Korea. That's a 'two-fer' for them; they hit South Korea, their mortal enemy ... and they hit our military very hard at the same time."

"They simply believed the best way to combat the U.S. was to hit us first, hard, with a nuke ... figuring if you can't win, get in the first licks," Ortiz said. "Their nuclear deterrent, they said, was entirely defensive. They'd seen the invasion of Iraq, and figured they were next. Iraq didn't actually have WMD. They certainly did."

"I thought this was awfully interesting – I was under the impression that North Koreans were rigidly agnostic," Ortiz said. "Sunday morning, we were supposed to talk to the trade minister. But it was illegal for the U.S. to trade with North Korea. We bagged the trade minister meeting."

"So the guide asked us what we wanted to do, and we asked if we could go to church," Ortiz smiled. "I thought the guide would just suggest something else. Big surprise, they took us to a Christian church. There wasn't time to plan it. They had no idea we would pass on the meeting with the trade minister. We didn't talk about it in the rooms. They sang the same hymns we sing, but, you know, in Korean."

The amount of time the Koreans knew in advance the Americans wanted to go to a church: 20 minutes.

"They had us down front, the Koreans were so excited to have Christians from the United States worship with them," Ortiz said. "Everybody wanted to touch us. Bunch of them gathered around us to pray for us. It was so moving. It was altogether unexpected."

"Interesting place to see," Reyes added. "We went on a metro, went to a Baptist church – a Baptist church there in North Korea. Who knew? It was so poverty-ridden and barren, and fascinating to be in a place so closed off from the world."

"Winter there was hellaciously cold," Reyes shivered. "The temperature in the airport terminal was 24 below zero. The heat was always turned off unless somebody was in a room."

"The hotel rooms were empty on both sides of each of our rooms," Reyes said of the accommodations in Pyongyang, North Korea's capitol.

"But they weren't really empty," confided Reyes, then a senior member of the House Intelligence Committee. "At one point, I saw inside one of the rooms next to mine and there was quite a bit of electronic equipment."

"In every meeting, I reiterated again and again my personal conversations with President Bush to tell them two things," Weldon said. "First, that the president said he did not seek regime change in North Korea; and second that he said he had absolutely no intention of a preemptive attack on North Korea, despite his earlier assertions in terms of the Axis of Evil."

State Department translator Tong Kim was in a strange place. The White House and State Department had not wanted the delegation to go at all. But they sent him along, in part because he was the most experienced, and in part to bring back the best report of the events there.

"Kim told us that in all his meetings with the North Koreans, this was the only time he'd seen them be open and have actual conversation," Ortiz recalled. "In the 17 previous meetings, he said he'd never seen such candor and transparency as he saw with us. Mostly the diplomats argued over the size of the negotiating table and the height of the flags that sat on the table."

CATHY TRAVIS

"Before we left, we gave presents to our hosts," Weldon said. "I told their top negotiator about how we treasure our sports teams in the United States, and gave him a congressional baseball cap. He said: 'you want me to take off my terrorist hat and put on your baseball hat'?"

"I said: 'you better believe it, that's exactly what I want'," Weldon smiled. "These guys know a lot about us. This guy even nailed the language idiom we use in U.S., likening a vocation with wearing a hat."

"Now, we knew this was going to be a huge deal," Weldon said of the reception that awaited them in South Korea. "North Korea is the most closed, most unpredictable – nuclear – country in the world."

"We got to South Korea and briefed U.S. officials," Weldon said. "Then we briefed the South Koreans, and headed for a press conference. It was an enormous turnout. Even we were surprised at the interest. We looked out on sea of lights, as far as we could see."

"I've never seen that many reporters in same place – and I've seen huge groups," Weldon said. "Told them they'd seen the press release; that it was released after we left, but I knew what it said. We'd asked the North Koreans to only offer the facts of our visit, not to offer anything else. And that's what they did."

"I told the mass of reporters that we'd gotten what we wanted: we achieved a genuine interface with these guys," Weldon said proudly. "Nobody else had been able to do that. Then I made a mistake at this press conference."

"I asked Kim to share the impression he'd shared with me," Weldon winced. "He told the reporters what he'd told me earlier. He said, 'I have been with these people 17 times; this is the only time I have ever seen them laugh.' But asking Kim to speak was unwise."

"He got fired for his candor," Weldon said, shaking his head. "The Bush administration just wouldn't abide candor if it was to praise our efforts."

"All in all, Solomon and I led 60 CODELS [congressional delegations] to 100 countries," said Weldon. "I'm very proud of the diplomacy we conducted, of the example we showed the world about the 'other Americans' in the U.S."

20 – REDISTRICTING, 21ST CENTURY'S SIN

"Representatives …shall be apportioned among the several States which may be included within this Union, according to their respective Numbers … every subsequent Term of ten Years, in such Manner as they shall by Law direct."
-- Constitution of the United States, Article I, Section 2, graph 3

"CONGRESSIONAL REDISTRICTING" IS the most archaic, nuanced component of organizing how citizens in each state are represented in the U.S. Congress.

The Constitution established the House of Representatives as the branch of government most representative of the nation – and the national mood.

Redistricting in Texas – and in other states – was traditionally done once every ten years, the year following the National Census, as laid out in the Constitution.

An outgrowth of over a century of denying voting rights of minorities was addressed in the Voting Rights Act (VRA), passed in 1965. In an ironic quirk of history, Republicans have always been in power in Texas to defend the VRA.

A relatively young component of U.S. voting rights, the VRA has been in force for the redistricting efforts in 1971, 1981, 1991 and 2001. And 2003, 2004, 2005, 2006, 2007 … 2011, and 2012.

In 2013, in a disgrace to democracy and free elections, the U.S. Supreme Court invalidated sections of the VRA that were the only barrier between more and more radical Republican redistricting in Texas, with nothing to hold them accountable in a democratic nation … not even voters.

Under the Voting Rights Act of 1965, Texas and other states with a history of discriminatory elections were required (until June 2013) to submit changes in their voting systems or election maps for approval by the Justice Department's Civil Rights Division.

"Good and decent Texans should not protest the fact that the Justice Department notes that Texas has had a difficult history in terms of race relations – we have," Ortiz said. "Bear in mind, our state traditionally held 'white man's' primaries … like most of the South … but Texans had the audacity to name it that."

By 2000, Republican George W. Bush was the Texas governor, and Republican Rick Perry was his lieutenant governor. After the 2000 elections, Democrats maintained their majority in the Texas legislature when they redrew congressional districts in 2001.

In 2001, when Democrats and Republicans were unable to agree on a new congressional district map for the decade, the Republican minority recommended it be sent to a panel of judges, for them to draw a new map of congressional districts.

Republicans were arrogantly certain the judges would redraw the map their way.

The judges' re-drawn map maintained the 17 to 15 Democratic majority in the Texas delegation to the U.S. House of Representatives.

Republicans were furious. Their "in" with the judges didn't exist.

The motive behind what came to be a criminal enterprise to give the Texas Legislature a Republican majority in the 2002 elections was entirely so Republicans could control all the political power in the state.

They needed that in order to grease the skids for the legislature to go at redistricting all over again in 2003.

Before October 2002, U.S. House Majority Leader Texan Tom DeLay's state PACs spent $3.4 million on twenty-two races for the Texas House, an astounding amount to spend on state races.

On October 4, 2002, DeLay's federal PAC sent $190,000 to seven candidates for the State House. The following month, all seven were elected, and Republicans became the majority party in the Texas House.

DeLay's Achilles Heel, in this manifest exploitation of every facet of state and federal government, was his carelessness with the law governing campaign money.

The law forbade a direct influx of federal money in state campaigns.

He should have laundered the money through the state party, which was one of several legal options. But he did not.

In the spring of 2003, Texas Republicans, who were now dominant in both the State House and Senate, proposed a new congressional map that promised to add between five and seven new Republicans to the Texas delegation. But they failed to pass a final plan.

Democrats never figured the Republicans would go to such enormous lengths to impose a new federal legislative map on the state (running roughshod over campaign finance law ... revisiting redistricting mid-decade ... forgoing action on a state budget ... violating the rules of their own state legislature ... and abusing federal agencies from the Federal Aviation Administration to the Justice Department).

And Texas Republicans never figured the Democrats would fight back so hard ... in the state legislature and in hearings the legislature was forced to hold on their plans. They never expected that the legislators in the State House and the State Senate – would leave the state of Texas before a final vote on the redistricting package, rather than contribute to a quorum in which the plan could be passed.

Democrats treated it as the political campaign it was, and vigorously shined the light on the machinations going on in Texas.

What the Governor and Republicans in the Texas Legislature – and the U.S. Congress – were doing was extraordinary in scope and audacity.

It was also extra-constitutional. Redistricting was not a "do-over" proposition ... or it was not then.

In over 200 years of U.S. history, states didn't get second or third shots at getting it right. You get one shot, the year following a census, which was how the Constitution set it up.

The U.S. Supreme Court changed that in 2006, saying that the Republicans indeed did it wrong. But they also said, because redistricting is an inherently political exercise, states can do it as many times a day/month/year/decade as they want to do it.

In a democracy, voters choose their representatives; representatives should never choose voters. In Texas, this tyranny took a higher priority than the children, economy and future of

Texas.

Raw partisan power grabs are all about finding ways to take power outside elections.

After the final redistricting plan passed by the Texas Legislature in 2003 was signed into law by Governor Perry, Joby Fortson – a political aide to Texas Republican Joe Barton – sent a candid e-mail to a group of colleagues that laid bare the naked intentions of Texas Republicans.

The memo, disclosed in subsequent litigation, offered a "quick rundown" on the disposition of each of the seats in the delegation.

Fortson's memo unmasked the nature and scope of the plan: "This is the most aggressive map I have ever seen. This has a real national impact that should assure that Republicans keep the House no matter the national mood."

That was the first time any of the Texas Republicans spewed publicly that Texas was big enough to manipulate enough Republican seats to ensure the Republicans in the U.S. House of Representatives remained in the slim majority.

Party division in the House then was 221 Republicans and 212 Democrats. Winning a total of five seats would make the Democrats the majority. That was DeLay's constant fear.

On October 14, 2003, Texas Democrats challenged the new congressional districts under the Voting Rights Act, but three months later a three-judge panel – two thirds of them appointed by Republican governors and lobbied by state and federal lawmakers – ruled that the evolving lines had not diluted the voting power of African-Americans or Hispanics.

Three months later, while another three-judge federal panel dismissed the claims that the new congressional redistricting plan violated the voting rights of minorities across Texas, the judges did criticize the Republican's method to reach their political objective.

"We decide only the legality of Plan 1374C [the Texas redistricting scheme], not its wisdom," the judges wrote in their final order in January 2004. "Whether the Texas Legislature has acted in the best interest of Texas is a judgment that belongs to the people who elected the officials whose act is challenged in this case."

This federal panel, made up of Fifth Circuit Court of Appeals judges, said the process used to move congressional district lines that were in place just two years created greater potential for abuse.

In a searing look at how to repair the damage to the body politic, the judges wrote: "Congress can assist by banning mid-decade redistricting, which it has the clear constitutional authority to do, as many states have done."

Politics had gone nuclear – there was really no stunt the Republicans didn't employ.

In 2004, Ortiz realized how the scope of politics of personal destruction had co-oped people of faith. Priests around South Texas – indeed all over the country, at the behest of local Republican political operatives – told congregants they would go to hell for voting Democratic.

They'd go to hell. What an awful pairing of politics and hatefulness. In churches and in the name of God.

The political terrain in 2004 had begun to turn against Republicans. Bush's re-election was by no means a lock. Since no WMD existed in Iraq, his machinations in Iraq were becoming clear. The numerical division in parties in the U.S. House of Representatives was razor thin.

Nobody knew this until long after the election, but the Bush-Rove Ohio strategy and the manipulation of electronic voting machines there – along with the co-opting of the churches as an arm of the Republican Party and getting gay marriage on the ballots in swing states around the nation – were critical, and outrageously successful, components of the 2004 strategy. Albeit wildly unconstitutional … and which should bring shame to them and their legacy.

Still, the most sinister part of that was co-opting the churches for money.

"It was always more insidious for the churches to be used by the Republicans like that… given Jesus' instruction for His church to not be part of any government," Ortiz said.

On Election Day 2004, with the new congressional districts in place, Republicans gained five seats in Texas. The net increase was actually six seats, because one incumbent Democrat, Ralph Hall, switched parties. (After the Democrats won back the House in 2006, Ralph Hall was heard asking – jokingly: "where do I go to change back?")

"In early December, 2005, we found a pivotal memo where Justice Department lawyers said that DeLay's redistricting plan violated the Voting Rights Act, one of our central contentions all along," Ortiz said.

But senior Bush Justice Department political hacks overruled the non-partisan lawyers and approved the plan despite those violations.

The memo, unanimously endorsed by six lawyers and two analysts in the department's voting rights section, revealed that the redistricting plan illegally diluted black and Hispanic voting power in two congressional districts.

It also said the plan eliminated several other districts in which minorities had a substantial, though not necessarily decisive, influence in elections.

These Justice Department lawyers in the Bush administration also revealed that they consistently contacted Republican lawmakers and state officials who helped craft the proposal to be sure they were aware it was discriminatory compared with other options.

The 73-page memo, from Dec. 12, 2003, was kept under wraps for two years. Lawyers working on the case were subjected to an unusual gag rule.

On June 29, 2006, the U.S. Supreme Court found that Tom DeLay's Texas redistricting plan had unconstitutionally diluted the voting power of Hispanics in the vast southwest district held by Republican Henry Bonilla, who did not traditionally vote for him.

The map for the 2006 races went back to the three judge panel to redraw the boundaries to fix the problem. Again.

In the summer of 2006, in the wake of the Supreme Court's ruling that the Texas redistricting plan violated the voting rights of Hispanics in South Texas, Republicans – for once – were on the hot seat in redistricting.

Proposed maps flew like a blizzard around Capitol Hill and Austin.

"The House Republicans from Texas asked for a meeting with us Democrats to try to agree on a map that would preserve the existing districts for both parties," Ortiz chortled, remembering how the Republicans had scorched the earth, and then begged Democrats to help put out the fire.

"We knew we weren't going to get in bed with the wolves that helped bring us to this place," Ortiz said. "But – we were curious, and figured it could be entertaining."

While the members sat together uncomfortably inside the Speaker's Dining Room in the Capitol, staff members for the meeting participants stood together uncomfortably outside the room.

Finally, a long-time advisor for a Texas Democrats approached a Republican staff member and asked, "So? What kinda map are they talking about?"

The rather junior Republican staffer described the map as one that was "fair to all the members."

He went on to say that – if the Democrats and Republicans all agreed on the map then being proposed; an impossible hurdle – the Governor, the Attorney General, and the Texas State Legislature's House Speaker would all ask the judges to adopt this particular map.

"The Governor, the Attorney General, the Speaker – they all gave their word of honor they'd all support this map," the Republican staffer huffed importantly.

"Just so you know," the Democratic staffer said evenly, "All through this redistricting crap, any time the Governor, the AG, the Speaker – any of the Republicans – gave their word, publicly or privately, they never kept it. Never. Not a single one of 'em … not a single time. What's the definition of insanity? It's doing the same thing over and over and expecting different results. AND judges always resent being strong-armed to do something."

It was a remarkably dumb idea.

The embarrassed Republican staffer followed his red-faced boss who bounced out of the meeting unceremoniously.

That was as far as that "Republican map" went.

If people wanted to fix most of the political abuses that brought us such dysfunction in government and national conversations, "They would focus on the sin of redistricting," Ortiz said. "Money in politics keeps it going, but it is the hyper-partisan redistricting that lays the foundation for the institutional abuse."

"In all candor, elected members of Congress look for an easy re-election; Republicans want more solidly Republican voters, and Democrats want more reliable Democratic voters," Ortiz said. "The only thing the Supreme Court was remotely right about was that it is an inherently political exercise. That doesn't mean it needs to be unfair. Or more frequent than once a decade."

DECADES IN THE MAKING

While agreeing with Ortiz that the money in politics is the constant engine, "Redistricting is not the original sin," in today's broken-down Congress, said Meredith McGehee, Policy Director for the Campaign Legal Center.

"Our nation remains closely and starkly divided in our political views," said McGehee. "Certainly 'demographic sorting,' partisan news outlets, and north/south and urban/rural divides are among the factors playing significant roles in the current polarized politics but redistricting and the flood of money unleashed by the Supreme Court's ill-advised *Citizen United* decision are key contributors to the dysfunction that has gripped Washington by the throat."

To some degree, McGehee said, the redistricting effort was put in motion in the 1980s and 90s when Democrats in Congress joined Republicans in an all-out pursuit of corporate money. Tony Coelho (D-CA) was the 1980s Democratic Congressional Campaign Committee (DCCC) chairman who tirelessly and effectively courted corporations and the business community for Democratic campaign coffers.

That's where the money was. And there were a number of policies on which the business community and Democrats agreed, primarily on the need to pay the national bills, keeping interest rates low. Southern and western Democrats often supported expanding trade throughout the Americas.

In an attempt to win battles and wars, Coelho and the House Democrats utilized all the tools – and corporate money – available under the law.

Since the beginning of money in politics, the shameless push to raise money by all campaigns makes odd bedfellows, and affects public policy once a candidate becomes an officeholder. The 1980s were a period of solid Democratic control of both houses of Congress; but consistent Republican control of the White House in actor Ronald Reagan.

Coelho's Democratic alliance with corporate America – and the proliferation of "leadership" Political Action Committees (PACs) – enriched Democratic campaigns, elected more Democrats, and entrenched control of Congress for the Democrats.

He was a folk hero to Democratic partisans and the political world of campaigns … and a Johnny-come-lately to Republicans, who knew that Democrats could never get to equity with Republicans in campaign contributions from the business/corporate community.

Again, that's where the money was.

Coelho rose quickly to House Majority Whip, where he was an inventive, tireless, and hardnosed vote counter for the Democrats in Congress.

But big money got him in the end, when he purchased $100,000 in junk bonds, underwritten by the investment firm Drexel Burnham Lambert. Failure to disclose that he had received the help from a savings and loan executive in buying the bonds, made the events worthy of a House Ethics investigation.

Ever the uncompromising pragmatist on the direction of blowing political winds, in 1989, Cohelo promptly resigned his seat. The Newt Gingrich Republicans were trying to "burn down the House to rebuild it" and had successfully persuaded the House Ethics Committee to investigate House Speaker Jim Wright (D-TX).

Where they weren't winning with elections, the Gingrich warriors drove out anyone they could.

Looking back at the politics of the time, Meredith McGehee said a confluence of events conspired to make corporate campaign contributions the be-all-end-all for both parties, and signaled the supremacy of money – for the sake of money – in all parties equally.

Two things were going on, McGehee said, that were both gradual, but obvious.

"As the military industrial complex realized the value of government contracts, they helped fuel the growing breadth of government spending," McGehee said. "Health care; Medicare and Medicaid services. Defense, all kinds of support services. Law enforcement. The list goes on and on, but more and more corporations desperately wanted pieces of the gigantic – growing – opportunities to win government contracts."

Business concerns, as always, were clear-eyed about their biggest concern: making more money.

The need to win back Congress in the 1990s led the corporate community to finance campaigns of state judges, to advertise on a faux news network (Fox News Channel), to finance campaigns of state legislators, and finally to finance campaigns of Republican congressional, senate and presidential campaigns.

Their money came in hundreds of thousands of dollars per contributor.

"The sheer amount of money changed how members – particularly Democrats now – ran, and how they made decisions once they were in office," McGehee said. "K Street [Washington's downtown avenue of top tier corporate lobbyists] grew exponentially."

The 1990s – with the Clinton-ian business Democrats sometimes winning the chase for corporate money – the field was set entirely as corporations wanted it.

"Manipulating the redistricting process for partisan benefit was not new, but in the 1990s, these efforts, assisted by new technologies, became part of the all-out pursuit of big money," McGehee said, "After the 2000 census, redistricting became a way to artificially expand mostly Republican congressional delegations in the House of Representatives."

ANY WAY OUT?

Knowing about the extraordinary manipulation by political forces to predetermine elections, voters should want to have an even-handed way to redraw congressional districts.

One option for state legislatures is to ban mid-decade redistricting in their states and create a commission to judiciously – and transparently – study the communities of interest in their state and divide the state accordingly.

Some states could also pass a referendum, forcing state legislatures to create a commission, McGehee said. "Greater transparency in the redistricting process and independent redistricting commissions like the one created in California are the first steps to moving forward. And Congress should not only pass updated campaign disclosure laws, but also laws to address the ills of a campaign finance system that is dangerously tilted in favor of the wealthiest in our country."

The United States Congress could ban mid-decade redistricting and require states to redistrict through independent commissions.

If the U.S. Congress passed a law to ban mid-decade redistricting, states could focus exclusively on finding a fairer way to apportion their delegations to Congress. But that will not happen; it would undermine corporate interests in government and there is no political will in Congress or the general public to address it.

The Fifth Circuit Court of Appeals judges said in a decision regarding redistricting, "Congress can assist by banning mid-decade redistricting, which it has the clear constitutional authority to do, as many states have done," they wrote.

Congress is wary of doing that, for individual political reasons inside their states. Usually, members of the state legislatures are eyeing the primaries for Congressional races themselves, so there is always a subterranean jockeying for position.

The best way for state legislators to lord it over the incumbent U.S. Representatives is to dinker with the district lines of that member.

Congress has the authority to give states the parameters to follow in carrying out congressional redistricting after the Census in a couple of different places in the Constitution.

Rep. John Tanner's (D-TN), Fairness and Independence in Redistricting Act (in 2007) – to ban mid-decade redistricting and require states to redistrict through independent commissions – got quite a bit of support in the U.S. House of Representatives. It never passed.

Obviously, Congress can reiterate the Constitution's instructions to the states to redistrict their states every 10 years – and no more – despite the Supreme Court's capitulation on that point.

In Article I, Section 4 of the Constitution, the framers gave Congress the power to enact laws governing the time, place, and manner of elections for members of the House of Representatives.

In the Constitution's 14th Amendment (Section 5) – the amendment that the nation passed in the wake of the Civil War, giving every person in the nation equal rights – gives Congress the power to enact laws to enforce the fair apportionment (redistricting) of its members.

"The tsunami of things that are in crisis – our economy, our military, our foreign policy, the earth beneath our feet, and dozens of other serious matters – will not be solved by the two parties continuing to snipe at each other, and fix elections," Ortiz declared.

"Solomon knew when it came to redistricting, that either we had to hang together, or we'd all certainly hang separately," Texas Rep. Charlie Gonzalez (D-TX) smiled, repeating a well-worn Ortiz mantra during the decade of Texas redistricting.

"His style in leading the delegation was the same style he brought to all things … he tried to keep us together," Gonzalez said. "In doing so, he instituted a mechanism for all of us to be in on major decisions, a way to make decisions together."

"Believe it or not, that was a little unusual in the delegation leadership when it came to redistricting," Gonzalez said.

Ortiz took the delegation leadership – which is based on seniority within parties – after the 2003 redistricting plan ended the long-time service of Representative Marty Frost.

"The DeLay plan in 2003 was just awful for Texas," Gonzalez said. "It only existed to help the Republicans retain the majority in the House of Representatives."

"Solomon told us together and separately: we have got to get along … none of us can only push our self-interest," Gonzalez said. "He made all of us focus on the big picture."

J. Gerald Hebert (Gerry) is the longtime Executive Director and Director of Litigation at the Campaign Legal Center, in Washington, DC. Hebert was the lawyer for the Texas Democrats in the long decade of Texas redistricting.

"When Congressional redistricting occurs, it is important for members of a state's congressional delegation to understand the politics and pressures of redistricting," said Hebert. "Congressman Ortiz understood both, and did so while protecting the voting rights of his constituents."

21 – POLITICS, NOT JOURNALISM

RIGHT AFTER ORTIZ' first re-election campaign in 1984, the local paper, the *Corpus Christi Caller Times*, started what would be a long tradition of investigating him. The much-ado-about-nothing probes of Ortiz repeatedly landed with a very loud thud. Every time.

The *Caller Times* had supported the paper's attorney, Jorge Rangel, in the 1982 race – and never got over the fact that Ortiz beat Rangel, and then went on to win increasingly higher and higher percentages in elections until well into the 21st century.

More than a little insidious, the paper's habit of running stories about dinky issues, but presenting them as important, tended to telegraph the message: you may be helping constituents, but not the right ones.

It annoyed Ortiz to no end when the paper took his press releases, and ran the story as though the reporter gathered the information, omitting Ortiz' name altogether.

That was the little stuff.

The *Caller Times'* forays every few months to "investigate" something related to Ortiz came to be called "proctology reports" by Ortiz and his team.

The measure of whether or not a news story is the real deal, is in if the story moves to the newswires, and is published by other newspapers. Reports on Ortiz by the *Caller Times* never got picked up by other news organizations.

They just landed with a very loud thud. Every time.

The local paper had lost many subscribers, even in the mid-1990s, before the print press started losing readers to the Internet. Most local subscribers bought the paper for the sports, obits, and coupons.

The "news" section was distrusted by so many readers by then, that if the Ortiz campaign took out ads in the paper, they were placed on page three of the sports section, to target white male voters.

Commissioner Oscar Ortiz reflected on how the community saw the *Caller Times'* repeated hack jobs on his brother. "Back then [1970s-80s], the *Corpus Christi Caller Times* wasn't the only voice around," Oscar Ortiz said. "The media was more diverse … there were strong community leaders in journalism. Local radio voices were local celebrities."

"When the paper would denigrate Solomon, he would respond on local radio," Oscar Ortiz said. "Now it's all Clear Channel and Fox. The only thing not owned by corporate interests – so far – is the Internet."

Probably the primary example of the "investigative" stories concerned Amtex, a company Ortiz founded, with Lencho Rendon in 1982. Ortiz remained the principal owner of Amtex until 2007.

Mike Rendon, an Army veteran with a degree in law enforcement – and Lencho Rendon's younger brother – ran the business for his brother and the former sheriff.

"Amtex was a good business, but we were hobbled from the start because Solomon decided early on that we would not compete for federal contacts, which are usually the most lucrative for private security companies," Mike Rendon said. "He wanted to draw a clear line between the company and federal contracts."

Smart politics, Mike Rendon said, but that decision meant the pool of potential business for Amtex was significantly shallow.

Nevertheless, a security company owned by two South Texas natives, known as swashbuckling drug warriors, was quite a calling card. The security company, first called South Texas Industrial Security, Inc., began to pick up work among businesses, schools and other clients.

In 1983, right after he first took office, Ortiz asked the Ethics Committee for guidance regarding whether he could use his name on brochures for the security company.

In a letter dated Oct. 11, 1983, the committee responded, "There is no federal statute or House rule which expressly prohibits a Member from engaging in outside business activities. House Rule XLIII, clause 3, however does provide that a member may not receive compensation for outside work…. Since you are not involved in the daily operations and are not identifying yourself as a Member of Congress, there seems to be a sincere effort on your part not to 'cash in' on your position as a Member of Congress," the committee told Ortiz.

The letter advised him to ensure that the company and its employees did not use his official title in his identification as company owner.

To that end, shortly afterwards Ortiz informed all the employees in writing: "Every effort must be taken to ensure the possible appearance that as a Member of Congress, I am not 'cashing in' on my position in the Congress. It is imperative that my title is not used under any circumstances during meetings or negotiations with potential clients."

Ortiz' instruction to employees at Amtex continued: "There must be careful monitoring of all other employees to see that they do not use my title or position for the financial benefit of the company. There must be no confusion of the two positions. I expect all parties of the company to abide by the instructions in the letter from the [Ethics] Committee."

"I always scrupulously kept a careful distance from Amtex, and made sure that my title was never used in any conversation or discussion associated with any business dealings," Ortiz said. "This rule was set up [by the House of Representatives] long before I got there and was to protect the institution of Congress, and kept really big business owners from taking a vow of poverty when they were elected to Congress. I was hardly a big business owner, but this covered me, too."

In 1984, Ortiz and Rendon took the company public, and re-launched South Texas Industrial Security into Amtex Security, Inc. As Amtex president, Ortiz was compensated in Amtex stock; he owned 55% of those shares, but he drew no salary.

Rules in the House of Representatives governing ownership of a company or publicly traded stocks were – as they should have been – very specific about owning a company or stocks, and outside income. Ortiz followed those rules to the letter.

He disclosed his ownership and earnings, and the House Ethics Committee verified that Amtex was allowed to use Ortiz' name only; but not the titles "Congressman" or "Member of Congress" on company documents.

Amtex complied completely with those requirements.

Ortiz' stock ownership of the company netted him around $15,000 annually by 1985.

It was tough to find both clients that needed the level of security Amtex provided … and contracts that were lucrative enough to keep the company in business.

Amtex won its most significant contract – for security at the Port of Corpus Christi – in 1995.

"You know how we finally won the contact for security at the port?" Mike Rendon asked. "The most expensive part of our bid included our insurance, which we had through Loyd Neal and which was $160,000. When I found another company that would insure us for $68,000, I sat with Loyd to see if he could match it, and he was pissed."

"He even left the room in a huff at the prospect of losing our business," Mike Rendon said. "I asked him what he'd do in my place, as a businessman. That didn't help, he was just so mad."

That moment may have been when Loyd Neal – local insurance salesman, Corpus Christi Mayor, County Judge, and once an ally of the Ortiz organization – began to pull away. Neal eventually came to epitomize the local opposition to Ortiz, siding with the interests of the downtown business cabal and a minority of commissioners for the Port of Corpus Christi to keep the prosperity in the county clustered tightly around the old-money Corpus Christi crowd.

Neal's separation from the Ortiz organization was final and complete when he became a tool of those narrow business interests in their quest to close Naval Station Ingleside – in 2005 – a major naval base adjacent to Corpus Christi.

The Port of Corpus Christi is governed by commissioners; at the turn of the century, the division of seven commissioners was this: four commissioners were appointed by Nueces County and three by the City of Corpus Christi.

The political interests of the county usually collided with the political and financial interests of the city.

When it was time for the port to renew the Amtex security contract in 1998 – another firm – Asset Protection and Security Services, Inc., owned by Scott Mandel, submitted a lower bid. But the port's qualifications required that a security firm have been in business for at least five years, Mike Rendon explained.

Mandel's firm was relatively new, in business under five years – so the Mandel bid was disqualified. The next lowest bid was from Amtex, which won the contract for port security again.

Then-Port Commissioner Bernard Paulson objected to the port following its own rules for security contracts in 1998, and told the *Corpus Christi Caller Times* four years later that "the port has a difficult time being objective when Ortiz is involved."

When Amtex won the contract again in 1998, port commissioners – including Paulson, Ruben Bonilla, and Bill Dodge – began to agitate over the security contract and the fact that it was owned by Ortiz. The port had every reason to be grateful to Ortiz for his work in Congress, since he had secured over $40 million in federal funding for the port during his tenure of congressional service.

But the downtown business community – with whom the port mainly worked – was unhappy about two things: that Ortiz was a benefactor for the port, and that the company he co-owned was a major contractor there.

Pleased with the security Amtex provided, the cabal at the port nevertheless seemed to view Ortiz as unworthy of repeated reelection, or the admiration of so many people in the community.

Banker Yolanda Olivarez – the 1999 chairwoman of the Port of Corpus Christi Commission and a fan of Ortiz – pushed for the port to name its new facility the "Congressman Solomon P. Ortiz International Center."

That only made matters worse with the three commissioners who were opposed to Ortiz and who had opposed the company he co-founded winning the port security contract. Whining to the *Corpus Christi Caller Times* produced a few stories that criticized Ortiz, and which included allegations from "confidential sources" who said Ortiz worked to win the security contract at the port.

Ortiz was never involved in conversations about the contract, and the sources were only "confidential" in the newspaper stories; many, many people knew the sources were one of the three unhappy port commissioners, or their agent.

By 2001, the decade-and-a-half ownership had added nearly $100,000 to Ortiz' portfolio.

On September 11, 2001, port officers watched the attacks on Washington and New York City and asked Mike Rendon that morning to double the security guards, which also doubled the price tag for them.

The first $40 billion Congress spent after September 11 was to clean up the attack sites, to begin the war in Afghanistan, and to ratchet up security around the nation. After September 11, the port asked Ortiz to champion its request for federal anti-terrorism grants, as they had done dozens of times in the past 20 years.

Ortiz got the port $2.27 million to heighten security around the ship channel and the waterfront facilities. "Certainly, he helped us on the security grant we just got," the *Caller Times* quoted then-port executive director John LaRue.

But the three port commissioners, who remained unhappy that Amtex was their choice again for port security, saw an opportunity to say that Ortiz and Amtex were profiting from 9-11, a nuclear accusation in the months following the al Qaeda attacks on the United States ... an attack Ortiz saw from Capitol Hill, and dealt with the after-effects of it daily.

Ortiz was furious.

The unhappy commissioners proposed using part of the new funding to install new automated cameras, so as to reduce the number of actual guards the port would need from Amtex.

"Of course cameras would enhance our security efforts," Mike Rendon said. "But cameras also require guards to watch, repair, and ensure they're all working. Anybody who's ever been in the security business knows a target is not safer with more cameras and fewer human eyes watching the place."

"Remember the context of the times," Mike Rendon said. "The next great threat we were expecting was coming through the ports which had so much tonnage coming through them. It was impossible to scan every single container for a threat."

The Port of Corpus Christi was a strategic seaport, through which war materiel passed 24 hours a day for much of 2002, headed to Afghanistan and (later mostly to) Iraq.

It was the summer of 2002 when *ABC News* smuggled a 15-pound cylinder of depleted uranium metal into the United States through the water port of New York, and then televised the story on the first anniversary of the September 2001 terrorist attacks.

"You better believe if something awful happened at the port, all fingers would have been pointed at Amtex saying what an awful job we did," Mike Rendon said. "Now, as a contractor, my contact with the port was primarily with the staff there, but this was too big a matter to leave with the staff. So I took it directly to the commissioners."

"A terrorist attack at a seaport could result in mass casualties, shut down the shipping industry," Mike Rendon reminded the port commissioners by letter. "At this moment, Congress is negotiating the final complex elements of legislation that will require enhanced security operations at all seaports."

"The Federal government is in the process of conducting a nationwide port assessment to determine the country's overall port needs … the Port of Corpus Christi is scheduled for its security assessment in July [that month]," Rendon's letter said, urging the commissioners to at least wait another two weeks, until after the assessment, before cutting back on security.

Days later [July 2002], the *Corpus Christi Caller Times* found someone at a nonpartisan foundation in Washington to say they saw "serious ethical questions in U.S. Rep. Solomon Ortiz's role as president of the company that provides security for the Port of Corpus Christi, and in the way the company has lobbied the port for a post-Sept. 11-fattened contract after Ortiz helped the port win anti-terrorism funding."

The *Caller Times* got the director of the Center for Public Integrity to question Ortiz's ethics and to call Mike Rendon's warning "heavy handed." The 2002 story included a reference to a Congressional rule, saying Ortiz was "… potentially in violation of House ethics rules."

That was untrue, and Ortiz was fully compliant with the House rules governing ownership of a company.

The day after the story ran, Monday July 29, a House Ethics Committee lawyer told Ortiz' staff that a *Caller Times* reporter called that day and misrepresented herself as having obtained permission from his office to talk to them.

"This manner of investigation after the fact, and outright lie by the reporter to the Ethics Committee, was not surprising to me," Ortiz said. "Still it was reprehensible. And the paper didn't report that part. They didn't report a whole lot."

The paper made a huge accusation against Ortiz, saying ownership of the company violated House Ethics rules and ran the story *without ever talking to the Ethics Committee.*

That's how the paper rolled.

Since their reporter [Tara Copp] never bothered to talk to the Ethics Committee, she extrapolated what she thought she knew about the law and ethics rules in the House. Plus she misrepresented the essence of the facts to the Center for Public Integrity so their director could be a validator for the paper's bullshit.

The center of the charge by the paper was to confuse "earned income" (a paycheck from a company, which was a violation of House rules) with "annual dividends" (a division of company profits at the end of the year, *which were allowed* under the House rules).

The minority of port commissioners then – and their patrons, the downtown business bureau – didn't have to like it, but Ortiz was on the right side of a bright line established by the House of Representatives in terms his relationship with the company he and Lencho Rendon founded and owned.

The other component of the paper's charge against Ortiz was that House rules forbade his company (Amtex) from using his name on company documents. Again, the paper's/reporter's information was false.

House rules didn't allow members who owned companies to use the terms "Congressman" or "Member of Congress" in association with their names on company letterhead, literature and documents.

"It was such bullshit," Mike Rendon said. "This crap was just that much more proof that the paper was either instigating a malicious effort to demean Solomon – or the paper was an active, manipulated agent for the instigators. Either one of those, that's a poor place to be for people who say they are journalists."

"They wanted to punish Solomon," Mike Rendon said. "Simple as that. They wanted Solomon get down on his knees and either give up his stake in the company, or make the company give up the port contract. I mean, we were in business to do business, but our business was security – at a major economic engine in our hometown. We took that seriously, every day."

"I categorically detest and think it is a terrible thing if there are individuals trying to politicize this . . . it's just muckraking that you and your paper need to do," the paper quoted then-port commissioner Tony Pletcher.

Ortiz owning Amtex, and Amtex having the port security contract, Pletcher was quoted saying in the paper, was "not any more surprising to me than that Senator (Phil) Gramm's wife was a shareholder of Enron. I think it is asinine for people to try and make a political point about congressmen, senators, elected officials' actions that are well within the law."

Port Commissioner Yolanda Olivarez said that she had not heard Ortiz' name used in conversations about the security contract. But as a native of Corpus Christi, she knew Ortiz owned Amtex.

It wasn't a secret. Ortiz and Lencho Rendon served Nueces County as heroic lawmen 20 years prior. Only the very young, or newcomers to the area, were lost on Ortiz' security credentials.

But the 2002 Port Commission chairman Ruben Bonilla, the *Caller Times* reported, "Said this push by Amtex may have been inappropriate."

Bonilla, whose sister challenged Ortiz for the Democratic nomination for his congressional seat in 1996, was an early sympathizer with *La Raza Unida*, and later, more formally, with the local League of United Latin American Citizens (LULAC), the more liberal Hispanic activists in Corpus Christi.

While Bonilla was an Ortiz campaign contributor, he and Ortiz were on opposite sides of most questions in terms of how to make change in the community. Bonilla, a lawyer, seemed to see Ortiz as an upstart, not quite 'good enough' to represent the community, according to a number of South Texans.

Those who thought there was anything inappropriate about the conduct of Ortiz or his company was a very small number, generally right around the three port commissioners, their megaphones in the editorial offices of the *Caller Times*, and parts of the Corpus Christi business community.

Other commissioners were candidly angry about the move to embarrass Ortiz, and try to make him and/or his company look bad, for crass political reasons … and for financial ones. The security contract was now a significant chunk of money and they preferred for one of their friends to get the contract, security professionalism notwithstanding.

Olivarez, the *Caller Times* said, had questioned the move to cut back security at the port. "I was not pressured," she told the *Caller Times* [when asked if Mike Rendon's letter influenced commissioners to keep Amtex's contract at the same level].

"I was concerned about port security," the *Caller Times* quoted

Olivarez saying. "I am a port commissioner with the Port of Corpus Christi, and I take that position very seriously. We were cutting port security, and right now, we are in a state of high alert. And I was very concerned about that."

Continuing the drumbeat two days later, after the grievous mistakes in reporting had been pointed out to the paper, the *Caller Times* editorial board said, in a moment of extraordinary exaggeration: "Congressman Solomon P. Ortiz willingly chooses to be blind to the conflict of interest in his involvement in the firm that provides security services to the Port of Corpus Christi. This is not surprising; to do otherwise would mean acknowledging he has profited from the national concern over terrorism in a blatant abuse of his political office."

Bullshit. Hyperbole. Employing the very political machinations they accused Ortiz of. Forced to be the mouthpiece for the hack job, or lose valuable advertising dollars as the print journalism industry was going under.

Whatever it was, what the *Caller Times* was doing was nowhere near journalism.

After that, every political story about Ortiz went chapter and verse back through what had long before been discredited … but when you tell the lie long enough, it becomes common belief. Fox "News" has raised that to an art form.

Ortiz and Lencho Rendon sold Amtex for $300,000 in 2007. In 2012, Amtex was a multimillion dollar global security company holding significant contracts with the U.S. military in Afghanistan and elsewhere, the types of contracts Ortiz forbade the company to compete for while he served in Congress.

In a discouraging analysis of the present journalism dynamic in South Texas, Oscar Ortiz said, "There is such viciousness on the local radio talk shows. No Hispanic radio to respond – no progressive radio to offer context. Freedom of speech is no more – since the Supreme Court ruled that money is speech, speech is bought and paid for. People that aren't rich can't compete."

22 – TRADE DIPLOMAT

BY VIRTUE OF his international travel with the Armed Services Committee, Ortiz was intimately familiar with what other countries wanted and needed – in terms of economic expansion.

On a swing through Asia in the late 1980s, Ortiz met businessmen from China, a nation whose economy was the fastest growing in the world. Investors there were making money hand over fist.

Ortiz began talking to them about the possibilities of marrying South Texas economic opportunities with Chinese manufacturing needs. He didn't do that just in China. Ortiz had similar discussions all over the Far East. Singapore, Japan and Indonesia were other opportunities Ortiz explored.

By 1990, Ortiz emerged as an ambassador-without-portfolio, leading trade delegations repeatedly to the Pacific Rim to rustle up opportunities for industry to re-locate to South Texas. That move was about bringing jobs to South Texas, and to leverage the contacts he was making in other nations to that end.

The North American Free Trade Agreement (NAFTA) was a major card for Ortiz to play as he trolled for business opportunities around Asia. NAFTA rules of origin were valuable for investors.

The rules of origin said that when a non-NAFTA nation compiled a certain percentage of a product inside a NAFTA country, it would have the same market considerations in North America as a product designed entirely within a NAFTA country.

So a Chinese widget – made to some degree in Mexico, the United States or Canada – could be sold in the U.S. without tariffs and many other incentives.

As Ortiz pitched opportunities with South Texas business owners around Asia – telling them that they could make and sell their products in the lucrative North American markets without tariffs, and without transportation costs. The NAFTA rules of origin were a valuable consideration for the Asian businesses and corporations.

"I will always believe that trade is the best diplomacy the U.S. can offer," Ortiz said, repeating his lifelong philosophy of how the U.S. should position itself in the world. "Trading with other nations – exchanging money – makes us more understanding of each other's culture, each other's needs, and each other's abilities."

"It's taking a small stake in each other's country," Ortiz said. "Everybody wins there. Democracy can change the world, and free trade is the best vehicle to export democracy and capitalism around the world."

Ortiz played an important role in passing all the free trade agreements in the late 20th century and early 21st century.

In 1993, NAFTA was supported by a Democratic president (Bill Clinton) but opposed by most Democrats in Congress, who then controlled the House and Senate.

It was supported by Republicans in Congress, but they had zero interest in helping a Democratic president accomplish such a big win on a policy matter.

In one of the true bipartisan moments on (non-military) policy in Congress, the players who supported streamlining the trade across Mexico, the U.S. and Canada (the original NAFTA countries) took an unconventional path.

With the Democratic leadership opposed to the treaty, even Republicans so inclined could not bring NAFTA to a vote.

Since the Democratic leadership opposed the treaty, its formal vote-counting organization (called the "whips") was unavailable. President Clinton and NAFTA Congressional supporters were flying blind.

You should never fly blind when controversial votes are in play.

So Clinton met with all the stakeholders: congressional supporters in both parties, labor unions, and the lobbying organizations for the national Chamber of Commerce, the Business Roundtable, and other lobbyists for the business communities around the nation.

Labor unions and the workers they represented would take the greatest hit under NAFTA. So the unions – long and steadfast supporters for Democratic candidates around the country – bitterly opposed the trade deal.

The central issue for unions, and for those in Congress who supported them, was that NAFTA would allow cheaper labor to be used in making products – even automobiles – and sold in the same market without tariffs.

For consumers and those who sold products, that meant prices for products would come down, and more foreign products would have easier access to U.S. markets.

For workers and unions, that meant that their way of life, their ability to earn a living, was slowly going away. Gone would be the days when U.S. workers could bargain as one force with the corporations for whom they worked.

If businesses could make their products with cheaper labor, the theory went, why would they continue to pay very good salaries with generous benefits to U.S. workers?

The globalization of the U.S. economy had already begun – well in advance of NAFTA – but the trade agreement was a pivotal realization of that advancement in terms of U.S. economic and trade policy.

It just completely screwed unions and the middle class workers they represented.

But for Ortiz, and South Texans, NAFTA held the promise of new jobs in terms of both production and transportation of products compiled in South Texas or in northern Mexico. Labor markets were shifting, and they were shifting towards South Texas.

Ortiz was determined to help find a way through the political tangle of the NAFTA vote and make South Texas the "front door" for NAFTA's lucrative markets.

Ortiz passionately pled the case for NAFTA to his Democratic colleagues, the greatest opponents to the trade treaty. They rarely moved, given their next elections were at stake.

The coalition of forces supporting NAFTA created their own vote-counting organization, which included Ortiz. In the frenzied lobbying effort leading up to the vote, the *New York Times* ran a front page picture of Brownsville Port commissioners in a congressional hallway, combing lists of members as they lobbied for NAFTA.

That underscored the importance of the trade agreement to South Texas, particularly the Rio Grande Valley.

NAFTA eventually passed the House in a close vote, and Ortiz' personal lobbying was given credit for pulling in several Democrats who'd earlier opposed it.

"Free trade changes the world," Ortiz said. "That's not hokey – peace and prosperity move people and nations together … and away from war. In any trade agreement, there are what we call 'winners' and 'losers.' That means somebody will lose some part of their livelihood, however unintentional that is."

"You have to look at these things as a whole, and judge if it helps more or hurts more," Ortiz said. "I respected my colleagues who opposed it because many times it hurt the people that they represented. I always respected that so many of my colleagues disagreed on NAFTA; I understood the political dynamic for them."

"That was what made my decision to support NAFTA easy; the people I represented would – on balance – be helped by the agreement," Ortiz explained. "The Rio Grande Valley had an unemployment level of 17% while we were debating NAFTA. A couple of years after NAFTA was implemented, that dropped to just 7%."

That meant more South Texans had jobs and income to pay for homes, schools, food, education, and all the things families need to climb the ladder of prosperity.

"Our votes on NAFTA – and later CAFTA (Central American Free Trade Agreement) – illustrated that partisan voting patterns on trade is not the way to make trade policy," Ortiz said, emphasizing trade in Central America is the key to combating poverty there.

Ortiz, and another Democratic vote he delivered, proved to be the decisive votes on CAFTA.

"A hemispheric trade relationship between Latin American nations and the U.S. means we keep more money in this hemisphere … it means we can attack the problem of illegal immigration and poverty at their root causes," Ortiz said on the House floor during deliberations.

"We heard some pretty awful anti-trade rhetoric in the trade debates," Ortiz remembered. "International trade and market integration will force nations to either be players and competitors in the global village … or losers watching from the sidelines."

Free trade – plus paying the nations' bills – were the foundation of Ortiz' economic philosophy. He later headed an ad hoc caucus in the

Congress – along with Republicans Pete Sessions and Curt Weldon – to pass the Singapore Free Trade Agreement.

Weldon and Ortiz included a swing through Taiwan on one of their forays in Asia.

"In Taiwan, Solomon was so well known," Weldon smiled. "He'd been going there with businessmen for almost two decades. Once we were there as a leg of a delegation trip and Solomon was taking us to meet a city council member."

"It was clear that everybody knew who Solomon was," Weldon said. "This was funny. We passed a church where there was a wedding going on. Somebody yelled at Solomon. It was the bride. She knew Solomon, ran over to hug him. The rest of us were laughing our ass off. So very typical Solomon."

23 – THE PERFECT STORM

"SOLOMON'S LOSS WAS a surprise," Nueces County's Republican Sheriff Jim Kaelin reflected. "His defeat [in 2010] was not so much a defeat, as a conglomeration of what was going on all over the country. The thing about serving in D.C. is you can't see what people are doing in D.C. So it leaves an opening for people to infer."

"What you hear [from Capitol Hill] is usually skewed, but you don't know," Kaelin said, indicating that when the people you represent can't personally witness your service, political opponents can portray that service dishonestly.

In 2010, a perfect political storm was brewing in South Texas.

"What happened in the Texas 27th is an object lesson in gerrymandering and big money run amok," said Meredith McGehee, with the Campaign Legal Center, in a 2013 *Huffington Post* article titled: "Poster Boy for Dysfunction: Redistricting and *Citizens United* in the Texas 27th."

"Texas' 27th Congressional District offers a perfect rebuttal to those trying to pretend that gerrymandering and big money did not play a huge role in the [2013] government shutdown and gridlock in Washington in general," said McGehee.

"In 2000, many Texas Democrats were gerrymandered out of their seats and either lost their elections or retired before they even took place," McGehee explained. "Ortiz was one of the lucky Democratic few whose seat was gerrymandered to be a safe Democratic seat. His district was an astounding 71.6 percent Hispanic, 24.2 percent White/Anglo and 2.2 percent Black/African-American. Going into the 2010 election, the district was considered safe for [Ortiz]. President Obama won the district in 2008 with 53 percent of the vote, and Nate Silver, formerly of *FiveThirtyEight* fame, had the district as leaning Democratic. He put Ortiz's chances of reelection at 76 percent. Ortiz enjoyed incumbency, more money, and favorable demographics."

But the 2010 elections were a difficult year for Democrats all across the country. "Obamacare" and the unpopularity of the sitting president, fortified by the Koch-Brothers-plus-Fox-News-financed conservative Tea Party movement, resulted in a landslide for Congressional Republicans.

KOCH BROTHERS

Charles and David Koch – famously known as the "Koch Brothers" – own Koch Industries, a privately-held firm with revenues estimated at $100 billion. While they have long funneled money into politics, it was the 2010 *Citizens United* ruling at the U.S. Supreme Court that allowed their billions to do even more damage to this democracy.

In *Citizens United*, the Supreme Court held that money is equal to speech, and therefore unlimited campaign contributions are protected speech under the Constitution.

Crap, of course, but that was the decision of the Supreme Court, as it struck down decades of campaign finance laws.

According to multiple news organizations, the Kochs and their firm are the central conspirators in an informal coalition of corporate executives, conservative thinkers and members of the government (including Supreme Court Justices Antonin Scalia and Clarence Thomas) all of whom – after the 2008 election – began meeting twice annually to strategize over how best to:

- dramatically lower personal and corporate income taxes,
- minimize government oversight of industry, and
- end public assistance for the poor.

The U.S. Supreme Court's January 2010 decision in *Citizens United v. Federal Election Commission* (supported by Koch friends Justices Scalia and Thomas) allowed corporations and unions to spend unlimited amounts of money to advocate the election or defeat of political candidates. The ruling triggered a flood of new campaign spending to sway even more elections, showcasing the possibilities in the 2010 midterm elections.

Since that ruling, contributions of more than $1 billion by special interests poured into campaigns by 2013 though new "Super PACs" which are financed by undisclosed donors, according to Common Cause, a nonprofit dedicated to shining the light on money in political campaigns.

"There's strong evidence that much of it was provided by corporate interests, including hedge fund managers, Wall Street financiers, defense contractors, energy companies, and private health insurers, all determined to prevent sensible legislative action on health care reform, financial reform, and climate change," according to a report on the Common Cause website.

"Koch Industries' top executives David and Charles Koch are major stealth funders of efforts to fight reasonable government regulations," the Common Cause report continued. "They're also leaders in a national campaign to roll back campaign finance laws that for a century have served as a check on corporate power."

David Koch is head of Americans for Prosperity, which conceived, organized and financed the tea party "movement." Americans for Prosperity is a political group that is not required to disclose its donors, most of whom are bankers, financers, corporate affiliates and individually wealthy people who favor paying fewer taxes.

The Kochs also help finance the 60 Plus Association, and would soon have an outsized voice in Ortiz' last campaign.

The tsunami of money in campaigns most often buys a sledgehammer of negative ads designed specifically to keep traditional voters from voting out of sheer disgust.

"The race for the 27th was actually not close until the end," explained the Campaign Legal Center's Meredith McGehee. "The proverbial straw that broke the camel's back in the Texas 27th apparently was a late surge in outside spending against Rep. Ortiz. Conservative groups, most prominently the 60 Plus Association, ran last-minute TV ads to unseat the incumbent."

"In an election where Democrats lost dozens of seats and control of the House, Ortiz lost by [just over 600] votes to Blake Farenthold, a Tea Party Republican from Corpus Christi who served as a 'side kick' on a conservative talk radio program," said McGehee. "Given the obvious advantages Ortiz enjoyed, his loss in 2010 was a shock — even in a year when the Democrats went down in flames."

So what is there to know about the 60 Plus Association and the role it played in this seat switch for the 27th district of Texas?

The 60 Plus Association is a political group that fancies itself as "the conservative alternative to the AARP," according to its website, and it played a deciding role in Ortiz' 2010 campaign.

Slate, an online magazine, reported in an October 7, 2010 story: "60-Plus does not have to disclose its donors .... In 2006 and 2007, it spent $1.2 million and $1.9 million [in campaign contributions]. Now [2010] it's dumping $6 million on ads?"

The actual source of 60 Plus' sudden source of millions of dollars to drop in congressional campaigns around the country – at an average of $400,000 per race – was a "mystery," according to the *Slate* article.

"Its [60 Plus] founding head was James L. Martin who formerly worked for the National Conservative Political Action Committee (NCPAC)," McGehee explained. "60 Plus issued a press release in 2010 stating it had spent $10 million on TV ads in 2010 targeting House and Senate members who supported health care legislation. The contact person for 60 Plus on the 2010 release was Carl Forti, now the political director of Karl Rove's American Crossroads Super PAC."

In January 2014, the *Washington Post* analyzed a blizzard of tax returns and declared: "The political network [of] Charles and David Koch has expanded into a far-reaching operation of unrivaled complexity, built around a maze of groups that cloaks its donors, according to an analysis of new tax returns and other documents."

"The resources and the breadth of the organization make it singular in American politics: an operation conducted outside the campaign finance system, employing an array of groups aimed at stopping what its financiers view as government overreach," the *Washington Post* concluded. "Members of the coalition target different constituencies but together have mounted attacks on the new health-care law, federal spending and environmental regulations."

Its funders remain largely unknown, the analysis revealed. This coalition was carefully and specifically built with extensive legal barriers to shield the donors.

"But they have substantial firepower," the analysis found. "Together, the 17 conservative groups that made up the network raised at least $407 million during the 2012 campaign, according to the analysis of tax returns by the *Washington Post* and the Center for Responsive Politics," a nonpartisan group that tracks money in politics.

OTHER FACTORS

Other conservative groups – pro-life groups that agreed with Ortiz on opposition to abortion – had been including votes on campaign finance to judge the pureness of candidates since the turn of the century.

But they had not weighed in against Ortiz financially; he believed that was because he agreed with them on their core issue: abortion.

Nevertheless, in 2010, pro-life groups punished Ortiz for voting for more stringent campaign finance laws … all of which the Supreme Court struck down in time for all these outside influences to depress the voter turnout through negative advertising in Ortiz' campaign.

Their ads inferred Ortiz was no longer against abortion.

In addition to health care as an issue that propelled voters to stay home, for the first time in his career, Ortiz was on the wrong side of anti-abortion groups, but not because he had wavered in his opposition to abortion.

"That made me so mad," Ortiz said. "Abortion had nothing to do with how we finance campaigns. But they wanted an outsized voice. They wanted to squeeze members on campaign finance votes. But, you know, I didn't belong to them either, no matter how much I agreed with them on that singular issue [being anti-abortion]."

That hurt Ortiz politically, said Lencho Rendon. "Politically, Solomon's voting percentage on pro-life issues dropped a lot, gave his opponent an opportunity to say he'd abandoned his principles."

At a logistical level, Ortiz – a senior member of the House of Representatives – was hurt by having a relatively rookie team going into 2010. He had a new chief of staff, Denise Blanchard, and in 2009, he lost both his talented legislative director and his military expert.

Blanchard, Ortiz' long-time district director in South Texas, was promoted to chief of staff in 2008. Regarded as a talented district director, she found that operating on Capitol Hill was a wildly different animal.

"Denise was an excellent district director for Solomon, but her expertise was in Texas, not Capitol Hill," Rendon said. "She was out of her element there."

In an election year when Ortiz' fundraising had to be both exceptional and flawless, the fundraising was simply insufficient.

In the end, with outside groups injecting hundreds of thousands of dollars – no matter how much Ortiz' campaign might have raised – they likely could not have overcome the damage done by the outside organizations.

"Denise had tiny fundraisers around the country, usually only raising enough money to cover the cost of the fundraiser and travel there," Rendon said. "Most wound up wasting time and energy. By the time September rolled around, she had no money for the beginning of the campaign. The campaign was really in trouble – and it never recovered."

Ortiz realized that as the election approached. He did two things. He asked Rendon to run his campaign full time in the months leading up to Election Day; and – for the first time since his mother took out a loan on her house in the first election for constable – Ortiz borrowed money for his campaign.

As the 2010 campaign heated up in late September, Blanchard was sidelined after a car accident. On a late night drive from Corpus Christi to Brownsville, Blanchard's car flipped and doctors benched her for the duration of the campaign.

Ortiz' long-time Capitol Hill friend, Transportation Committee staffer Jimmy Miller, lamented that his old friend was not well served in the year before the election. "In the last campaign his people were not doing him right," Miller said. "His chief of staff kept telling him everything was OK. That chief had zero political savvy. Denise [Blanchard] had no clue about how Congress works."

"Denise' job was to protect the boss," Miller intoned. "But getting past the bullshit on health care took getting into the mess and doing it on TV," Miller said wistfully. "I felt the worst about Solomon more than any of the members that fell in 2010. Clearly, the good guys do not always win."

"The people in his office were not tending to business," Miller said. "It was the kind of year you have to pull out every stop and gamble a little bit to win by a little bit."

"That plus all the crap people were making up about the health care law ... followed at the end by all those negative ads – in

Solomon's district alone – by that Koch Brothers group really drove the last nail in the coffin," Miller said of the 2010 campaign.

"Solomon is just a wonderful guy," Miller said. "But he should have gotten outside help. He could have survived despite all that, but the foundation wasn't laid."

Ortiz did get outside help at the end. Lencho Rendon, by then an international businessman, had put his business on hold for the last five to six weeks of the campaign in order to devote his efforts to Ortiz' campaign.

"Even that wasn't enough," Miller said. "2010 was the kind of political year that you had to have hit all the right notes, for the previous two years.

Blanchard chose not to talk about her tenor as chief of staff.

"Denise did things as well as she could," said Ortiz. "She was very loyal to me."

"The stories that were written, most were unfair but there was a little speck of truth to it," Richard Borchard said. "It all conspired to make people stay home. It was terrible the way it ended. I was – everybody was – in total disbelief."

"People just figured he was in no trouble and they didn't go vote," Esther Oliver said. "Even traditional Solomon supporters didn't go vote. Robstown just didn't come out to vote – again, they figured he would win by so much it would never matter. It always matters."

"The 2010 political dynamic was the culmination of what the Republicans have been trying to do since the 1990s," Oscar Ortiz said. "Redistricting is constant now, not a once-a-decade endeavor. You've got Karl Rove with all his unlimited money … and the super PACs blessed by the Supreme Court. This is a war, and it's gonna get worse."

"The 2010 elections were just months after the Supreme Court decision, and still they [Republicans] were remarkably prepared and successful in targeting anybody they saw as unfriendly to their financial interest," Oscar Ortiz said. "The negative campaigning on the Republican side was the result of the watershed moment when the Supreme Court decided money equaled speech."

Money is most certainly a megaphone, but it is not speech and does not deserve the high court's declaration that corporations are equal to individuals in this political system.

"In 2010, Solomon didn't lose, so much as the political

environment shifted altogether," Oscar Ortiz said. "Politics and campaigns are no longer a community activity in backyards. You couldn't get people to do that anymore."

"Solomon's [2010] loss was devastating to me," said Rep. Walter Jones (R-NC), Ortiz' friend on the Armed Services Committee. "It was personally devastating because he was my friend, and it was a rare friendship, across party lines. And it was devastating to this institution because in order for democracy to work, members must work together. Solomon could make that happen."

"The Hispanics in Congress – and we weren't alone in this – were confident that Solomon didn't have a problem in his re-elect," Rep. Charlie Gonzalez said, brow furrowed. "2010 was a terrible year politically, but still we were shocked. Solomon had told us he had a tight race on his hands. It was so sad."

ELECTION NIGHT AND RECOUNT

Corpus Christi native Gloria Caceres first met Ortiz in 1992.

"On Election night 2010, when I realized the numbers weren't there, I felt like I was going to throw up," Caceres said. "2010 was so hard, hard to get money, and even harder than usual to get people out to vote."

"We'd redoubled our efforts in block walking and phone banking," she said, but shoe leather just couldn't stack up against the hundreds of thousands of dollars in negative ad buys.

"That night, I had such a knot in my stomach; when the numbers were all in, it was just numbness," Caceres said. "I felt like I needed to be strong to support Sollie [Ortiz, Jr.], for Solomon. People always ask about the recount: so few ever get it, most thought it was a waste of time."

In that Nueces County recounted ballots like Republicans in Florida in 2000, maybe the recount was a waste of time since it was preordained. There wasn't an accounting of ballots.

"We only recounted mail-in ballots only; it was so frustrating," Caceres said. "One of the Republican counters couldn't count," she explained, saying they were keeping up by the traditional method of four slashes crossed by a line to signify five votes.

"This lady was doing five slashes, then crossing them," Caceres said. "It was maddening. Then closing down was hard, they had so much stuff to organize from their offices. Solomon had stuff from 40 years of service."

"Solomon is so beloved, he is so excellent at one-on-one encounters," Caceres said. "Anybody says anything different, it's just because they have not had a one-on-one with him – they didn't know him."

"The very low – I mean LOW – Hispanic turnout in 2010 was a huge contributor to Solomon's defeat," Robstown's Sam Keach said. "My view is that one of the things that hurt Hispanic turnout here was Obama. Elections workers told me people would come in to vote and say, 'I usually vote for the straight democratic ticket, but not for Obama'."

"The Republicans did that very successfully in 2004, but racial undertones were also at play in the 2008 and 2010 elections," Keach said. "We had a retired bishop here who went on TV – said 'if you vote for Obama you're going to hell.' Manipulating people of faith is despicable."

People will always disagree about politics. Some people's judgment will always be colored by race. Can't change that. But manipulating people of faith is a special sin for those who purport to speak for Christianity, or any single religious faith.

24 – LEGACY

THE BREADTH OF Ortiz' legacy is deep and wide – and impossible to adequately characterize. He had a profound impact on his community in South Texas, in Congress, in the military, and in nations around the world.

SOUTH TEXAS

"I wasn't involved in politics until 1991," campaign worker Gloria Caceres said. "I was just a little girl when Solomon was first elected, and I was from Corpus, so I didn't have the relationship people in his hometown had with him."

"But I was so intrigued by this little Hispanic guy from Robstown being sheriff – by then I was a young adult," Caceres said. "I was so impressed by him. I got to know him better when I worked in his campaign headquarters, and on his annual campaign fundraising dinner."

By 2003, Caceres was a pivotal player in the Coastal Bend Democratic Party and was the president of the local Texas Democratic Women, going on to work for Solomon Ortiz, Jr. when he was the local party chairman and later for the younger Ortiz' office after he was elected to the Texas legislature.

"Coming from that era, Solomon was as well known here as a Kennedy was in Massachusetts," Caceres said. "Over the last couple of decades, I've met people all over South Texas who love him so much. The things he has done, the man that he is, he means so much."

"You can still go to a small town around here, all the way down to the Valley, and they will still talk about Solomon, all the things he has done," Caceres said. "This is a shame, but today we have gotten away from the grass roots campaigning that elected public officials who made a real difference in peoples' lives."

"What I really admire about Solomon is that somebody that comes from where he did, to go so far, to be so fearless," Caceres said. "I can't tell you what it's like to see him wade into a crowd. People gravitate to him in a room. The impact that he has here is palatable. It is so moving to see the respect he had earned."

"He is respected and revered, not so much because he was a congressman but because he is so kind, always," Caceres said. "He gives to the churches … well, religiously."

"Every day, we still get messages and notes to the congressman," Caceres marveled. "A woman asked him if he remembered a song she wrote for him long ago. He's just still so loved."

Corpus Christi native Esther Oliver first met Ortiz at the County Courthouse, where Oliver worked in bookkeeping. Her friend, whose husband worked in the Sheriff's Department, "Took me to coffee with her," Oliver said, and when Ortiz swept in, "I met him for the first time."

Oliver said, "I got the famous Solomon hug and kiss, I almost expected him to have the white Stetson hat," having been familiar with the Ortiz 'David-and-Goliath' legend.

"But there was no white horse," she smiled. "He was just like a regular man, treated me so kindly. He even sent me a sympathy note when my husband died – I didn't know him well then, we'd only met."

"When he was sheriff, I noticed that little by little there were more Hispanics getting elected to different political positions," Oliver said. "His election broke the dam; he was a trailblazer. I worked in the tax collector's office for decades, so I saw more and more Hispanics as officeholders come into the courthouse. After he was elected, people saw that things could change."

"Back then, people saw Solomon as a doorway to better things," Oscar Ortiz said. "They identified with him. He literally began a movement. Some of the activism in the 1960s was channeled into his campaigns."

"Solomon could bridge the diverse community of Robstown back then, which had more middle class Hispanics and whites then," Oscar Ortiz said. "All sides trusted him. Now Robstown's almost entirely Hispanic; we simply don't have economic engines there to stimulate the local economy."

"A lot of people don't want to live in Robstown now," Oscar Ortiz said. "Even the property owners live elsewhere and rent their houses, meaning the people who live in Robstown today, many times do not have roots there."

"Truthfully, today people are just not that interested in politics," Oscar Ortiz said. "The dynamics that existed then don't exist in Robstown anymore."

"As a society, we don't communicate anymore, either left or right … just no middle ground anymore – it is all lost to ideological purity," Oscar Ortiz said. And anger.

"Solomon got so much for his South Texas congressional district," Rep. Charlie Gonzalez said. "I never understood why he never got credit in his district. People in Congress were constantly amazed at the things he managed to do, to get for his people."

"Corpus Christi has such great potential – but it has never been realized," Rep. Gonzalez said, shaking his head, repeating a common lament about the Coastal Bend of Texas.

The Grand Canyon of political disconnect – between the area business community and the large Hispanic and middle class community – in Corpus Christi stymied practically every major economic opportunity.

When Ortiz brought giant manufacturing companies to the table in the Corpus Christi area, the downtown business community and Port of Corpus Christi routinely opposed it. It was beyond frustrating.

"Solomon's contribution to the Corpus Christi/South Texas economy was never appreciated," Gonzalez said. "The sheer tonnage of people whose job is there because of Solomon Ortiz would stun most people. If they even know, it seems they don't care," Rep. Gonzalez shrugged.

"My dad [former Texas Rep. Henry B. Gonzalez] used to say 'you gotta toot your own horn, nobody else will.' For a Member of Congress, Solomon was not the guy who took all the credit," Gonzalez said. "He loved to share credit – he knew everything was teamwork. But he would push other members to the camera."

In the end, Gonzalez acknowledged, being a gentleman didn't work for Ortiz in his home county.

"He'd put out a press release, but people never really knew all the things he did, all the things he brought to South Texas that would never be there – if not for Solomon," Gonzalez thundered, still amazed at the lack of popular understanding at Ortiz' extraordinary success.

"Solomon paved the way for Hispanics in Nueces County to take on the power brokers in this county," Sheriff Kaelin mused. "Where he came from, to go to Congress and rise to where he did, it was just a fairy tale. A glorious fairy tale."

"His background shaped him entirely," Sheriff Kaelin said. "Solomon grew up with no money, no influence. He didn't know anybody with influence. For him to have come from such a humbled upbringing, then to rise to the level he did … it was just a remarkable, amazing journey."

"He has a true concern for the people he represented, he always has," Kaelin said. "That was Solomon's secret. That was his strength."

Caceres was anxious about closing the offices of Ortiz and Ortiz, Jr. after the 2010 elections, merely because she knew so many people would be blown back when they called and another officeholder was there.

"When we closed offices, we arranged to keep the numbers for local offices and redirect them to the nonprofit we started," Caceres said. "So many people still call, asking for help with VA issues, Social Security issues, immigration, and more. We can't officially help, but we can give them advice about how to proceed."

Sam Keach reflected on another legacy Ortiz left in Robstown, this one both aesthetic and emotional.

"There is a big park on the edge of town. It was a farm labor camp operated by the federal government until sometime in the 1960s," Keach said. "It was for migrant workers transiting this area. It was squalor. The county operated it for several years after that."

"When Solomon was County Commissioner, it was about to be closed, but he wanted to completely change the face of it, he wanted it to be a public park," Keach said. "The work to make it a different part of the community was continued by following county commissioners, but it was Solomon's vision … his initiative. Now it's a wetlands park, with biking and hiking trails."

"When I ran for sheriff [2006], I was a Republican," Kaelin said, describing how Ortiz saw past party and politics. "One of the major Democratic candidates was Pete Alvarez, who Solomon was supporting. When Pete lost the Democratic Primary, he called to tell me he was endorsing me, a Republican."

"I still remember what Solomon said on TV when he was asked what he thought about Pete endorsing me," Sheriff Kaelin said proudly. "Solomon said, 'I respect his [Alvarez'] decision'."

When it came to representing South Texans evenhandedly or serving his constituents effectively, Ortiz was a champion, Kaelin said.

Seeming to refer to the racial tensions in Nueces County, Sheriff Kaelin spoke glowingly about Ortiz service in Congress. "Some think that he [Ortiz] represented only some people. But he represented me [in Congress] as well as anybody who's ever been there."

"He was always available to people, he never shunned a conversation about politics or legislation," Sheriff Kaelin said. "Solomon was always honest with me. He was always candid about what he could do, what would be very hard to do, what he couldn't do."

"He was a mentor," Sheriff Kaelin said, describing Ortiz' political skills as unequaled. "Solomon always knew how to play the cards he held."

In politics knowing when and how to maneuver inside a governmental body is a tricky dynamic, but Ortiz knew better than nearly everybody about how to proceed to get what his constituents needed.

"Of the commissioners on the Court at the time, of all power brokers, Solomon was the only one who looked after public safety, and the people who worked for taxpayers," Sheriff Kaelin said.

At the time, Ortiz was breaking barriers on a daily basis as the only Hispanic County Commissioner, meaning that racial equality in South Texas had become more real to Hispanics who had long had their faces pressed against the window of local government.

Also at the same time, that racial equality had become uneasily real to the Anglo population and powerbrokers, whose control in South Texas previously had been absolute. But for Ortiz' innate skill, that moment could have been just temporary.

Yet Ortiz' political talent – and genuine ability to connect with people and solve problems – made him far more than a representative of just the Hispanic population.

Many Anglo business people appreciated his sensibility on economic development, and the larger Anglo community eventually appreciated Ortiz' consistency on solving problems.

"I am a proud Republican, but I was an Ortiz supporter, my whole family supported him," Sheriff Kaelin said. "And Solomon Junior. There is such a kindness in that family, and that just overflowed onto my family."

"Every year he had an annual barbecue," Sheriff Kaelin said. "He always brought us free tickets. He never, ever forgot where he came from, or who his friends were. Even today, when I see him, he calls me 'Jimeeeeeee.' He is always so gracious to give me that 'Solomon hug'."

"Solomon's enduring legacy was his inspirational success in representing his district in Congress," Silvestre (Silver) Reyes said. "He is so unselfish, so creative. With Solomon, what you see is what you get."

"It was never about credit," Reyes said. "He was all about changing things for the better. Solomon was a workhorse, not a show horse. That's not just my opinion; that was Solomon's reputation in Congress every moment he was here [Capitol Hill]."

MILITARY, LOCALLY AND NATIONALLY

In the Corpus Christi-Kingsville area of South Texas, the hub of military installations has been a tremendous economic engine throughout the decades. That has been all-important sustenance for South Texas families as the community stagnated economically.

Ortiz' consistent support, careful planning, tremendous attention to detail in the House Armed Services Committee, and persistent Pentagon lobbying ... was all part of the heavy lifting that protected the Coastal Bend military community.

That daily effort even added – ADDED – jobs and missions to the bases in the Coastal Bend, even as the nation was closing military bases in the 1990s.

That was an enormous – unique – accomplishment. Every single other military community around the nation – communities that fought just as hard as the Coastal Bend – lost missions or bases over the course of four national base closures.

"Solomon's influence in Washington was what saved our military bases, every single time," Borchard said. "They [four base closure commissions] were always coming down hard, and the competition was fierce. There was little else the *Caller Times* liked about Solomon – but they did give him credit for that. There was no doubt in our minds; the bases here would have been closed down in the early 1990s, except for Solomon."

"The other big part of his legacy in Congress is his dedication to having a national defense that is second to none," said Congressman Charlie Gonzalez. "Solomon was dedicated to a strong national defense, more than most people would ever guess."

A veteran, Ortiz had an inherent understanding of the military, from the concerns of the privates to the anxieties of field commanders or generals at the Pentagon. That understanding came through at each hearing and mark-up of the House Armed Services Committee.

His greatest service to the military he so loved was his clarion call in 2006 that the readiness of the U.S. military was so precarious that the military was almost as hollowed out as it was after the Vietnam War. Only in 2006, the U.S. military remained actively engaged in two separate wars.

His heavy lifting ... his personal contact with other Members of Congress ... his consistent and alarming behind-closed-doors briefings ... all led to reconstituting the bulk of the U.S. military.

It was a gigantic feat, one which was done largely behind closed doors, and eventually in the Readiness Subcommittee he chaired after the Democrats took control of Congress in 2007.

INTERNATIONAL DIPLOMACY

"Solomon really was the example of what a member of Congress should be," Amigo Rep. Curt Weldon [Ortiz' international travel companion] said. "He was always himself, with whoever we talked to, on the battlefield or in a meeting room with tough looking guys, in a nuclear facility – wherever."

"Congressional travel today has almost vanished, and that is a huge shame," Weldon said. "Our nation needs every advantage we can get on the world stage. I've heard that only a third of the current members of Congress even hold passports. We did good things, and also had fun."

And the "Amigos" made a difference.

There were very few international leaders Ortiz had not personally met and very few – if any – places on the planet Ortiz did not walk upon.

In 2007, Californians in Congress (with a sizeable community of Armenians) got a resolution through the House of Representatives' Foreign Affairs Committee – a high-profile moment – picking Armenia's side in the century-old tragedy.

The resolution said that the U.S. agreed with the Armenian version of events at the end of the Ottoman Empire. The Armenians maintain that the present-day Republic of Turkey is responsible for a genocide on Armenians.

It was known as the "Armenian Genocide Resolution," and it was deeply opposed by the Turkish government, populated by people who weren't even born when the disputed events occurred, in an empire that predated their republic.

Ortiz knew how much Turkey despised being held to account for events long ago, before Turkey was a nation. Just a couple of years earlier, on a congressional delegation mission with the House Armed Services Committee, led by Committee Chairman Ike Skelton (D-MO), the delegation met with Turks who complained bitterly about being subjected to events that occurred over a century before.

After the resolution passed the Foreign Affairs Committee, Ortiz, Skelton and other members heard from the staff at the U.S. Embassy in Turkey, echoing the need for Congress to stay out of the genocide debate, saying it was creating a dangerous atmosphere.

As the only Muslim member of NATO (the North Atlantic Treaty Organization, the western military alliance), Turkey is a pivotal player in international security efforts in a very dangerous neighborhood.

Turkey borders Syria, Iraq, Iran, Armenia, Azerbaijan and Georgia, the former Soviet Republic. Russia and Turkey have consistently sneered at each other, over centuries of a mighty brutal and bloody past.

Russia invaded Georgia in 2008.

A very dangerous neighborhood.

So Turkey is a frequent stop for members of the House Armed Services Committee (and Foreign Affairs Committee). The U.S. Air Force base near Incirlik, Turkey, is a major projection of American forces in this dangerous neighborhood.

"So few people realized what it meant to pass a resolution calling out our ally over events adjudicated over a century ago," Ortiz said. "The United States carries great influence in this part of the world, but diplomacy is a delicate dance. The Armenian Genocide Resolution was like throwing a match in a pool of gas. It was a really, really bad idea. A dangerous one."

Rarely can sudden international danger be contained in the Halls of Congress. "But when we can get involved to avoid deeper diplomatic damage, you gotta do it," Ortiz said. "Ike and I were talking to friends in the Turkish embassy here the day the resolution passed in 2007, my friends in Turkey – everybody saw this as a shot across the bow, something that put NATO in real trouble."

Ortiz understood the nature of members of Congress. The Californians – and several other state delegations – had a sizeable Armenian population.

For all their work, for all their votes, for all their campaign contributions, all the Armenian-Americans asked of the candidates they supported was to vote for/support the Armenian Genocide Resolution.

For years, that included putting their names on letters to the State Department and the Foreign Affairs Committees.

Throughout those years, the resolution routinely failed in the House Committee on Foreign Affairs – until October 10, 2007, when it passed and was sent forward for a vote in the full House of Representatives. The next day House Speaker – and Californian – Nancy Pelosi vowed the resolution would be brought to a vote on the House Floor.

Publicly, the Turks talked angrily … privately, they spoke candidly and urgently with Ortiz and other friends on the Hill.

"They were in a very bad place," Ortiz said. "They actually spoke of breaking with NATO. I didn't think that would happen, but if the House had passed the stupid thing, that would have been the public conversation. In a very dangerous neighborhood … where we have so many interests. It was a precariously bad idea."

Ortiz and a small number of other members with a nuanced understanding of diplomacy – and Turkey's importance to the national security of the United States – began a frantic behind-the-scenes lobbying campaign to stop the bleeding at that point.

"A lot of damage was already done," said Ortiz, rolling his eyes.

"The best we could do was contain the damage. Ike and I talked to the Speaker [Pelosi] and laid out the security implications. To her credit, she was receptive. It took a couple of days, with others weighing in, including Silver [Reyes; then the chairman of the Intelligence Committee], before she was entirely convinced. But in the end she did the right thing."

On October 26, 2007, in a letter addressed to the House Speaker Nancy Pelosi, four key sponsors of the bill requested that the debate on the Armenian Genocide Resolution in the full House of Representatives be postponed.

International crisis averted. Quietly.

"A big part of Solomon's legacy is his lesson about the necessity of international relations," Rep. Gonzalez said. "This was his political theory writ large, writ globally: talk to each other, friends and enemies."

LAW ENFORCEMENT

Ortiz' professionalization of the law enforcement in Nueces County is his legacy in the Coastal Bend, said Justice of the Peace Bobby Balderas.

"Solomon was the first sheriff to put us in uniforms and marked units," Balderas said. "It's crazy I know, but when I was younger, I knew about the Police Department, but I didn't know the Sheriff's Department existed. When he came in, he did great stuff. He started crime prevention and drug education programs. All that sounds simple now – everybody does that. But in the 1970s, Solomon started that here."

"Solomon made a difference here," Balderas said. "He just really structured and professionalized the department – and he did it so well, that subsequent sheriffs pretty much kept the same structure. He brought real law enforcement to the county."

He took the Nueces County Sheriff's Department from anonymity and associations with the Bandidos drug cartel – to a modern professional law enforcement agency that left the Bandidos a broken organization by the time he left.

In only six years, Balderas said, "Solomon's boys did a lot. We knew we were out there to enforce the law. Period."

Ortiz' great legacy as a drug warrior in the 1970s was twofold, said Lencho Rendon. "On the one hand, he was the guy who stood up to the Banditos, and reversed their reign of terror and drugs. Plus – and this was fundamental to clamping down on the drug trade in South Texas – he went after the money the drug guys were dropping around. Wherever it was. And it was everywhere."

REDISTRICTING

"Solomon always had the practical view of things," Congressman Charlie Gonzalez said. "He was an ambassador to bridge differences. If he were still here in Congress, he could have kept the Democrats together in redistricting fight of 2011. He always kept us together – and he could talk to anybody."

"The commonality of all the parts of his legacy is in how people of opposite views can talk to each other, reason together," Rep. Gonzalez said. "His core belief was that if you disagree with somebody – either in domestic politics, or international diplomacy – you talk to them. He didn't think that solved 100% of a problem, but he knew it solved most of it."

"Solomon – and his brand of reasoned talking to each other here – are gone," Rep. Gonzalez said sadly. "His 2010 race represented what has happened to the institution now. National interest got trumped by selfish parochial interests."

The Campaign Legal Center's Meredith McGehee agreed with Gonzalez, "Partisan gridlock in Washington is not new. Neither is gerrymandering. Here is what is new. Gerrymandering has reached new heights as technology has allowed ever more precise line drawing and the courts have chosen to sit on the sidelines."

"The constraints on huge sums of money from corporations and wealthy individuals have almost been eliminated," McGehee said. "Money from anonymous sources is pouring into key elections and playing a crucial role in both outcomes and political discourse.

"Solomon's race may have marked the sea-change in what happened in this country during the last few years, in politics and government," Rep. Gonzalez said. "It's almost like meanness is an ideology."

Politics at the national level has always been hard, very tough – as it should be.

But frequent, partisan redistricting, unrestricted money in politics blessed by the Supreme Court, and a round-the-clock information TV network for Republicans – have conspired to remove conservative Democrats, moderate Republicans and the workhorses of both parties since the turn of the century.

"After the 2010 elections when it came time to draw the congressional district lines for the next decade, the state's Republicans, secure in holding most of the districts, focused on solidifying their hold on the Texas congressional delegation," wrote Meredith McGehee in a *Huffington Post* article. "Of the three seats that the Texas Republicans picked up from Democrats in 2010, only two of them were at all close. Republicans decided to make one of them – the Texas 27th – safe for 2012 and to pour money into the other one – Texas 23rd – in hope of keeping that one in the Republican camp as well."

"As a result of the lines, the Texas 27th has morphed into another solidly Republican district," McGehee continued. "In addition to the geographic differences, the demographic breakdown was significantly different from the original district. The Hispanic/Latino population dropped from almost 72 percent to 49 percent, and the White/Anglo population jumped to 42 percent from 24 percent."

"The end result is that now Rep. Farenthold has a safe seat in Congress for the next decade, certainly insulated from Democratic challenge in the general election," McGehee went on. "As a Tea Party Republican, it is not surprising that Rep. Farenthold has taken positions considered to the right of mainstream politics. In August of this year, Rep. Farenthold called for the president to be impeached on the grounds that his birth certificate was a fake."

"More recently, Rep. Farenthold was a strong supporter in the House Republican Conference of shutting down the government over the Affordable Care Act," McGehee continued. "When asked about the shutdown, he told KRISTV.com that the stalemate in Washington was necessary to achieve party goals. 'I feel like my mandate when I was elected was to go reduce the size of government, lower taxes, and increase freedom, and freedom isn't free, and sometimes you have to make a small sacrifice to move forward with what you're after.'"

"In this new, safer district, the likelihood of a primary challenge to Rep. Farenthold in 2014 is slim," McGehee said candidly. "Given his positions, however, there is likely to be little daylight between Rep. Farenthold and another Tea Party challenger. A challenge from the middle by a more moderate Republican candidate currently appears unlikely."

"The Texas 27th congressional district is just one story of how *Citizens United* and redistricting are having an impact on our politics, but it is an illustrative story nonetheless," McGehee said. "If a seat is competitive it is going to see a flood of outside anonymous money and odds are it either has been or will be gerrymandered or both."

"The bad thing about carving out the middle is that it makes the House [of Representatives] dysfunctional – government can't work like that," Rep. Gonzalez said. "People – good people – who are even remotely interested in government, are looking at this mess with their hands up. Knowing every wart you ever had will be examined in minute detail makes people run away from public service in horror."

So the Supreme Court's devastating decision in *Citizens United* leaves a giant footprint in South Texas.

"Control of the House in recent years has rested on about 10 percent of races," McGehee said. "Those 30 to 45 competitive contests determine what goes on or doesn't go on in Washington. The 27th congressional district in Texas is one of those races and stands as a testament to the corrosive impacts of gerrymandering and the Supreme Court's disastrous *Citizens United* decision."

HISPANICS IN CONGRESS

"Solomon was a fixer," Rep. Gonzalez said, even in the midst of unwieldy Congressional Hispanic Caucus meetings. "We'd have a big fight, and there would be all this high tension. Solomon inevitably relieved the moment with humor, broke up the bad feelings."

"Solomon was the Hispanic Caucus chairman in the early 1990s," Rep. Curt Weldon said. "I came from a poor family in Pennsylvania; I knew nothing of Hispanic issues. One of the ways my friends influenced me in Congress: Solomon and Silver made me appreciate the Hispanic community, their needs and influence."

"I became friends with Solomon when I came up to D.C. as a rookie congressman – but I knew who he was before then," said Rep. Charlie Gonzalez. "There's a picture of him with my dad [pioneer Rep. Henry B. Gonzalez, D-TX] from his first campaign for constable."

Their friendship began, Rep. Gonzalez said, when he joined Ortiz in Congress. "By the time I got to Congress, Solomon was a senior member, that's when I got to know him well," he said. "He gave me sage advice – but then he gave everybody sage advice."

Ortiz was all about teaching the rookies the ways of Congress.

"I learned from him – the legislative process of course – but more importantly, he helped me understand how decisions get made, how decisions sometimes reflect the quality of the relationship," Gonzalez said.

"Solomon's gift, his strength in Congress, was that he was friends with everybody, liked by everybody, worked with everybody," Gonzalez said. "He was the last of a breed, the guys that worked to solve problems regardless of party."

Shaking his head in frustration, Gonzalez noted, "You can't even have a conversation with so many of the members here now [2011]."

In 2011, Gonzalez announced his intention to retire from Congress.

Ortiz offered a Ph.D. in how to work in Congress, Gonzalez said. "From Solomon, I learned the necessity of personal relationships … not that decision makers would do you a favor. Wasn't like that. But when you really know somebody, they will listen, give your arguments credence."

So simple. Work hard, be nice.

But that was Ortiz' driving philosophy. He always knew that race and ethnicity fundamentally influenced underlying political dynamics. If he was the only Hispanic somebody were to meet, he wanted to leave a good impression.

"Solomon was a visionary for the Congressional Hispanic Caucus (CHC)," Reyes said. A member of the Hispanic Caucus for a decade, Ortiz chaired it in the early 1990s.

"Solomon's goal was to flat out get more Hispanic members elected to Congress," Reyes said. "He called us both pioneers. He was usually the only Hispanic member in a room on Capitol Hill, and there was only one Hispanic at my level in the Border Patrol."

"Solomon always had one eye on history, even as it was happening … seeing opportunities for other Hispanics," Reyes said. "Solomon wanted to change the face of the organs of government by inspiring them to hire incredibly talented people who were minorities."

"'We the People' only really works when all the people are included," Ortiz said. "But race can't ever be the only factor."

"When I got promoted to [Border Patrol] Chief, I was there in a room with white guys, all pissed at me for getting the job they'd coveted," Reyes remembered. The new chief was a helicopter gunner in Vietnam; tough as nails, fearless, and a practical jokester with wicked sense of humor.

"Silver's ethnicity was the last thing that distinguished him in law enforcement," Ortiz said. "He was the perfect profile for a border chief."

"Insights and contacts associated with being Mexican helped that way, but Silver was just so smart, so tough, so practical in his approach to border enforcement," Ortiz smiled. "And he wasn't afraid of anything. Ever."

PUBLIC SERVICE, ORTIZ STYLE

Kaelin eventually went back to the Department of Public Safety (DPS) after working for Ortiz' Sheriff's Department, but remained good friends with Ortiz, who had been elected to Congress. "Our paths just kept crossing," Sheriff Kaelin said, including at the annual Charro Days Festival in Brownsville, Texas. "Solomon was a good friend, and he never forgot his friends."

"Here's what I mean," Kaelin continued. "I have two sons, both also went into DPS. One, a veteran, tried to buy a new home on the G.I. bill [a federal bill to provide veterans with college, home and business loans]."

"My son was told by the developer that the floor plans he'd selected were not approved in conjunction with the G.I. bill," Kaelin said. "The exact same plans were approved in other cities around Texas, but not this city in Jackson County. So my son was in a bind, he had a loan rate to lock in and time was running out."

"So I called Solomon, who was in Congress by then," Kaelin said. "Solomon always took my call; or called me back when he got back to the office. Don't know who he talked to, but suddenly my son's G.I. home loan was approved."

Jackson County, Kaelin noted, was nowhere near Ortiz' congressional district.

"Solomon established a middle class party that drew from whites that wanted reasonable change, and conservatives," Sam Keach said. "Solomon went to everybody – all the stakeholders. He wanted to include everybody, and made sure people knew that from the beginning. Of course it was in his political best interest, but it was also just how he operated."

"That tactic allowed him to earn respect from a greater percentage of the Anglo population," Keach said. "Some of the old Anglo farmers would say until they died that they didn't get the level of service from commissioners that they got from Solomon Ortiz." He hastened to add that the county commissioner system changed later.

"One of the biggest curses for Robstown is that we are in Nueces County," Keach said evenly. "They [Corpus Christi's business-political community] talked a good talk, but they never delivered. The legal establishment, the business establishment, they never owned him – they hated that they couldn't control him. The hushed conversations were 'we can't have a congressman that can't speak good English'."

While Ortiz had a GED (General Education Diploma or high school equivalency), and attended college while he was a county official, he had no college degree. That frequently became a matter over which people who opposed Ortiz focused their ire.

In 2012, Robstown native Roel Lopez, at the Monte Sinai Christian Church, in which Ortiz grew up, offered a story about his congressman's service at a time in his life when few people could have helped.

Lopez explained that when his son was in the service, his son and daughter-in-law were stationed far away.

While Lopez' son was away from his base during a training mission, a local girl said that Lopez's son had fathered her baby. With the soldier far away, it was a confusing circumstance with nobody there to refute or verify the story.

Like many people, Lopez asked his friend and congressman if there was something he could do.

"Solomon looked into it, and discovered quickly that the baby was born while my boy was still in high school, long before he had even been stationed at the base," Lopez said. It was a scam, and probably pretty successful, but "Solomon figured it out."

"People in South Texas have a tremendous example of public service from Solomon," Oscar Ortiz said. "He worked incredibly hard; he included everybody, even former opponents. Remember Willie Vaden [Ingleside Republican who twice challenged Ortiz for Congress]? Solomon reached out to him during the base closure fight over [Naval Station] Ingleside; and they worked together for the community."

Despite their political opposition, when Ortiz heard that Vaden might be a willing partner in the fight to keep Ingleside alive, Ortiz wrote an op-ed for the local paper, praising his former opponent.

Senior Federal District Judge Hayden Head, Jr., of Corpus Christi, didn't meet Ortiz until the younger Head was a judge and Ortiz was already in Congress.

"That's when I got to know him," said Judge Head, the son and namesake of Ortiz' first big political supporter. "We would talk about judicial issues, growth in the region, and I'd keep him advised on matters in his district."

"In 1987, the clerk of the court came to me – said 'you need a new courthouse, you've outgrown this one' – and we had," Judge Head said. It was an age of deficits and federal belt-tightening as Head and Ortiz started the process.

"It got bumped off the track, but Solomon got it back on," Judge Head said. "He was in a position to see that his district got the facilities we needed. We've got a full courthouse now. We wouldn't have survived without more space. And we wouldn't have had it without Solomon – of course the senators helped, but it was Solomon who was a bulldog about getting it done."

"Solomon was very effective in getting this courthouse; he was positively looking for judicial efficiency and for justice," said Judge Head. Ortiz' legacy, he added, was that he worked hard for the region, did what congressmen are supposed to do.

"Solomon was just brilliant at understanding relationships, knowing what moved people and how that could be leveraged to serve South Texas," Keach said. "Once, there was a pivotal vote on the Choke Canyon reservoir. The vote was in a Senate committee, and [Senator] Bill Bradley (D-NJ) was on the committee."

Near the confluence of two rivers, Choke Canyon supplies the water to Corpus Christi; and the state of the reservoir is always of great concern to residents of the arid South Texas area. Senator Bradley, Keach said, was an old friend of his brother, Bill Keach; both men were Rhodes Scholars together.

"At the moment of truth, the vote was so close; they were worried that it would lose," Keach said. "Then Solomon remembered both Bills [Bill Bradley and Bill Keach] had been Rhodes Scholars at the same time."

"Solomon called my bother Bill, asked him to weigh in with the Senator on the Choke Canyon vote," Keach said. "Of course Bill did just that, and Senator Bradley voted with the South Texans' interest on the Choke Canyon issue."

Water in Texas is always feast or famine – drought or flood.

"When Oscar was commissioner, maybe 2002, there was a big flood in Robstown," Keach said, describing an exchange between the Ortiz brothers. "Oscar was trying to figure how to get the money to fix the drainage problem, as we stood on one of the few dry places in town, across from the high school, which was a lake."

"Solomon said people will never get the extent of a problem if they cannot see it," Keach remembered. "He said, 'photograph it; get some TV cameras over here so people who work at the courthouse can see what we are seeing, see people walking through the water.' Solomon just always knew how to act in the moment – how to solve a problem."

In 1995, Esther Oliver went to work for Ortiz in his Corpus Christi Congressional District Office as a caseworker, fielding all manner of requests to help with Social Security checks, veteran's benefits, and even the occasional very odd request.

"One day Solomon was in the office – he would spend time in the Corpus office at least once a week, always asking what's up, what are people asking about," Oliver said. "Right about then, I got a call from a man who was going to commit suicide. I wrote a note, so the others would know what was going on. Solomon said, 'give me the phone'."

"My brother, how are you? It's Solomon," Oliver remembered Ortiz saying, still overwhelmed at the moment. "He told this poor guy, 'Only God knows what's going on in your life. If your family is having hard times now, what will their lives be like after they lose you? This is not the answer. We'll try to help in any way we can, but you have to your part."

"I was just watching him, admiring his good spirit," Oliver said. "I just kept thinking, 'he talks to presidents and big shots, and here he is talking to this guy, who is at the lowest point in his life.' To me, that really illustrates his compassion, the kind of man he is."

Ortiz' impact on South Texas, in Congress – and in the world – is just barely scratched as this story ends.

The story of his life remains unfinished.

ORTIZ: THROUGH THE YEARS

Early congressional campaign rallies.

Ortiz in Iraq at a battlefield promotion ceremony (above), followed by a briefing (below) with Rep. Curt Weldon (R-PA).

Ortiz (above) posing at the "spider hole" where U.S. Forces captured Saddam Hussein in Iraq, and (below) eating with troops.

Ortiz (above) says the Pledge of Allegiance with veterans, circa 1985. Below, Ortiz details border security dangers to Lee Hamilton at 9-11 Commission hearing in 2004.

Ortiz (above) in Libya in 2004; below, Ortiz stands atop the U.S. Capitol, looking down the National Mall in the mid-1990s.

Above, Ortiz at his desk on Capitol Hill; below at his annual appreciation dinner in Corpus Christi.

At the White House Ortiz (above) with Corpus Christi native Eva Longoria and President Barack Obama; below with the first couple.

ABOUT THE AUTHOR

Cathy Travis worked on Capitol Hill for 25 years – the last 18 years as a communications director, senior advisor and political consultant for Solomon Ortiz, and later for the Texas Delegation Democrats. She left Congress to be a full time author in 2008.
A native of Jonesboro, Arkansas, Travis graduated from Arkansas State University and resides in Washington, D.C.
Her first book, the award-winning *Constitution Translated for Kids*, was hailed by partisans in all major political parties as an even-handed, non-ideological rendition of the founding U.S. document.

OTHER BOOKS BY CATHY TRAVIS:

Remember Who You Are (a novel): From a Capitol Hill confirmation hearing, Judge Jodie Davis – a U.S. Supreme Court nominee – tells the U.S. Senate about her childhood in northeast Arkansas in the turbulent South of the late civil rights era. The lives of young Jodie's neighbors are thrown into turmoil – first when a black family tries to buy a house in their neighborhood, then by a monster tornado roiling through their town. But none of that prepares them for the chaos in the aftermath of a murder on the football field of the high school. The decisions that everyone makes have enormous consequences for each one of them.

Elected (a novel): Inaugurated after a bitter recount in Florida, following the 2000 presidential race, President Hal Cord leads an angry and divided nation. White House Press Secretary MJ Bennett watches in horror as her country is brutally attacked, and careens into a Central Asian war that threatens the life of her new love, a legendary Special Forces commander. After September 11, 2001, Cord calls for a creative "worldwide war." Sending an overwhelming military force to Afghanistan badly damages Osama bin Laden's force there; and Cord's focus on eliminating the combustible engine forces al Qaeda to morph quickly, with dangerous results for Saudi Arabia … and the United States.

Target Sitting is a heartbreakingly candid journal written when Travis was a Capitol Hill staffer. Beginning the week after the September 11, 2001 attacks – ***Target Sitting*** carries readers through that heart-pounding day, the anthrax attack on the Hill, and the full body shudder associated with working at the seat of government in the ensuing years. ***Target Sitting*** is a stark look at life in the target that al Qaeda missed in 2001.

Constitution Translated For Kids – winner of the 2011 Gelett Burgess Children's Book Award for Education (Government and Politics), the "Mom's Choice Award" and a "Best Books Award" – is a simple, widely acclaimed, non-ideological translation of the entire U.S. Constitution, side-by-side with the original 1787 text. Teachers hail the accompanying free Teacher's Guide, and a classroom Toolkit, as extraordinary resources to offer lessons on Constitution Day in September.

Reunion (a novel): Wicked international peril lurks in Karabakh, the corner of Azerbaijan occupied by the Armenian military. Iran has built underground nuclear weapons depots there to evade U.N. inspections. The kidnapping of a Peace Corp worker in Azerbaijan propels several friends to Central Asia to find her. There, they stumble into a dangerous brew of international criminals and transnational weapons smuggling … that promise the weakened al Qaeda terrorists a huge victory. "Reunion" is a story of love, of friendship, and of a national reunion in Azerbaijan.

9115768R00133

Made in the USA
San Bernardino, CA
04 March 2014